# THEME FOR REASON

It was a theame
for reason, much too strong for phantasie.
—JOHN DONNE

# THEME FOR REASON

BY
JAMES WARD SMITH

PRINCETON UNIVERSITY PRESS
PRINCETON, NEW JERSEY
1957

Copyright © 1957 by Princeton University Press
London: Oxford University Press
ALL RIGHTS RESERVED

L.C. CARD 57-10322

Publication of this book has been aided by a grant from the
Princeton University Research Fund

Printed in the United States of America
by Princeton University Press, Princeton, N.J.

# CONTENTS

| | |
|---|---|
| Chapter One: Orientation | 1 |
|   I. Three Needs | 1 |
|   II. Distribution of Emphasis; and Its Justification | 7 |
| Chapter Two: The Problem in Political Philosophy | 14 |
|   I. Piecemeal Engineering | 15 |
|   II. Justification by Deduction | 28 |
|   III. An Example | 39 |
|   IV. The Conditions of Sound Advice | 49 |
| Chapter Three: The Problem in Moral Philosophy | 60 |
|   I The Categorical | 60 |
|   II. Ought and Is | 71 |
|   III. Intuitionism | 81 |
|   IV. The General Problem and the Moral Problem | 99 |
| Chapter Four: Outline of a Solution for Political and Moral Philosophy | 107 |
|   I. Towards a Solution | 107 |
|   II. Political Philosophy | 109 |
|   III. Moral Philosophy | 121 |
|   IV. The Nature of Man | 131 |
| Chapter Five: The Present State of Philosophy: Analysis | 137 |
|   I. Self-Correctiveness and the Analysis of Analysis | 137 |
|   II. The Range of Analysis (Part One) | 142 |
|   III. The Range of Analysis (Part Two) | 169 |
|   IV. The Musts of Science | 177 |
| Chapter Six: The Present State of Philosophy: The Grand Tradition | 190 |
|   I. Metaphysics as Critique | 190 |
|   II. The Nature of the World | 196 |
|   III. Ultimate Matters: Religion | 203 |

# THEME FOR REASON

# CHAPTER ONE: ORIENTATION

## I. *Three Needs*

THOSE who differ in opinion are likely to be in agreement in more ways than they are aware. The conscious focus of our thinking is usually upon our disagreements with others, upon what they say which we think is wrong, and upon our reasons for believing otherwise. Constructive ideas are generally introduced amidst a maze of polemic. But beneath the polemic the parties of a dispute are almost certainly making common assumptions, focusing attention on the same kinds of question, agreeing that such questions are the important ones; and they are generally failing to be self-critical at common points. This is why the task of future historians is so often one of shifting the focus of attention from disagreements to agreements, from the points at which disputants differed to the points at which they agreed. When the dust of disputation has settled, a perceptive historian may learn more about us by examining the unnoticed and unheralded ways in which we have thought alike than we ourselves have learned in our preoccupation with dispute. Both what is best and what is worst in our intellectual life may lie embedded in the common assumptions which we have taken for granted and failed to discuss.

No one conversant with recent philosophical literature can fail to be impressed by certain standard disagreements; but there may be many who fail to recognize the common assumptions on which some of these disagreements are based. We are no more omniscient than our forbears; and we, like they, may do well to ferret out the unconscious assumptions on which our conscious disagreements rest. In particular, there are three primary needs which have become increasingly evident in the midst of current philosophical disputations. Each involves a refusal to be complacent about the common assumptions which underlie our differences. I begin by citing these three needs.

*First*: There has been a great deal of talk in recent years about "reducing" philosophy to "analysis." Much of this talk is critical, indulged in by those who do not like the philosophical tendencies by which they find themselves surrounded; some of it is proclamation of a gospel. In either case, it is important to be on our guard. The word "analysis" is extremely vague and often illusive. A great many different ways of approaching intellectual problems may properly be termed "analytic." There have been several tentative attempts at differentiating these ways and examining their interconnections, but nothing thorough or entirely satisfactory has yet been done. Under the circumstances it is dangerous to proceed on the assumption that there is any clear-cut difference between "analysis" as a genus and something else which is wholly different. If many of those who advocate "reductionist" programs are guilty of an over-generalized conception of available alternatives, so too are many of those who reject "analysis" in favor of philosophy "in the grand tradition." The idea that competent analysis on the one hand and problem-solving in the grand tradition on the other hand are two conflicting and incompatible undertakings will simply not withstand careful scrutiny. Yet many people, on both sides of a variety of arguments, assume that there is really a forced alternative here. There is certainly truth in the impression that some who most persistently practice various of the "analytic" methods provide in the long run little enlightenment with respect to the important problems we have inherited from the grand tradition. There is equal truth in the impression that some who most vigorously discuss the problems of the grand tradition either ignore or consciously flout the valid findings of recent "analysis." It is possible, however, that each of these regrettable facts is in part the result of assuming a dichotomy between "analysis" and "something more." An analytic philosopher who thinks in terms of such a dichotomy may delude himself into believing that the problems handed down to us through the grand tradition do not need solving. His method does not justify ignoring them; his ignoring them confines his application of his method. A philosopher in the grand tradition who thinks in terms of the same dichotomy may shun what the analysts are doing as irrelevant to his own purposes.

## THREE NEEDS

In so doing he may commit very real errors which the analysts have rightly sought to expunge; but it may well be that it is not facing those problems which necessitates committing these errors. Committing the errors may simply be the result of a mistaken notion that facing such problems is somehow an undertaking generically different from careful attention to analytical detail. Much that has recently been done in the name of analysis lacks any guiding sense of what problems are important; much that has recently been done to reinstate the problems of the grand tradition has been done in a spirit hostile to, and often in ignorance of, the valid findings of analysis. But this justifies no impetuous theory about irreconcilability.

The first need in the present situation is to break down the uncompromising distinction between "analysis" and "something more." In no generic sense can analysis be properly contrasted with speculation, or divorced from methods appropriate for handling the problems of the grand tradition. "Analytic philosophy" is neither a self-contained panacea to be adored, nor a temporary aberration to be vilified. There are many ways of analyzing. The best results achieved along each of these ways may provide keys to speculative progress. There is no clear-cut contrast between two ways of doing philosophy. There are many different kinds of philosophical problems, and many different ways of approaching them. Between "reductionism" and flagrant repudiation of analysis we must find a middle ground. Only so will we avoid the kind of analyzing which lacks all sense of proportion and importance; only so will we avoid a treatment of the great problems which tends to be sterile, retrospective and unimaginative. This is the first matter to which I shall seek to draw attention.

*Second*: A more specific distinction—a more precise either/or —has been widely discussed in recent decades. We are forever talking about the distinction between analytic and synthetic propositions. Here again is a distinction which has on occasion led to the dangerous idea that we must under certain conditions do either one or the other of two opposite things. We talk as though no middle ground is available. In questioning this idea I shall wish to refer not only to the technical worries of Quine, Goodman, and others to the effect that a clear and unassailable dividing line between analytic and synthetic has never been drawn. This is, to be sure, an important and troublesome problem; and yet in one sense we all know perfectly well what has been meant by those who have drawn the distinction between logical truth and truth by experimental test. The voice of wisdom has always warned that not everything we say with sense must be one or the other; that indeed most of what we intelligently say is not in the nature of propositions at all, and that talk about truth or falsity is as often Pickwickian as it is technical talk either about theorem-deriving or about probability statistics. But what I wish to discuss, though it bears on all this, goes beyond it. It concerns that very puzzling phrase "synthetic a priori." This phrase (or, in its absence, practices to which as a label it has seemed applicable) was very common in the grand tradition. In recent decades, the tendency to sharpen the distinction between analytic and synthetic has had the result of rendering the phrase, in certain uses, well-nigh self-contradictory. In certain uses the a priori simply *is* that which is analytic—i.e., that the truth of which can be demonstrated independently of reference to empirical matters. The synthetic simply *is* that the truth of which depends upon what specific matters of fact are found to be. If we decide to use words in this way we may with reason be suspicious of the phrase "synthetic a priori"; but we may in the process blind ourselves to a more important problem. For it remains as important as it ever was to clarify the status of those things we want to say which do not conform to either of the very special models—theorem-deriving and fact-stating. These two very special kinds of utterance do not exhaust the scope of either our daily or our theoretical discourse, and there is much need for further consideration of the rules which should govern our reasonable and intelligent use of kinds of utterance less often discussed in a precise and technical way. So long as we assume that there are two and only two clear-cut alternatives before us—that

## THREE NEEDS

either we accept or reject the notion of the synthetic a priori—we may unwittingly sidestep the most important issues which that mere phrase was once invented to discuss.

The second need in the present situation is to move more boldly in that vast middle ground which stretches between theorem-deriving and experimental induction. A sensible man must be tenacious of his opinions in many contexts where "proof," either deductive or inductive, is out of the question. Justification of one's opinions in such contexts involves problems both very like and very unlike those which have generally been discussed in the context of the tradition of a "synthetic a priori." There is a sense of certainty which is far from logical and yet equally far from the tentativeness customarily assigned to piecemeal predictions of matters of fact. There are "musts" in our intellectual life which are neither the "musts" of logic nor the "musts" of incontrovertible evidence. We ought neither to enshroud such "musts" in technical jargon and jeopardize the intelligibility of what we say, nor allow our passion for simplicity and exactitude to blind us to real problems that may resist treatment in terms too simply and too exactly defined. Opinions must be justified in context; and if there is any coerciveness about an opinion the character of that coerciveness must be described in context and in detail.

Now, these first two matters to which I shall be calling attention are closely related. It is from work that has generally been classified as analytic philosophy that we are discovering what a vast range of problems falls between problems of defining and deducing on the one hand and problems of fact-stating and predicting on the other. Witness the growing influence of the closely analytic (in one sense) work of the Oxford philosopher John Austin. An intelligent contemporary approach to problems in the grand tradition must grow out of this kind of careful analytic work. As we shall see, analysis itself (in various of its senses) may make us aware of new ways of conceiving of the insight required to shed fresh light on old problems. Witness the almost legendary influence of the Cambridge philosopher Ludwig Wittgenstein. The language of isms, dichotomies, and impasses is often a very wrong-headed kind of language in which to express the problems of philosophy if we are to understand what is involved in them. Analysis itself is making us suspicious of many of the stereotyped models in terms of which we have been conceiving the most important problems that confront us. A fresh approach to the problems of the grand tradition cannot with impunity continue to operate in terms of some of these inadequate models. This fact leads to the third matter to which I wish to draw attention.

*Third*: Perhaps nothing so confines and encumbers our ways of approaching philosophical questions as our tendency to conceive of the demands of rationality on inadequate standard models. No need is more pressing in the present scene than the need for reinterpreting what we mean by "rational opinion." We persist in operating in terms of two ideal models of rationality: on the one hand, the model of logico-mathematical deduction; on the other hand, the model of piecemeal inductive engineering. We feel that we are being rational only to the extent that we confine ourselves to the enunciation either of demonstrated theorems within deductive systems or of empirical hypotheses which sheer weight of evidence will tend to confirm or confute. Though we may be aware that we cannot confine ourselves to these two ideal ways of talking, we continue to approach intellectual problems as though doing anything else is either careless or at best an unfortunate necessity. Reason is tacitly conceded to be a faculty for seeing everything in system; if an opinion can be shown to be a theorem deducible from axioms it is conceded to be a rational opinion, if it can be shown to be an hypothesis made probable by experimental evidence it is conceded to be rational; opinions of any other sort are (whether frowned upon or hailed) conceived to be somehow not rational.

It is worth asking whether it is proper to have *any* model for rationality. A reasonable man is one who is capable of providing for his opinions such justification as is appropriate; but the concept of justification is complex and many-sided. It may be better understood without preconceived models. Models may tend to blind us to the crucial fact that what would constitute appropriate justification under very ideal conditions will constitute wholly inappropriate and misleading justification under conditions less ideal. The two standard models take insufficient account of the fact that a reasonable man must decide in the face of his own fallibility, ignorance, and confusion. A man's ignorance and confusion consists precisely in his uncertainty with respect to axioms and his inability to predict; but this does not render him irrational. Rationality consists in a certain temper of deciding which is perhaps more important in just these circumstances than in any other. To conceive of rationality in terms of models which derive from ideal conditions will mislead us when we operate in the middle ground of doubt and uncertainty within which most important decisions are made.

The third and final need is thus closely parallel to the second, for to think in terms of what rationality *requires* is to think in terms of "musts." With respect to any problem, the question "what must I do if I am to adopt a rational stand?" is one of the most important we can ask. And it is by no means a merely verbal question.

## II. *Distribution of Emphasis; and Its Justification*

I have begun by stating these three needs briefly and dogmatically. In so doing, I have really been predicting themes that will constantly recur as we proceed. The central task to which I set myself is the task of clarifying the concept of responsible justification where standard models are inadequate. The thing to do, of course, is to begin with a specific *kind* of problem, a specific *kind* of context, in connection with which the concept of responsible justification stands in need of clarification. Chapter Two will begin with a discussion of justification in political theory. Starting with a description of the unsatisfactory character of standard justification models in such a context, I shall try to isolate the unanswered questions which a satisfactory concept of justification would require. Such questions, however, will carry us far beyond the confines of political theory. Before we are through, we will find that our attempt to clarify the concept of justification will force us to reconsider the very notion of philosophical activity itself.

It is the common practice of mankind, when asked to justify practices or recommendations, to respond by enunciating theories. Now, reflection is generally a source of puzzlement, and nowhere more so than here. For reflection may suggest a question we seldom ask, and a question which, when we do ask it, is extraordinarily difficult to answer. What is the relation between a theory on the one hand and our practices, our decisions, and our recommendations on the other, such that the former is offered, and sometimes accepted, as a "justification" of the latter?

As it stands, such a question is no doubt too general and too vague to admit of any definitive answer. You cannot clarify the concept of responsible justification in a vacuum. For one thing, you will have to begin by achieving some degree of clarity as to *what* you are trying to justify. We often speak of justifying our "opinions" or our "beliefs." And it is probable that we usually assume that our opinions and beliefs must be stated in propositional form before we can undertake to justify them. Formulate your belief as an unambiguous proposition; and then we can proceed to "justify" it either by deductive or by statistical techniques. These are our two models of "theory"; and with the models we associate our attempt to justify respectable beliefs and opinions by appeal to "theory."

But, when we seek to justify our actions, our decisions, our recommendations, and our hopes, fears, and purposes, is it fitting to assume that our concern is "really" a concern for the justification of propositions? And even where we are concerned with justification of the propositions we utter, are there not decisions and recommendations and hopes as it were *behind* those propositions? And is our justification of a proposition complete until we have justified the decisions which lie behind it?

Every word we use when we allow ourselves to talk in this way must be guarded against association with standard models which may be misleading. The most general and noncommittal term

## DISTRIBUTION OF EMPHASIS

which we can use to designate the object of such justification as we shall seek to render responsible is the word "interpretation." But noncommittal and vague though it is, this word too is associated with various standard models. We must loosen it up before we begin. The two most persistent models in terms of which we think of interpretation are a pyramidal model which is based on the notion of relating particular to general, and a synonymy model which is based on the notion of linguistic translation. Each of these models has serious limitations, and neither should function as an unvarying standard. We should be prepared to recognize that there are many different ways in which interpreting can proceed, and that no single model, nor even a limited set, can do full justice to the entire range.

There are many occasions on which we speak of interpreting the more particular by subsuming it under the more general; and there are also many occasions on which we speak of interpreting the general by applying it to the particular. Note that this is a two-way affair, and that interpreting may refer to proceeding in either direction. Even if we keep this in mind it is far from clear that when we refer to relating the particular and the general we have always the same kind of relation in mind. Applying a generalization about dogs to a particular cocker spaniel may involve thought processes quite unlike those involved in applying a general logical principle to a particular argument; and when we "apply" general theories about the nature of man by making specific proposals as to how we should act, we may be doing something importantly unlike either of these things. To say that interpretation involves relating particular and general may on occasion be singularly uninformative.

We often speak of interpreting as though it were essentially a search for synonymous expressions. Much of the preoccupation of philosophers in particular seems to be with the enterprise of saying in unfamiliar ways things that are generally accepted or taken for granted in their own way. On the whole, this is a two-way affair involving technical language and ordinary discourse. Some philosophers preoccupy themselves with translating the so-called truisms of common sense into highly technical and supposedly logically prior terminologies. Only so, it may be maintained, can we accurately interpret what is meant by those truisms. Other philosophers, who incline to distrust of technical terms, insist upon continuous translation of the deliverances of technical disciplines into ordinary English. Only so, it may be maintained, can we intelligently interpret the sense of what those disciplines are trying to say. In either case, interpreting is conceived as being rather like trying to say in German something that has been said in highly idiomatic French. We interpret by finding an entirely different way of saying the *same* thing.

Now there is a very broad sense of the word "interpretation" which neither of these models clearly represents. Most of the situations we seek to understand, and most of the problems we set ourselves to solve, are extremely complex. What is more, the background out of which we select the problems which interest us, the total mass of partially understood fact amidst which we isolate those segments which we seek to understand better, is nothing short of cosmic. There is a sense in which nothing so characterizes any attempt to interpret anything as the simple notion of distributing emphasis. *What* do we select to be precise about? *Which* particular facts and *which* generalizations interest us? When we emphasize deductive techniques we have to choose the axioms from which we will start; when we emphasize inductive techniques we have to focus our attention on certain facts rather than others; when we seek to translate meanings with precision we must start by meaning *something*, by focusing our attention somewhere.

The way in which we interpret anything is largely determined, is indeed constituted by, the way in which we distribute our emphasis. This may lie embedded in the very questions we ask; it may lie unnoticed in every willingness to accept a solution *as* a solution. The core of our way of interpreting generally lies behind our explicit efforts at deductive or inductive demonstration; it generally lies behind our attempts to sharpen up the language we use; indeed, it seldom reaches the level of explicit verbaliza-

## DISTRIBUTION OF EMPHASIS

tion. It is not accident that philosophers so often seek to state in words what functions in our thinking beneath the level of verbalization. *How* we interpret is largely a matter of *what* we focus our attention upon.

Justifying an interpretation in this sense is a task of justifying our distribution of emphasis. There is an analogy for this sort of thing which has been found increasingly attractive in recent years; but it must be stressed that the analogy is partial and may in its turn be very misleading. The analogy is found in the concept of the basic rules of a game. The basic rules of any game specify or determine what is thenceforth crucial in any attempt to play the game. Most games involve many optional rules as well—conventions which we may decide to use or not to use on occasion. There is generally much more talk about the conventions than about the basic rules. When we begin a game we *discuss* the conventions to be used; we *assume* that the basic rules will be followed. Similarly, if we set ourselves to engage in science or in art criticism, or, more vaguely, to provide a rational account of anything whatsoever, we operate both in terms of conventions which we announce with care and in terms of basic rules which we often simply assume as operative. These basic rules, whether we discuss them or not, are the key to what we are doing. We must justify *them* if we are to justify our science or our criticism or our rational undertaking.

There is much to be said for this analogy, and we will examine it in detail in the sequel; but a warning must be issued at once. Games are arbitrary. It does not matter whether we play them or not. The question what we must do if we are to play bridge properly arises only if we have already agreed to play the game. This is why we are satisfied to consider the basic rules of bridge either as a set of axioms from which we can deduce what any competent bridge player will do or as the result of an inductive empirical description of what all competent bridge players have as a matter of fact agreed to do. (This strange willingness to take *either* line will be of interest later.) It is because bridge is arbitrary that we can nonchalantly assume that unless you know the rules you simply cannot play the game.

Engaging in science, or undertaking to provide a rational account of something, is not quite so simple. If we persist in the game analogy, it is as though we must agree to play the game of science before we have any clear conception of which rules are basic. The attempt to find out what rules are basic is *part of the game* of trying to adopt a rational standpoint. This difference is connected with the fact that the attempt to adopt a scientific approach, or the attempt to achieve rational understanding, are not arbitrary goals. We formulate them with important purposes in mind, and if we conceive of them as games at all we must conceive of them as games which we are forced to play before we know what is involved in playing them well. This is why we are less inclined to accept a description of what all scientists *have* done as a prescription as to what we as scientists *must* do; and it is why we are less unanimous in specifying in advance a set of axiomatic rules from which we can deduce what any rational thinker will concede.

Justifying the way in which we distribute our emphasis in our intellectual undertakings may be both importantly like and importantly unlike justifying the basic rules of games. The background of any attempt to justify our way of interpreting is always ignorance, uncertainty, and fallibility. We simply do not know how best to understand the world; and when we seek to say what we must do to understand it better our "musts" are neither logical entailments nor testable hypotheses. They are simply *our* ways of calling attention to the coerciveness involved in certain kinds of emphasis. Justifying those musts will be a matter of justifying emphasis in the midst of confusion.

A closely related point is this: if we conceive of interpretation as a way of distributing emphasis, any attempt to justify an interpretation will involve us in a circle. Clearly, the way in which we interpret will determine what we will and what we will not accept as a justification, for in this sense the core of any interpretation is a series of commitments as to what justification will

## DISTRIBUTION OF EMPHASIS

involve. You cannot justify distribution of emphasis without distributing emphasis. If we are frightened by the notion of circularity we may shy clear of any question which forces circularity upon us. But the idea that all circles are vicious is a myth. On the contrary, we face here a circularity from which will emerge our principal insights into the nature of sound philosophical method. There is nothing frightening about the fact that all justification must be internal to an interpretative context.

All of this will bring us back to the three needs which we have cited. To begin with, we must continuously indulge in careful and painstaking analysis, but we must do so with an eye to what is important. We must never delude ourselves by thinking that analysis can be "mere." There is no such thing as a piece of analysis which avoids committing itself, however far beneath the surface, on all the issues which are important. To analyze *is* to distribute emphasis. Every analytic movement *is* a *Weltanschauung*. Secondly, the clarification of the "musts" of our intellectual life will require that we break down the supposition that analytic propositions and synthetic propositions are our only ways of talking good sense. When we commit ourselves, and especially when we seek to justify our commitments, we cannot confine ourselves to the logicians' boxes. Of all the problems we will face, none will surpass in importance that of clarifying the rules which should govern the proper use of such expressions as "must," "entails," or "we have no choice but." Finally, it will emerge in the doing of all this that we must drastically revise some of our most cherished preconceptions about the nature of rationality.

## CHAPTER TWO: THE PROBLEM IN POLITICAL PHILOSOPHY

A political proposal is a way of interpreting a complicated human situation; and the central problem of political philosophy is simply this: how are we to justify the political proposals we wish to make? We must face the fact that human problems are complicated enough to be read in wholly different ways. There is never one and only one proper way of reading them; but there are surely wrong ways of reading them; and we must try to state as clearly as we can our grounds for considering certain ways wrong and for rejecting them. We must try to state as clearly as we can the differences between political proposals which are rationally justifiable and those which are not.

The need for political philosophy arises from our own shortcomings. We do not know how to live together. We understand neither others nor ourselves. We are seldom able to state clearly what we "stand for." We are constantly forced to base our decisions on hunches, guesses, and hopes rather than on demonstrations, proofs, or certainties. Political philosophy is misconceived as a search for demonstrations, proofs, or certainties. What we need from political philosophers is sound advice as to how to make rationally justified decisions when we are dealing with hunches, guesses, and hopes.

There are two standard ways in which we have tried to conceive of justification in political theory. On the one hand, we have tried to show that our proposals "are logically entailed by," "can be deduced from" elaborate metaphysical theories concerning the nature of the world and the nature of man. On the other hand, we have tried to show that our proposals can be somehow supported by "scientific induction," "experimentalism," or "social engineering." These two standard ways of approaching the problems of political theory are in constant conflict. The pendulum swings from one to the other. But each way of approach, insofar as it recommends itself as the only alternative to the other, rests upon the same fundamental mistake—the mistake of supposing that there are only two ways of talking sense, two ways of rationally justifying our opinions. Political philosophy can learn much from increased application of scientific methods to social problems; but it cannot be reduced to a science. Political philosophy can always be stimulated (for good or bad) by bold metaphysical speculation of the traditional sort; but it cannot be reduced to a string of deduced theorems. The models of geometry and/or engineering simply will not do. We must get rid of the tacit assumption that proposals can only be rationally justified either by deductive demonstration or by experimental proof. If political philosophy is to succeed we *must* talk sense in ways other than tautologies and/or empirically testable hypotheses. We are dealing with a world of mottled grays; and we will continue to wreak havoc so long as we persist in mapping it out in black and white.

## I. *Piecemeal Engineering*

On the whole, political philosophers in English-speaking countries have been in recent years highly skeptical of any attempt to justify political proposals by deduction from elaborate metaphysical systems. The two most obvious exceptions are communism and Roman Catholicism. Each of these, of course, makes much of the distinction between means and ends. Both are remarkably flexible in their approach to questions of means, but both conceive of the end of political action as determined by or as deducible from large metaphysical doctrines. We shall be concerned to examine this practice in due course: to ask what dialectical materialism has to do with the attempt to "justify" the communists' proposals that we act in certain ways; to ask what a theocentric "two-layered" Christian view of man has to do with practical politics. Let us begin, however, with the other side of the picture. Let us begin with those who have no time whatsoever for the idea of justifying practical proposals by deduction from large and moving *Weltanschauungen*.

In a recent book by T. D. Weldon there occurs the following

remark: "I do not myself think that democracy or communism have foundations in any significant sense. By this I mean that the types of political organization called 'democracy,' 'fascism,' and 'communism' are usually said to rest on, or to be the expression of, distinct political philosophies or ideologies." The author thinks that this popular supposition is a mistake; types of political organization do not have foundations in any significant sense.[1]

What is meant by the word "foundations" here? Weldon consistently associates the idea of "foundations" with the idea of deducibility within an axiomatic system.

> What then are these foundations or principles which are so important and the subject of so much disagreement? . . . I have already suggested that they are closely connected with axioms and postulational systems. . . . Essentially the search for foundations is a search for proofs.[2]

Proofs are being thought of here in the mathematical sense. We are being told (do we really have to be?) that political proposals cannot be justified in the same way in which mathematical theorems are justified. Mathematical theorems are "justified" by demonstration that they can be deduced from given axioms; and one way in which we have conceived of the "foundations" of our beliefs has been on this analogy. There are of course very persuasive reasons for rejecting the idea that a proposal to act in one way rather than another can in any literal sense be "deduced" from any axioms whatsoever. We will ourselves be critical of this idea. But if we reject the idea that the foundations of political proposals are properly conceived on the geometrical model, we must take care lest we think we are rejecting more than we are. We often use the word "foundations" in a looser sense. Though we may be unable to deduce proposals to action in any strict sense, we most certainly do try to provide them with rational justification. Rejection of a misleading geometrical model

---

[1] T. D. Weldon, *The Vocabulary of Politics* (London: Penguin Books, 1953). See p. 84.
[2] *Ibid.*, p. 86.

PIECEMEAL ENGINEERING

of justification by deduction is not tantamount to the rejection of any and all attempts to justify.

Where does Weldon take us? His argument is that since political proposals cannot be justified as logical entailments of large and moving philosophical theories, they can only be justified, if at all, as confirmable empirical hypotheses.

> ... when verbal confusions are tidied up most of the questions of traditional political philosophy are not unanswerable. *All of them* are confused formulations of purely empirical difficulties. This does not mean that these are themselves easy to deal with, but it does mean that writers on political institutions and statesmen, not philosophers, are the proper people to deal with them. As empirical questions they do have answers, but the answers are neither simple nor demonstrably and incorrigibly true, nor can they be discovered by any process of non-empirical intuition.[3]

Weldon may here commit an error which is more disastrous than the error he is combatting. Even if it is an error to believe that political proposals can be justified by deduction, it is a more serious error to suppose that they must *either* be so justified *or* justified as empirically testable hypotheses. A large part of the defense of experimentalism in political theory consists simply in the rejection of aprioristic absolutism. We are presented with a dichotomy: either aprioristic absolutism or experimentalism; and when sufficient scorn has been heaped upon the former we are presumed to be faced with a new alternative: either experimentalism or no rational defense of our proposals at all.

Perhaps nowhere has this tendency been more evident, and incidentally more influential, than in the writings of John Dewey. Throughout his copious and repetitive writings Dewey has based the defense of his experimentalism upon the unargued claim that it is the only alternative to "absolutism," to "mere definition and classification," to "dogmatism," to the "anti-empirical," to "ex-

[3] *Ibid.*, pp. 192-193. Italics are mine.

clusive concern for a presumed superior reality." Dewey says of his philosophy:

> It breaks completely with that part of the philosophical tradition which holds that concern with superior reality determines the work to be done by philosophical enquiry. . . . It holds that not grasp of eternal and universal Reality but use of the methods and conclusions of our best knowledge, that called scientific, provides the means for conducting this search.[4]

The same implied dichotomy runs throughout his defense of experimentalism in moral theory—one of his most constant concerns. He insists that any rejection of his point of view

> . . . would involve the commitment to a dogmatic theory of morals. The alternative method may be called experimental.[5]

> The alternative is . . . between a morals which is effective because related to what is, and a morality which is futile and empty because framed in disregard of actual conditions.[6]

Now, nobody wants to be told that his cogitations on moral theory "disregard actual conditions," but it is sheer nonsense to claim that *either* you disregard actual conditions *or* you concede the game to experimentalism. Experimentalism insists upon treating all respectable theories as empirically confirmable hypotheses. Surely we can share the fullest possible regard for actual conditions and yet deny that all respectable theories are empirically confirmable hypotheses. Dewey's position rests upon the unexamined premise that unless we are testing propositions which evidence will confirm or confute we can only be indulging in empty definition and word-play.

Dewey's general attitude toward philosophy and toward moral theory sets the stage for his treatment of social theory. Here again he rests his case on the assumption that we must either

[4] John Dewey, *Problems of Men* (New York: Philosophical Library, 1946), pp. 10-11.
[5] John Dewey and James H. Tufts, *Ethics* (New York: Henry Holt and Co., 1932), p. 364.
[6] *Ibid.*, p. 367.

## PIECEMEAL ENGINEERING

consider social theory as a search for empirically testable hypotheses or give way to the horrors of absolutism. He insists that

> ... policies and proposals for social action be treated as working hypotheses, not as programs to be rigidly adhered to and executed. They will be experimental in the sense that they will be entertained subject to constant and well-equipped observation of the consequences they entail when acted upon, and subject to ready and flexible revision in the light of observed consequences.[7]

If this is done

> The social sciences ... will then be an apparatus for conducting investigation, and for recording and interpreting (organizing) its results.[8]

The upshot of all this is that social experimentation must *precede* social theory; and it will be noted in the above quotations that the "experiments" on which social science is to be based are in fact experiments with our policies. Dewey is quite unambiguous about this. The policies which emanate from Washington, D.C., should be provisional (as all good hypotheses should be) and social theory must follow upon, rather than precede, actual trial and error.

> The point I am making may be summed up by saying that it is a complete error to suppose that efforts at social control depend upon the prior existence of a social science. The reverse is the case. The building up of social science, that is, of a body of knowledge in which facts are ascertained in their significant relations, is dependent upon putting social planning into effect.[9]

---

[7] John Dewey, *The Public and Its Problems* (London: Allen and Unwin, n.d.), pp. 202-203.
[8] *Ibid.*, p. 203.
[9] From *The New Republic*, July 29, 1931; reprinted in *Intelligence and the Modern World*, ed. Joseph Ratner (New York: Random House, 1939), p. 951.

Now, there is no doubt something attractive about this. When we remember that Dewey was reacting against an age of Hegelianism, we are inclined to applaud. His proposals seem down-to-earth and hopeful. By and large, the American nation responded; or perhaps Dewey himself was responding to a national temper already clamoring for his articulation. Unfortunately he—and the nation—went too far.

Experiment requires the context of a theory. Dewey's version of empiricism rests upon an oversimplification. It is simply false to suppose that we must choose between two clear-cut alternatives: either an unanchored theory prior to any experiment, or no theory at all until the results of experimentation are in. There is as much reason for saying "no experiment without a prior theory" as for saying "no theory without prior experiment"; and both admonitions can be misleading. In one sense, no one could recognize this more clearly than Dewey himself. He knows perfectly well that experiment requires the context of a theory. Yet his insistence that no theory is respectable, that no theory is deserving of attention, unless it is related to "actual conditions" is continually metamorphosed into the demand that theories must be treated as hypotheses. This shift conceals the error which invalidates most of what Dewey has to say. In concerning ourselves with actual conditions we do not have to confine ourselves, indeed we *cannot* confine ourselves, to experimental hypotheses.

Few things are easier than the pouring of scorn upon deductive absolutism. Yet, because deductive dogmatism is barren, it does not follow that inductive generalization is a panacea. Dewey hypnotizes his audience into believing that we really do face a clear-cut choice between what he often calls "working down from above" and "working up from below." Once they are in this hypnotic state he convinces them that the *only* respectable intellectual quest is the search for testable empirical hypotheses. He assumes that to deny this is tantamount to endorsing deductive absolutism. That is simply a mistake; it ignores the vast middle ground. Must we overestimate social science in order to applaud it; and must we assume that the only alternative to social science is dogmatic absolutism? There are more than two ways of talking sense. It is a fantastic mistake to suppose that if our political proposals are not demonstrable consequences of eternal verities they must either be empirical hypotheses or wholly irresponsible.

It is a mistake, moreover, which has caused untold practical harm. We have been blinded by the general term "experimentation." There are experiments and experiments. The parallels between social science and physics can be overdrawn. When you are "experimenting" with national and international policies, the "stuff" with which you are dealing may alter the whole notion of experimenting. We have been rather fascinated with the idea that conducting an international policy is something like experimenting; and we have been tempted to say that we (the United States) will justify our policy abroad by showing that it works. It takes time to learn the lesson (it has taken the United States several decades, and the lesson is still not fully assimilated) that in international politics our policies simply *will not work* unless we put them into operation on the basis of independent grounds of conviction. National policies must be capable of withstanding the shock of apparent failure. We cannot wait upon experiment. We are here dealing with human beings. The very material we are experimenting with is demanding justification from us. It is as though the neutrons and electrons in a physical laboratory stopped and proclaimed: "See here, we won't budge in cooperation until you give us some ground for supposing that your experiment is going to work." The influence of pragmatism in American political life has been disastrous. We had lost our faith in ideas; and now that we realize how desperately we need them, we find that we have lost our hold upon them. We have been so intent upon making our policies work, that we have let slip the convictions which are the prior condition of their working.

Karl Popper, in his influential book *The Open Society and Its Enemies*, has manifested a greater sensitivity to the complexity of the situation than Dewey did. Popper has been severely criticized as a bad historian. There can be no doubt that his treatment of Plato and Hegel, and to a lesser degree of Aristotle, is based on extremely careless scholarship. At the same time, the learned attacks upon his scholarship invariably leave his main points untouched. For all his textual errors he is, in general, correct about the insidious tendencies in Platonism, in Hegelianism, and in Marxism.

Popper is sensitive to the problems we have in mind. He is aware that we have overplayed the game of justification in political theory. Unlike Dewey, he is a superbly clear writer, careful in his analysis of science and perceptive of the differences between the physical and the social sciences. Unfortunately he ends by committing the same fundamental error as Dewey.[10]

Popper is a member of what is usually called the "positivist" tradition. This tradition has been varied and changeable, and one generalizes about it at one's peril. But historically there can be no question that much of the tradition has hinged upon an attempt to formulate technically the same dichotomy which we have noticed in Dewey. The so-called "verifiability theory of meaning" has been the clearest example in twentieth-century philosophy of the tendency to insist that there are only two ways of talking good sound sense. The original expressions of that theory boldly asserted that anything other than the tautologous-analytic or the empirically verifiable is "meaningless." While later developments have conceded a wider range to the word "meaning," they have generally persisted in the assumption that other kinds of meaning are "non-cognitive" or "merely emotive." The dichotomy persists in one's conception of what constitutes rational and respectable discourse.

Popper has been unable to break away from this tradition. The assumption of a clear-cut alternative for respectable "cogni-

[10] I have, in general, little good to say about Dewey. In all candor, therefore, I think it should be pointed out how far ahead of his time he was. Recent positivists, and especially the linguistic philosophers, are repeatedly making "discoveries" with their elaborate methodological machinery which Dewey, in his no doubt blundering and heavy-footed way, made long ago. For all my antipathy to Dewey, and for all my conviction that many of these very points are utterly wrong-headed, I must concede that this is a measure of Dewey's greatness.

## PIECEMEAL ENGINEERING

tive" discourse hamstrings him again and again. Because of it, he repeatedly fails to grasp the importance of the very conclusions to which what he is saying points. In the end he commits himself to an approach which is indistinguishable from Dewey's. Compare, for example, the following passage with those already extracted from Dewey:

> The only course open to the social sciences is to forget all about the verbal fireworks and to tackle the practical problems of our time with the help of the theoretical methods which are fundamentally the same in *all* sciences. I mean the methods of trial and error, of inventing hypotheses which can be practically tested, and of submitting them to practical tests. In other words, *a social technology is needed whose results can be tested by social engineering.*[11]

Elsewhere, and more often, he calls what he is recommending "piecemeal engineering." The key word in the passage quoted is the word "hypotheses," which Popper is clearly using, not in a vague uncritical sense, but in the technical sense of propositions capable of experimental verification. Like Dewey, he is working with the dichotomy: *either* mere verbal fireworks, *or* testable hypotheses. The middle ground is again ignored.[12]

And yet not wholly ignored. Popper's assumptions seem to conceal from him the importance of what he himself sometimes says. That this is so comes out nowhere more clearly than in his remarks on the issue between rationalism and irrationalism. I have suggested that it is a mistake to assume that we are rational only when we enunciate tautologies and empirical hypotheses. If one makes that mistaken assumption, and then recognizes that we simply cannot confine ourselves to those two ways of talking, one begins to think that something called "irrationalism" is in-

[11] *The Open Society and Its Enemies* (London: Routledge and Sons, 1945), Vol. II, p. 210. [Princeton: Princeton University Press, 1950, p. 407.] Italics are Popper's own.

[12] As usual in matters of this kind, the key words ("only" and "hypotheses"), on which the argument hinges, are not among those placed in italics. It is simply false that the *only* course other than verbal fireworks is inventing testable hypotheses.

23

escapable. In fact, our inability to confine ourselves to tautologies and confirmable predictions has nothing whatsoever to do with the issue between rationalism and irrationalism. That issue concerns our ways of justifying the decisions we make and the advice we give, and it is an issue which is most pressing precisely when we are *not* concerned with questions which we can answer as logicians or as scientists.

Let us examine Popper's remarks about rationalism. He begins with a general statement of what he means by the word. I find nothing to criticize in this general statement:

> We could then say that rationalism is an attitude of readiness to listen to critical arguments and to learn from experience. It is fundamentally an attitude of admitting that "*I may be wrong and you may be right, and by an effort, we may get nearer to the truth.*"[13]

Obviously, Popper is not here defining the word "rationalism" as it is ordinarily used in histories of philosophy, where it is used as a label for Descartes, Spinoza, and Leibniz as contrasted with Locke, Berkeley, and Hume. That is a special usage of the word which does not here concern us. Popper is defining "rationalism" as a synonym for the phrase "the attempt to be rational," which, I agree, is a more important use of the word.

Now, there can be no objection to including in one's account of any attempt to be rational the idea of readiness to learn from experience. What is more, so long as we are talking in a vague and imprecise way, it is natural enough to be led by the phrase "learn from experience" to use of the word "empiricism." Popper, at any rate, begins to use the words "rationalism" and "empiricism" as synonyms. If "empiricism" continued to mean (very vaguely) "readiness to learn from experience" the shift would be innocuous, but in Popper it does not so continue. It soon becomes evident that empiricism is being conceived as the demand that *all* non-tautologies be treated either as testable hypotheses or as emotive trimmings. The moment this more precise

[13] *Ibid.*, II, 213 [Princeton, p. 411]; Popper's italics.

## PIECEMEAL ENGINEERING

version of "empiricism" comes into use, "empiricism" and "the attempt to be rational" cease to be synonymous.

One may surely be as worried as Popper by "irrationalist" tendencies in recent philosophy, without agreeing that we face as clear-cut a choice as he seems to suppose. Popper means by "rationalism" piecemeal engineering; he means by "irrationalism" irresponsible emotionalism, sometimes called by him "mysticism." There is no doubt *a* sense in which we face no more basic choice than that between rationalism and irrationalism; but it is simply misleading to talk as though we must either be visionary mystics or scientists, irresponsible emoters or engineers.

Drawing the contrast as sharply as he does, Popper runs into difficulty. He recognizes that in his limited sense rationalism (i.e., empiricism) is not self-sufficient. In short, we *cannot*, when we leave the happily barren fold of logic, confine ourselves to testable hypotheses. The fatal conclusion results that rationalism is itself irrational.

> ... whoever adopts the rationalist attitude does so because without reasoning he has adopted some decision, or belief, or habit, or behaviour, which therefore in its turn must be called irrational. Whatever it may be, we can describe it as an irrational *faith in reason*. Rationalism is therefore far from comprehensive or self-contained.[14]

Popper is far from happy about this conclusion, and calls himself a "critical rationalist" in a spirit of compromise which may be disappointing to one who has applauded the earlier and looser definition of "rationalism."

The core of his difficulty is his own unconscious shift from a vague sense of the word "rationalism" (willingness to change one's mind and learn from experience) to a technical sense of the same word (confining oneself to the results of precise inductive tests). Consider how one might rephrase the passage just cited:

> Whoever adopts a careful inductive approach (to political

[14] *Ibid.*, II, 218 [Princeton, p. 416]; Popper's italics.

problems) does so because he has made certain decisions (i.e., has distributed emphasis in certain ways) which cannot be treated as testable hypotheses. Is there any reason for conceiving of these decisions as irrational? No doubt we must admit that an inductive empiricist approach is far from comprehensive or self-contained; but a careful rational attitude will in that case require attention to the kind of justification which can be provided for decisions and attitudes which are not properly expressed in propositional form at all.

We can approach a problem rationally without demanding that all sense is either definitional or verifiable; and when we recognize that much of what we say—with sense—is neither, we need not sadly admit an element of "irrationalism." We are not irrationalists because we admit the need for more than testable hypotheses. The distinction between rationalism and irrationalism is mainly apparent in the way in which we interpret just those elements in our theories which are neither tautologous nor "strictly" empirical. Freed from its entanglement with a fatal sense of dichotomy, Popper's "critical" rationalism could be read as an endorsement of this. He could reject irrationalism more boldly and with less compromise, if he were willing to abandon the mistaken idea that *only* tautologies and empirical hypotheses are rational.

The same fundamental point could be illustrated again and again, but I shall confine myself to one further example. When he discusses the study of history Popper seems prepared at first to grant the intelligibility of something very close to what I have briefly described as "interpretation." He seems to recognize that historical interpretations, rightly conceived, cannot be treated either as deductive or scientifically inductive.

> I shall call such historical theories, in contradistinction to scientific theories, *interpretations*.
>
> Interpretations are important since they represent a point of view.[15]

[15] *Ibid.*, II, 252 [Princeton, p. 449]; Popper's italics.

## PIECEMEAL ENGINEERING

This is very hopeful; and yet within four pages hope is dimming. By "hopeful" I mean that promise is given of recognizing that often an interpretation which is irreducible to the simplified canons of deduction or induction may nonetheless count as rational justification. Consider, however, the following:

> Instead of recognizing that historical interpretation should answer a need arising out of the practical problems and decisions which face us, the historicist believes that in our desire for historical interpretation, there expresses itself the profound intuition that by contemplating history we may discover the secret, the essence of human destiny.[16]

This is discouraging. Once more we are back with the dichotomy. We must either be pragmatists or mystics. We must either engage in inductive engineering or dogmatically proclaim God's-eye visions. Popper constantly leads us to the vast middle ground of mottled gray, then doggedly maps it out in black and white.[17]

This is discouraging; for Popper does not, I think, commit such absurdities as either Weldon or Dewey. Weldon, in a passage I have quoted, denies to philosophers the privilege of solving the "purely empirical difficulties" to which "all" of the "questions of political philosophy" reduce. He confines philosophers to the role of straightening out linguistic muddles, a role which, if we are to judge from his own practice, may blind them to the limitations of the scientific approach to political problems. Dewey, not being a linguist, preferred to change philosophers into social scientists. Both agree that political proposals must always be treated as empirical hypotheses. Popper, for all his devotion to the "piecemeal engineering" of social science, recognizes that

---

[16] *Ibid.*, II, 256 [Princeton, p. 452].

[17] Perhaps I will be forgiven one additional example in a footnote. Often a single sentence is sufficient to indicate the presupposition in terms of which Popper is working. In Volume II on page 208 [Princeton, p. 406] he says: "Both Kantians and Hegelians make the same mistake of assuming that our presuppositions . . . can neither be changed by decision nor refuted by experience." Notice the two alternatives. Popper clearly means by "decision" the decision involved in setting up axioms and definitions. He is once again working with the idea that, *if* they make sense at all, what Kantians mean by "presuppositions" must be either tautologies or testable.

27

there are limits to this. He is sensible enough to see that we cannot empirically test everything. He rightly conceives of the philosopher's role as one of constant "moral decision."[18] Earlier he has boldly admitted that his rejection of Platonism rests upon commitment to certain principles of procedure, and he lists those principles. They are not definitions, and they are not empirical hypotheses. But unfortunately his devotion to an arbitrary mode of classification makes him treat moral decisions as emotive rather than cognitive.[19] If we sense that this is a mistake, the whole problem of "justifying" political proposals will be reoriented for us. It comes then to this: that there is no excuse for dubbing what is untestable as " merely" emotive; and a philosopher should do more than announce his decisions, he should justify them.

## II. *Justification by Deduction*

Thus far we have been assuming without argument that there is something wrong with any attempt to solve the questions of political theory in a strictly deductive way. We have conceded this to those who advocate a program of inductive engineering; and we have argued solely that the inappropriateness of a deductive model of justification is no guaranty that the problems of political theory must either be settled by inductive engineering or not at all.

As a matter of fact, the model of justification by deduction has been subject to attack not only by those who worship at the shrine of inductive engineering. Albert Schweitzer, for example, in his *The Philosophy of Civilization* insists that neither one's conception of the world as a whole nor one's commitments as to social action can be defended on the model of mathematics. He also insists, however, that they cannot be supported on the model of inductive engineering. This is the real force of his argument

---

[18] *Ibid.*, p. 227 [Princeton, p. 425].
[19] I shall have more to say about recent uses of the labels "cognitive" and "non-cognitive." See below, pp. 164ff. They are examples of a kind of label which one finds puzzling in this respect: that one is never certain whether they are intended as *defined by* the tables of classification in which they are used or *add something* to the import of such tables.

## JUSTIFICATION BY DEDUCTION

throughout the first volume of *The Philosophy of Civilization*: that *neither* induction *nor* deduction can serve as a model for what is required in order to justify a man's basic commitments in any attempt to solve or to answer broad cultural or moral or metaphysical problems. In one sense there is nothing new about the idea that philosophy errs whenever it restricts itself too exclusively to the models either of mathematics or of experimental physics or of both. But even where these models have been considered most suspect their spell has not ceased to exert influence. Thus Schweitzer in the preface to the second volume of his work, when summing up the general conceptions expressed in the first volume, repeatedly announces that the force of his conclusions is somehow to demonstrate the necessity of the "non-rational."

> If rational thought thinks itself out to a conclusion, it arrives at something non-rational which, nevertheless, is a necessity of thought.[20]

Now, to express the conclusion that the justification of our beliefs and commitments cannot always be on the models either of strict logical deduction or strict experimental induction, by saying that the non-rational is a necessity of thought, may be very misleading. It might be less misleading to say that we have misconceived what the requirements of reason are. We have been oversimplifying. We have been mistaken in supposing that we are rational only when we are either deducing or inducing.

Schweitzer reveals that he is as influenced by the models of mathematics and engineering as is Popper. The step from "non-rational" to "irrational" is very short; and to say that either is unavoidable simply because we cannot prove what we need to say in either of the traditional senses of "prove" is to reveal a rigid conception of the requirements of reason which is certainly a mistake. Most of what we refer to as "existentialist" thinking at the present time plays upon a "hangover" conception of what

[20] Albert Schweitzer, *The Philosophy of Civilization*. II: *Civilization and Ethics* (London: Adams and Charles Black, 1949), p. xix.

being rational consists in. Most existentialist thinkers rightly see that philosophers have too meekly acquiesced in adopting the models of mathematics and/or empirical science; but most have wrongly used this insight as justification for a flight from reason. At heart they concede the game to those "positivists" who insist that there are only two ways of talking rationally. The concession is disastrous; for having rightly seen that there are other ways in which we must talk, the concession generates silence as to our crucial task. Instead of trying as clear-headedly as possible to specify canons for responsible justification, the existentialists revel in an orgy of freedom which masquerades under the disguise of the new respectability of "irrationalism."

All of this is a restatement of what we have already proclaimed as one of our major themes: the need for redefining the demands of reason. But beneath the surface there is a further problem which we cannot afford to ignore. The Weldons and the Schweitzers of the present time are at one in rejecting the model of justification by deduction. Our proposals concerning political action, and more generally the commitments we continuously make in deciding how to face any human situation, are somehow wrongly conceived as deducible in any strict sense from elaborate sets of metaphysical axioms. So much has been written in recent decades in support of the claim that programs of action cannot be deduced from over-pretentious metaphysical doctrines, that it would seem superfluous to add fuel to the fire. What may not be superfluous, however, is to ask why it is important that this be shown. Who says that political proposals *can*, in any strict sense, be "deduced" from general theories?

The problem may be briefly stated in the following way: A great deal of what passes as political theory is written in a tone which suggests the notion of strict logical deducibility. Political theory bristles with such idioms as "since (followed by some highly general metaphysical comment), therefore we must . . . ," or "unless (some large theory be true), there is no basis for doing so and so," or "if (again followed by an enormous idea), then we cannot avoid or we have no choice but. . . ." It is not

## JUSTIFICATION BY DEDUCTION

surprising that such idioms suggest the idea that what is transpiring somehow conforms to the model of mathematical deduction. It is therefore important that someone show in detail the failure to conform. The idioms we have cited virtually always function in political theory in a loose and inexact way. When you take the trouble to be precise, the "musts" involved are scarcely ever logical "musts." And this means that anyone who in using such phrases *thinks* he is deducing in any strict sense is just downright mistaken. What he is doing is not deduction at all but something else. This fact, however, cuts two ways. Demonstration that what is transpiring is not strict deduction in no sense demonstrates that what is transpiring is irresponsible hocus-pocus. The kind of phrases to which we are calling attention may have important and responsible uses other than the strictly logical. A political thinker who believes he is deducing in any strict sense simply because he uses such phrases may be grievously mistaken; but a political thinker is equally mistaken who believes he has rendered all such phrases obsolete by showing that in certain of their most important uses they do not express a logical relation of deducibility.

Candor is essential here. In the main, there are three ways of approaching the problems of political theory which philosophers have had in mind when they have attacked "justification by deduction." First, there is Hegelianism, which, though now relatively dormant in English-speaking countries, is recent enough (as a dominant force in political philosophy) to continue to evoke passionate reaction. Secondly, and not unrelated to Hegelianism, there is Marxism. Thirdly, there is Roman Catholicism. Now, if you look carefully at the writings of the leading representatives of these ways of approaching political problems, you will find that they seldom use the word "deduce," and when they do use the word it is generally pretty clear that they do not intend it in the strict mathematical sense. One does not find Hegelians saying bluntly that Hegel's theory of the state can be "deduced" from his metaphysics. They are more apt to say that a certain view of the state, or certain political proposals, "follow from" or "are entailed by" certain metaphysical beliefs. "Follows from" is a very vague phrase; and "is entailed by" is a much looser phrase than "is logically (in the strict sense) entailed by." Similarly, Catholic philosophers like Jacques Maritain do not say that the rights of man can be "deduced" from a Thomist world view. They are more apt to say that there simply "are not" any rights "unless" a Christian version of man's twofold nature is true.[21] Marxists do use the word "deduce" a great deal, but one finds on closer inspection that they usually use the word as a rough and ready synonym of "predict."[22] Much of the pseudoscientific character of Marxism rests upon entirely untenable assumptions regarding the relation between deducing and predicting;[23] but *it is surely unrealistic to think that one can silence a Marxian by demonstrating this.* In the last analysis, Marxists are trying to say that if you see the grand truths of dialectical materialism you simply *will* see the inevitability of certain political or societal ends. I cannot believe that they will be cured of saying this by demonstrations that it is not properly spoken of as "deduction."

[21] See, e.g., Jacques Maritain, *Man and the State* (Chicago: University of Chicago Press, 1951), p. 96: "In other words there is no right unless a certain order—which can be violated in fact—is inviolably required by *what things are* in their intelligible type or their essence, or by what the nature of man is, and is cut out for."

[22] See, e.g., Lenin's remark: "Marx deduces the inevitability of the transformation. . . ." *The Teachings of Karl Marx* (New York: International Publishers, 1930), p. 29.

[23] The Marxists' use of the words "deduce" and "predict" as synonyms shows a complete failure to understand the role played by deduction in predicting. It is true that in order to make predictions we must perform certain deductions; but it does not follow that predictions *are* deductions. If every man I have ever observed has in fact been mortal, I may generalize to the hypothesis that all men are mortal. (If I were *very* careful I would say "most men" rather than "all men.") Now, my prediction that John Jones is going to die depends in some sense upon my performing the deduction: All men are mortal, John Jones is a man, therefore John Jones is mortal. It does not follow, however, that my prediction that John Jones is going to die is itself a deduction. It is a *guess* (a very good guess) which is *based upon* a long train of argument one step of which is the deduction just cited. When Marxists refer to their predictions as "deductions" they slur over this difference. *No* prediction has the certainty of a deductive demonstration.

## JUSTIFICATION BY DEDUCTION

Suppose that you succeeded for once and for all in demonstrating the impossibility of "deducing" either specific proposals or general recommendations to action from elaborate *Weltanschauungen*. In one sense, such a demonstration would be doomed from the start; for it is inconceivable that it would convince any of the culprits at whom it was aimed. They would all obviously reply that in the strict sense, the impossibility of which you have demonstrated, they never said that you *could* "deduce." They will say that they have not been indulging in mathematical demonstrations; they have simply been providing their political proposals with a theoretical justification. They may even claim that what they have been doing is "interpreting" in the sense which I have briefly described in Chapter One. They may insist that the phrase "is entailed by" is not always synonymous with the phrase "is deducible from" (i.e., "is *logically* entailed by"); and they may claim that what their critics condemn as impossible deductions are not deductions in the strict sense at all. One way of putting all this is to note that the "musts" of political theory are generally closer akin to the "oughts" of ethics than to the "therefores" of logic and mathematics.

The reason political theory is such a difficult subject is that political philosophers are seldom precise, and when you *make* them precise they can always say that you have not understood what they meant. If a man says vaguely that one thing he says is entailed by something else he is saying, it is sanguine to suppose that you automatically silence him by showing that he cannot deduce the one from the other. "Is entailed by" has a wide range of uses.

One occasionally feels that those who attack the deductive approach to the problems of political theory are more inclined to proceed deductively than those whom they are attacking. Weldon, for example, insists (no doubt rightly) that in one important sense of the word "ought" there is no linguistic bridge between "is" and "ought to be."[24] He seems at times to talk as

---

[24] See *op.cit.*, p. 192. "In one sense of 'ought' there is no bridge from 'is' to 'ought to be,' and it makes no sense to say that there might be."

though one can "deduce" from this fact the conclusion that certain political proposals "ought not" to be made. No doubt Weldon would reply that the word "deduce" is out of place here, or he might insist (I think wrongly) that a different sense of "ought" is here implied; but it does not seem to have occurred to him earlier that the "deducers" he was attacking might have made the same kind of reply. It is always dangerous to criticize someone for "deducing" when he has not used the word.

Another criticism of the so-called "deductive" approach which seems to me to fail in its object is one which is popular among the pragmatists when they review the history of political ideas in the United States. It runs somewhat as follows: We note if we study American history that certain practical ideals in action lead a remarkably steady and constant life. We may, if we like, designate these constants by the usual slippery terms found in political orations, like "freedom," "equality," "justice for all," and so forth. These terms may be slippery, but if you study the facts of history they designate relatively constant purposes in action. We note also that at various times these purposes have been "justified" by the most amazing variety of totally unlike but equally pretentious "metaphysics"—in 1690 by the whole apparatus of Calvinist Puritanism; in 1750 to 1800 by a mixture of Lockeism, excessive Newtonianism, French Encyclopedism, and the shallow metaphysics of deism; in 1840 by the wild transcendental orgies of Emerson; in the late nineteenth century by the cosmic evolutionists, by Hegelian idealists, and by the early metaphysical pragmatists; to name only a few highlights. Clearly what is important here, so the argument runs, is the relative constancy of the practical aims; the metaphysical periphery, with all its kaleidoscopic change, is quite irrelevant. Sensible pragmatists will slough off the periphery as so much chaff and concentrate on the manageable kernel of the problem—namely, how best to put those practical aims into working effect.

Now, what does this argument accomplish? For the most part, the facts on which it rests are so obvious that one wonders why they need be pointed out. Certainly we have from decade to

## JUSTIFICATION BY DEDUCTION

decade sought to justify our practical ideals in terms of extraordinarily different metaphysical ideas; and yet, as certainly, there has been a discernible constancy about those ideals. What does this prove? In the first place, it has nothing whatsoever to do with the question whether from theoretical premises we can or cannot deduce specific proposals concerning action. If recommendations concerning action *were* deducible from metaphysical theories, there is not the slightest reason why the same recommendation might not be deducible from a variety of theories. Many geometrical propositions can be deduced equally well from Euclidean, Riemannian, or Lobatchewskyan axioms. In the second place, disregarding for the moment the question of supposed deducibility, the fact that at different times we defend our ideals in different ways in no way implies that at any given time we would have been better off had we attempted no theoretical defense at all. The fact that many different theories have been proposed as supports for democracy in no way implies that none of them does in fact support it, nor does it imply that no support is preferable to several.

It is true that if we use the word "deduce" strictly, it is an egregious mistake to suppose that recommendations to act in certain ways can be deduced from general theories. It is also true that when Hegelians, Marxists, and Thomists speak of their particular political and social proposals as "entailed by" or "following from" their large and pretentious metaphysical doctrines they are guilty of irresponsible hocus-pocus. But we must be alert to the fact that there are two points here, not one. The first is generally easy to show; the second may be difficult. When we examine these three ism-bound ways of approaching the problems of political theory, I believe that we can make short shrift of the claim (if anyone has ever made it) that political proposals are being deduced from metaphysical theories; but in each case it requires considerable care to see where the real hocus-pocus of the entailment recommendations lies.

There are then two quite different and equally important tasks which are forced upon us by the use of entailment phrases in political theory. There *is* the task of making clear the difference between the rules governing the proper use of such phrases and the rules of strict deduction; but this involves the further task of being clear about the rules which *do* govern their proper use. It is not enough to be clear only about the rules of deduction. Non-clarity as to the alternative rules may lead us either (1) to assume too hastily that there are no further rules and hence that where deduction fails no responsible thought is being expressed or (2) to capitalize upon the non-clarity of alternative rules in such a way that we really *are* irresponsible when performing something other than deduction. The latter alternative generates mistakes which a Weldon or a Dewey may properly expose; but the former alternative generates a different kind of mistake which a Weldon or a Dewey may unwittingly commit.

When the matter is put in this way, there might seem to be but one sensible method of procedure. The first requirement is to formulate and record the rules which do govern the proper use of these entailment phrases. We could then see at once the difference between these rules and the rules governing logical entailment; and we could easily spot any case in which the non-logical rules were themselves being violated. Unfortunately the matter is not this easy. Indeed, so to assume involves us in the mistake of *oversimplifying an intellectual problem and ignoring our own* inevitable shortcomings. We cannot *start* by listing the rules which govern non-logical uses of entailment expressions. Our problems are generated by the fact that we do not know those rules to begin with. The only course open to us is a course of careful case studies. We must see *in detail* first in what sense or senses such idioms as "must" or "entails" have uses other than those customarily labeled "logical uses," and secondly what the differences are between responsible and irresponsible use of such idioms in their non-logical contexts. Only then will we be in a position to formulate anything remotely resembling rules. At the moment we do not know what the rules are.

Hegelians, Marxists, and neo-Thomists are trying, like a great many other people, to justify certain proposals concerning action.

## JUSTIFICATION BY DEDUCTION

They do so by constant reference to elaborate systematic conceptions of the nature of the world as a whole. What rules govern this constant reference? Can we show clearly that there are mistakes of reasoning committed, and that in some sense rules of responsible reasoning are being violated? I shall begin in the following section with a simplified case study taken from the Hegelian or near-Hegelian tradition; but before I do so I must first record certain principles which will govern my own remarks. I shall have more to say about these principles in subsequent chapters. At the moment they are recorded not as fiats unopen to question, but simply as preliminary conceptions setting the tone of our initial investigations. I have in mind three such principles:

First: one of the primary characteristics of any *Weltanschauung* worth considering is its capacity to provide a linguistic recipe for describing *any* fact with which it is confronted. It is not an accident that we are unable to adjudicate between rival metaphysical theories by experiment. In one sense, the whole point of a metaphysical theory is that it provides, if it is successful, a set of terms general enough to enable one to discuss anything whatsoever. Some people are suspicious of metaphysical theories for this very reason; but such suspicion raises further questions which do not concern us at the moment. All that concerns us at the moment is that a *Weltanschauung*, if it *were* successful, would provide a linguistic recipe for discussing and describing anything whatsoever. (Note: I am not saying that this is *all* a metaphysical theory is; but that it is at least this is certain.)

Second: strict rules of logical entailment will govern much of what we do in working out the details of any *Weltanschauung*, but will be powerless as a leverage for recommending the *Weltanschauung*. By this I simply mean that if we accept a highly general terminology we will in applying it to specific cases invoke the usual canons of consistency with respect to discourse. But any of the standard metaphysical terminologies *can* be consistently employed. To *recommend* one such form of discourse as opposed to another requires more than the appeal to consistency.

Third: the problem of recommending any *Weltanschauung* as a whole and the problem of recommending any specific proposal (either descriptive or otherwise) with which one seeks to associate that *Weltanschauung* are not two different problems such that one passes from one to the other either deductively or inductively. To recommend a general conception of the world *is* to recommend making one's proposals in one way rather than another; but it simultaneously *is* to recommend just those proposals (descriptive or otherwise) rather than others. As we shall see, it is this fact more than any other which complicates the requirements for sound and responsible recommendations. It should be added at once that it is the enterprise of *recommending* which forces us into the use of entailment idioms. The "must" and the "no choice but" of speculation are closer to the "ought" of ethics than to the "strictly entails" of logic or the "weight of evidence" of engineering.

Anyone who seeks to communicate any idea must satisfy the canons of consistency. Weldon, Dewey, Popper, and Schweitzer will seek consistency no less than Spinoza. In this sense, the performance of any writer is governed by rules of deduction; and this will provide us with ammunition for accusing *anyone* of justification by deduction. And especially where one encounters any attempt to be consistent with a way of approach inimical to one's own, one will be tempted to assume that every "must" and every "entails" expresses merely a logical requirement imposed by an alien and avoidable terminology. When we try to isolate uses of "must" and "entails" which are not strictly logical, we must never forget that *any* use will have an element of logic about it. Such idioms will always say in part that once you adopt a certain kind of terminology you have the wherewithal for making proposals in a certain way. We need only grant this, and then see what *more* is being said.

I have said that one mark of a powerful *Weltanschauung* is the presence of a terminology such that one can formulate in it any proposal, descriptive or recommendatory, which one wishes to make. The choice between two conflicting proposals made in any such terminology cannot be adjudicated solely on grounds

AN EXAMPLE

of consistency; and this, as we shall see, is the principal reason why justification by deduction from *Weltanschauungen* tends to be barren. A proposal is not *justified* merely by showing that it can be expressed in any such highly general terminology. The kind of justification required in political theory is never *merely* a matter of showing that a specific proposal can be expressed in a special terminology; it is never *merely* a matter of justifying a terminology by showing that certain proposals can be stated therein. The kind of justification required is always one of justifying a terminology and a proposal *all at once* as providing in some sense a recommendation capable of eliciting our efforts and our energies. In this sense the "musts" of political theory are always "oughts." Not only in political theory, but in our intellectual enterprises generally, the non-logical senses of "musts" and of "we have no choice but" will derive what meaning they have from the force of things that are said upon our decisions as to what we are to do.

These highly general remarks are preliminary. Let us start now with a concrete example.

## III. *An Example*

I shall start with an example taken from post-Kantian political thought. Whether or not the word "deduce" occurs in such contexts, it has certainly been repeatedly said that the theories of the nature of the state and the political recommendations offered by philosophers like Fichte and Hegel in some sense "follow from" or "are entailed by" the metaphysic of post-Kantian idealism. This may well be called the standard conception of post-Kantian political thought in Germany. On the other hand, we all know that the general outlines of post-Kantian idealist metaphysics were accepted and vigorously defended by thinkers less inclined than the Germans to draw the supposed inferences of political statism. Ralph Waldo Emerson, for example, though perhaps not a philosopher of top-ranking importance, did accept and defend a general conception of the world which is strikingly like that of Schelling. So far as basic metaphysical conceptions are concerned, all his thinking bears the same marks as the post-Kantian Germans. Emerson, however, who wrote a remarkable essay entitled *Self Reliance* (too seldom studied with care by philosophical historians of this period), associated those metaphysical conceptions with an uncompromising rejection of statism and a defense of one of the wildest orgies of individualism and laissez-faire which the world has ever seen. What is more, Emerson insists that all this "follows from" or "is entailed by" the metaphysic he is propounding.

A philosopher who has been brought up in the German tradition, or who is simply conditioned to think of this phase of the history of ideas in its German setting, may too hastily dismiss Emerson as "inconsistent" or "confused." After all, he is not in any sense a rigorous or an original thinker, and one has learned to expect puzzling anomalies from him. On the other hand, the more closely one examines his attempt to defend laissez-faire in terms of romantic idealism, the more difficult it becomes to isolate any specific inconsistency or confusion. The more closely one examines in juxtaposition the political philosophies of Emerson and (let us say) Fichte, the more difficult it becomes to say that either violates the canons of internal consistency. Since they are offering wholly incompatible political proposals as "entailments" of metaphysical doctrines which are remarkably similar, it may be well to examine the sense in which each conceives of this "entailment."

It is difficult to examine this sort of thing briefly, for one is generally dealing with highly complicated doctrines, and when one treats them summarily one always runs the risk of oversimplifying. One will be accused of misrepresentation. On the other hand, unless one is brief one runs the risk of losing sight of the major point. Let us suppose two people agree on the following three highly metaphysical premises. We will begin by assuming that these three premises are all that are needed to make clear the essentials of their "world view."

1. The real essence of the world is a unified all-embracing spirit.

## AN EXAMPLE

2. This real essential unity expresses itself, or instantiates itself, in two distinct ways. Macrocosmically it expresses itself as the objectified world of Nature. Microcosmically it expresses itself in finite pinpoints of acute self-awareness or consciousness—i.e., individual minds.
3. All explanation ultimately involves appreciation of the underlying identity of these expressions in the unity which they are expressions of. The "knowing" of Nature by individual minds requires this real unity; the influence of natural processes upon our conscious life requires it; appreciation of the "meaning" of history requires it; and so on.

Now, what, we might wish to ask if we were happily ignorant of history, does all this have to do with politics? Well, let us look at our two philosophers (now hypothetical), who are in agreement on these weighty matters, and imagine some of the things they might do. In order to imagine this, we must give them contexts.

The first individual is an intelligent member of a nation which has just suffered a devastating military defeat. The history of that nation has been pretty discouraging on the whole, but he feels there is a tremendous wealth of ability beneath the disturbed and disorganized surface. What that nation needs is unity of effort and unity of purpose. Pondering, in the terms of his metaphysic, our thinker comes up with a remarkably suggestive idea. Suppose you conceive of the State (capital letter, mind you) as an intermediary unity inserted between the all-embracing unity of the spiritual reality and the scattered individual consciousnesses which are moored in the objective world of Nature. If one thinks of the matter in this way, one can call upon the individual to sink himself in the State and its purposes as a half-way house on the road to realizing himself as an expression of ultimate reality. This sounds excellent. The individual can be told that his path to real freedom and self-expression lies in subordinating himself to the will of the State. Statism is provided with the support of the metaphysic expressed in those three premises.

Now, the second individual is an intelligent member of a very different kind of nation. His nation is revelling in an orgy of individualism, success and unrestraint. It has just won a revolution against one of the greatest powers on earth; so far as can be seen, it has succeeded in setting up a working form of government; there is an expanding frontier which is to all intents and purposes limitless; it is a period in which the cult of the idiosyncratic flourishes. What does our intelligent friend do—he too thinking in terms of his metaphysic? One thing seems to him quite clear: that if we are all in fact *really* part and parcel of this all-embracing spiritual reality, if we are its "expressions" cosmically attuned to that great world of Nature which is its other manifestation, we should not, theoretically at least, require any constraint whatsoever at the social and political level. If we all dig deep enough into our idiosyncratic selves we should come out all right in the end. He has a pond-loving friend, indeed, who is a roaring anarchist on just these grounds. Our philosopher, however, is a bit more cautious. He is willing to grant that the state is a necessary evil. The state is a penalty we pay because many individuals simply will not dig deep enough. We need government because individuals will make the mistakes which their finitude permits; but it is a necessity to be deplored rather than a program to be preached. The program to be preached is self-reliance and avoidance of the pettiness which is implied in constant concern for conformity. Where our first philosopher reified the State at a level *higher* than the individual's particularity, our second grants the state an unfortunate necessity *at* the level of unenlightened particularity. In these terms he has provided laissez-faire with a justification expressed in terms of the three crucial premises.

What will we say if each of these individuals approaches us with the claim that his proposal—statism in the one case, laissez-faire in the other—is in some sense entailed by, or in some sense follows from, his metaphysical speculations? I have formulated the issue as briefly as I can because my analysis of it, brief as it is,

## AN EXAMPLE

is going to be rather complex. I should like to make five points, and I should like to summarize them before making them.

(i) As the matter stands, it is absurd to say that either proposal "is entailed by" the metaphysic in the sense that it "is deducible from" the three premises listed. In order to make the phrase "deducible from" intelligible, one would be forced in each case to add to the original list at least one additional premise (different of course in the two cases).

(ii) When we look closely, we will find that in each case the additional premise required simply *is* the proposal which one eventually wishes to make, worded in the highly flexible language prescribed by the metaphysic.

(iii) When we see this, we see that the important question at issue is not at all the question whether political proposals can be "deduced" from elaborate metaphysical premises. The important question is whether there is any reason why we *must* accept one new premise rather than another.

(iv) In the example under consideration, the answer to the latter question is obviously "no."

(v) If this is so, it means that what is bogus in both Fichte and Emerson is not that either one is violating the canons of deduction. What is wrong is that neither one of them is presenting us with a genuine entailment recommendation. Neither one of them has provided any convincing grounds whatsoever for claiming that we must approach political problems in one way rather than another.

I shall now consider these points *seriatim*.

(i) I am always puzzled when philosophers talk as though recommendations to act in a certain way can be "deduced" from anything whatsoever. I can conceive of no context in which such talk would make sense, unless it be a context in which we had occasion to say that "You now ought to do so and so" can be deduced from "All men ought always to do so and so under certain conditions, and you are a man now in those conditions." For many reasons this seems to me a very strange way of talking, but in any case it is irrelevant here.[25] I take it as perfectly obvious that from the three premises I have listed neither the proposal of statism nor the proposal of laissez-faire can be "deduced."

I do, however, envisage the following criticism. I have been talking so far as though we have here two individuals supporting incompatible political proposals in terms of the *same* metaphysic. Surely, however, someone will insist that the disagreement is metaphysical. One man reifies the State, the other does not; that is a metaphysical difference. In each case, were we to state the man's metaphysic adequately we would need a fourth proposition. The first would require a premise hypostatizing the State as a metaphysical entity; the second would require a premise negating this. That done, we would clearly be confronted by two different metaphysics, from one of which statism "follows," from the other of which laissez-faire "follows." I am still far from happy about translating the word "follows" here into the phrase "is deducible from," but I am willing to give it a try. I agree that if talk about deduction is to make any sense in such a situation something of the sort must be done.

(ii) Now, surely there is something seriously bogus about such a suggestion. The suggestion implies that, for example, reifying the State and the political proposal of statism are in fact two different things one of which "follows from" the other. And this seems to me quite false. There are not two things here at all. There is simply one thing (the proposal of statism) which is being said in a very peculiar way (i.e., talk about reifying the State).

We can make the political proposal of statism in a great many ways. Hobbes in the *Leviathan* certainly proposed statism without (as I think) in any way using the terminology (or the metaphor—if it is one) of "reifying the State." But when you are using the kind of metaphysical terminology which the post-Kantians used, reifying the State is simply the way in which that proposal is worded in your terminology. The proposal of laissez-faire can

[25] I shall discuss this problem at length in the following chapter. See below pp. 86-88.

## AN EXAMPLE

be made without any talk of microcosmic souls realizing themselves as portions of the absolute, as a great deal of Republican oratory proves; but if, like Emerson, you are using that terminology you can couch the proposal of laissez-faire in it. Any one of the traditional metaphysical terminologies is a powerful and flexible tool. All of them provide the linguistic wherewithal for describing any fact with which you confront them, and all of them provide the linguistic wherewithal in which to make any proposal you wish.

If we grant that Fichte's metaphysic contains a fourth premise reifying the State, and that Emerson's metaphysic contains a fourth premise negating this, it will be a complete mistake to suppose that in such case either one of them would then be "deducing" his political proposal from his metaphysic. For what we would have granted would in each case have been the *inclusion* of the political proposal *in* the so-called metaphysical premises.

(iii) The important issue between Fichte and Emerson has nothing to do with the question whether political proposals can be deduced from principles which in other, non-political, respects form the basis of romantic idealism. The important issue between them, in the terminology each is using, is whether the State should be conceived as more real than concrete individuals; but this is simply a highly metaphorical way of arguing about which of two attitudes one should adopt toward the need for subordinating one's own interests to contrary interests of one's political group. Fichte recommends that we rejoice in this need as an opportunity to improve ourselves; Emerson says that we should deplore this need as a symptom of our failure. There are two ways in which we can view this issue. We can continue to look upon it as a metaphysical disagreement, or we may shift our focus and look upon it as a practical disagreement as to which of two attitudes we should adopt in political life. The significant thing is that, viewed in *either* way, the issue has the same general characteristics.

If we continue to treat the issue as metaphysical, it is simply this: Is there any reason why we must accept one fourth premise rather than another? If we treat the issue as a practical one concerning which of two attitudes we should adopt, it is simply this: Is there any reason why we must adopt one attitude rather than the other? As a matter of fact, these are simply two different ways of formulating one issue—an issue which, as I say, has nothing to do with questions of deducibility. The "must" which needs to be justified is not a "must" of logic but a "must" of decision. We cannot assume that the decision to approach political problems in a certain way has already been agreed upon, and that *now* our "must" is one of mere logical entailment. If there *is* any "must" involved it impinges upon the very decision in question. What is more, that decision will be neither merely terminological nor merely a matter of evidence. It will of course require the consistent use of *some* terminology; and it may commit us whether we know it or not to what we will *count* as evidence; but as a decision it must in a certain sense precede our application of the canons of logic and of scientific inference. We must (and I use the word advisedly!) plunge *in medias res*, and if there is anything coercive about what we propose, that coercion cannot be justified as anything less than a requirement of sanity and reason.

(iv) The real difficulty both in Fichte and in Emerson is that neither one of them has presented us with a genuine "must." Neither one of them provides us with any reason for supposing that one recommendation rather than the other has any binding character. Each one is tricked into supposing that his recommendation "follows from" his elaborate metaphysic because of the relatively unimportant fact that his metaphysic provides a terminology in which the proposal can be stated. In allowing himself to be so tricked, each lays himself open to the attack of the "non-deducers." It *looks as though* each is trying to perform a feat of deduction, because neither presents us with any other kinds of reasons which are binding.

Philosophers like Weldon are fond of reading the "musts" of

## AN EXAMPLE

political philosophy on the analogy of the "musts" of games.[26] The success of the analogy, however, may focus our attention more upon a political philosopher's mistakes than upon his primary intention. In one sense it is true that Fichte and Emerson present us with nothing more binding than the rules of games, rules prescribing "musts" which are in the last analysis quite arbitrary. Each presents us with an elaborate set of terms, somewhat as we are presented with the kings, queens, knights, and bishops of chess, and then prescribes how we shall play the game of political theory. The radical difference between them hangs in mid-air. It is somewhat as though, having learned Fichte's two-dimensional version of chess, we suddenly find Emerson playing a three-dimensional version. The pieces are the same, certain basic rules are the same, but the field of play is differently laid out. Since each is inclined to provide justification in terms of what both share in common, the fundamental difference strikes us as arbitrary.

All of this, however, can be accepted as a fair account of Fichte and Emerson only if we ignore the question of what they are *trying* to accomplish. The similarity between what they *do* accomplish and the rules of games is the result of a mistake; it is not what they intend at all. Both Fichte and Emerson are trying to prescribe what we must do if we are to adopt an intelligent approach to political problems. In the same sense any philosopher of science is trying to isolate what we must do if we are intelligently to engage in an enterprise called "science." *If there are any*, the basic principles of political theory, like the basic principles of science, will be importantly unlike the basic rules of any game; for they will prescribe, as the rules of games do not, what we must do if our doing of it is to be rationally justified. The fact that Fichte and Emerson fail in the end to justify their basic principles in this sense does not indicate that there are no such principles. If Weldon is right, he shows no more nor less than that certain philosophers fail to achieve a purpose; he has in no sense shown that the purpose is suspect.

[26] *Op.cit.*, esp. Chapter 6.

(v) If we understand what is really bogus in Fichte and Emerson, we will stop talking about deducibility and about rules of games, and we will start talking about the question whether there are any genuine entailment recommendations in political theory. I mean by this: Is there anything we must admit, any method of approach we must adopt, *if* we are to approach political problems sanely and rationally? The fundamental issue between competing political philosophies is always an issue of this sort. Neither logic nor empirical science can ever be the final arbiter in such conflicts. We can of course eliminate considerable nonsense by uncovering logical fallacies and by showing that the evidence fails to support something offered *as* an empirical hypothesis; but in the last analysis the role of logic and experiment in political theory is largely negative. With their help we can uncover mistakes; neither can guarantee a program. The central questions of political philosophy are, as it were, pre-logical and pre-scientific. They concern our initial commitments as to what constitutes a proper way of approaching political problems in the first place. They concern our decisions as to how we will go about justifying our method of approach. Even where our decision is to place more confidence in logic and empirical science than the situation makes reasonable, that decision itself is extra-logical and extra-scientific.

Another way of saying the same thing is this: that political proposals are not propositions but recommendations, demands, admonitions—in a word, advice. A great deal of advice is conditional and tentative. It would not disturb us too greatly if we found we had to alter it. But unless we refuse to adopt any firm standpoint whatsoever, there must be some point at which the advice we give is not conditional and not tentative. Changing it ceases to be an interesting possibility and becomes a major castastrophe. How can we possibly justify this kind of thing? Essentially this question has nothing to do with dogmatism, apriorism, disregard of the facts, or anything of the sort. It is not a question of violating either the canons of logic or the factual information we possess; it is a question of what questions we are

## CONDITIONS OF SOUND ADVICE

going to be interested in before we even think of logic or science, what answers will satisfy us when logic and science fail to provide any leverage for choice, and how we are going to conceive of the demands of our own intellectual conscience.

I want in the following section to look more closely at the kinds of questions which we must face when we deal with such issues.

### IV. *The Conditions of Sound Advice*

I should like to begin by examining something easy and manageable as a prelude to tackling what is more complex and more difficult. I propose to begin by looking briefly at a certain kind of trivial and off-hand remark which we are accustomed to make with little or no thought. This may be of some help toward achieving an understanding of the more learned and professional things that we sometimes say. It surely makes a great deal of difference whether we say something solemnly and with thought, or whether we say something carelessly and without thought; but I shall take full account of that difference in due course. I want to begin with something off-hand, and I select as an example the familiar cliché "What you don't know won't hurt you."

If I were to utter this cliché, what would I think of someone who laboriously began to demonstrate either (i) that it is not an empirical hypothesis which the evidence will support or (ii) that it cannot be deduced as a consequence of a set of a priori axioms? I suspect that I would find it difficult to believe that anyone who undertook such profound tasks had understood the point of my remark.

Obviously, anyone who wanted to *might* read the words "What you don't know won't hurt you" as an empirical hypothesis of an excessively overgeneralized kind. So read, the words express a statement so plainly false that it is difficult to see how any man could be stupid enough to utter them. What-we-do-not-know most certainly does hurt us again and again, and we are all plainly aware of that fact. Similarly, anyone who wanted to *might* so interpret those words that they express a simple tautology. This could be done in several ways. Perhaps the most obvious would be to legislate that the phrase "what you know" means "that of which you are aware" (i.e., *any* awareness), and to point out that the words "hurt you" mean for anyone "to have a certain specific kind of awareness." Given all this purely definitional apparatus, the words "What you don't know won't hurt you" simply say that you cannot be aware of what you are not aware of. That would not be a very interesting comment. It is a tautology which says nothing.

Surely it is absurd to suppose that when we utter this remark, as we very often do, we mean either one of these things. We are being neither stupid nor ingenious. We are not ignorant enough to be supposing that a cancer in my liver of which I know nothing is doing me no harm; we are not clever enough to be trying to convince our auditors that *a* is *b* by saying that *a* is *a*. We are not *trying* to describe the facts truly, nor are we *trying* to enunciate tautologies. If we examine the kinds of situation in which we use such an expression we will find, I think, that we are trying to give advice. So interpreted, what we are saying may not only make good sense, it may also be perfectly good advice. If you and I are in an airplane together, and you begin to fret nervously about the condition of the motors and whether all the gadgets are in proper working order, I may very sensibly say "What you don't know won't hurt you." What I mean is "Stop worrying!"

Having seen this much about our cliché, let us begin to examine something more learned and more solemn. Let us examine, for example, a very well known political principle with which we are all familiar: the principle "All men are created equal." What are we going to say about those who try to demonstrate either (i) that this is not an empirical hypothesis which the evidence will support or (ii) that it cannot be deduced from a priori axioms?

Can we really believe that anyone ever intended this series of words as an empirical description? Is it possible that anyone could be unaware that some babies are born black, others white; that some are born geniuses, others morons; some born into wealth, others into poverty? Interpreted as a testable hypothesis, these words say what is so patently false that charity will refuse to allow that anyone ever intended them in that way. Suppose, then, we interpret them as expressing a tautology. This will not be difficult. "All men are created men"; that is true enough, saying as it does nothing whatsoever. Any member of any group shares the characteristics which define membership in the group. In this sense, all frogs are equal, all toadstools are equal, and all mountains are equal. Somehow these latter principles do not sound very interesting.

Surely something has gone wrong when we begin to talk as though intelligent men speaking seriously have been trying either to describe the facts or to utter tautologies when they have used the words "All men are created equal." Under what conditions would I use those words myself? Let me use this as a clue to what others may have meant. I am prompted to utter such words when I see Hitler exterminating Jews or when I read of segregation of races in Protestant church congregations. What do I mean? I mean: "You ought not to do that." I mean that there is a certain minimum decency with which you ought to treat any man. Do not try to tell me that I am "deducing" these latter proposals from the principle that all men are created equal; that principle *is* these proposals and nothing else. That principle is absurd as an hypothesis and empty as a tautology. It makes very good sense as a recommendation, a proposal, a protest, or a piece of advice. This is the first lesson we must learn: that reasonable advice may be turned into nonsense when interpreted in either of the two standard ways in which we ordinarily interpret propositions.

I now return to the cliché "What you don't know won't hurt you." If we agree that its intention is to advise, admonish, or recommend, what could we possibly mean by the claim that it is "binding"? Such a claim may seem *prima facie* inappropriate when we are dealing with an off-hand and generally un-solemn remark like this, but it may be helpful to ask what it *might* mean. And I think it might mean two very different kinds of thing. On the one hand, we might wish to say that our advice is binding simply in the sense that on *this* particular occasion it just *is* good advice. On the other hand, we might wish to claim that the sort of advice expressed by these words is *always* good advice, not just on this occasion or on occasions like this, but on any occasion whatsoever.

I should like to say that, however good the advice expressed by this cliché may be on isolated occasions, there is nothing to be said for it as a generalization. In short, it is sometimes good advice, sometimes bad advice. It is good advice to a nervous passenger; it is bad advice to a man with a liver ailment. The important point to be noticed is this: When I say that this cliché expresses advice which is not always good advice—when, in short, I say that such advice is overgeneral—I am not accusing it either of being a false empirical hypothesis or of being an unenlightening tautology. I am not treating it as an hypothesis; I am not treating it as a tautology. I am treating it as advice; and I am saying that as advice it is, when taken alone and out of context, too general.

I once heard the head of a prominent School of Divinity remark that the Golden Rule could be appealed to by any young man seducing any young woman. "I would do unto you as I would have you do unto me." This learned theologian was rightly pointing out that as it stands the Golden Rule is too general. It says too much. "Do unto others as you would be done by" is sometimes good advice, sometimes bad advice. It is not, the theologian argued, the core of the Christian ethic at all; and I hope he was right, for if it is the core of the Christian ethic the Christian ethic is a shambles. On the other hand, "Do unto others as you would be done by" is not a proposition which is true or false at all. In calling it overgeneral, we do not mean that it is a falsified empirical hypothesis, and we do not mean that it is somehow definitionally incorrect.

Let us now return to "All men are created equal." Taken as advice, what could be meant by the claim that it is binding? Now that we are talking about something solemn the claim does not seem, at any rate *prima facie*, absurd. There is an important difference, however, between the claim that it is binding in the sense that under special circumstances it just *is* good advice, and the claim that it is binding in the sense that it is *always* good advice. Surely "All men are created equal" is in this respect like "What you don't know won't hurt you." When Locke uttered this advice, or issued this warning, and when Jefferson later reiterated it, each was addressing an audience which faced a problem. England in 1688, and America a century later, were engaged in revolutions—whether bloodless or bloody. In each case, the tenor of the advice communicated by those words was unambiguous. You do not have to submit to tyrannical pressures; you are men, and as men you can resist. Under the circumstances this was excellent advice. It was important, and it was to the point.

On the other hand, it is of the utmost importance to recognize that these words do not always constitute good advice. "All men are created equal" is sometimes irrelevant, and it is sometimes positively bad advice. (In this respect it is exactly like "Do unto others as you would be done by.") We do not appeal to this principle in a scientific laboratory, and I believe that we ought not to appeal to it as much as we do in setting up our educational system. There are innumerable occasions on which saying that all men are created equal is precisely the wrong thing to say. We in the United States are often not as sensitive to this fact as we should be. In the last war, for example, we did not, as England did, make the proper use of our brain power. Philosophy PhD's were made foot soldiers, while football players were assigned to desks in intelligence. (I can document this among my own students.) Britain was notoriously more careful in such matters; and one sensed somewhat too much of the "all men are created equal" attitude in Washington, D.C.

There are several points which I am trying to bring out. The first I have already made: namely, that there is a sense in which we can condemn advice as overgeneral without reference to the irrelevant claims that it constitutes either a false hypothesis or an improper tautology. The second point, to which I am now turning, is this: that where the principles to which we appeal are in fact overgeneral we waste far too much time over the irrelevant question whether they express true propositions, and fail to spend enough time discussing the appropriate question—under what conditions do they constitute sound advice? The third point, which I want finally to face, is this: that there remains one all-important question which tends to get lost in much of our talk about political problems: the question whether there *is* any advice which is both general and sound; that is to say, whether there is any advice which we are willing to commit ourselves to as being *always* good advice.

The case of "All men are created equal" seems to me to be typical of one of the most persistent ways in which political theory can get side-tracked from an important issue into considerations which are entirely irrelevant. It is of the utmost importance that we ask ourselves under what conditions we should and under what conditions we should not treat different individuals with differing capacities in the same way. It is not important *at all* to discuss whether "All men are created equal" is a true proposition. In its important uses it simply is not a proposition; it is a recommendation to act in one way rather than another. Political theory bulges at the seams with arguments about the truth or falsity of bloated general propositions where in fact it should be examining the conditions under which one kind of advice is appropriate rather than another.

Nowhere does this seem to me more discouraging than in the way in which we discuss the problem of "*the* nature of man." Why is it that to be impressive we must exaggerate? Most of the giants in political theory are giants because they have caught hold of some genuine insight into the ways of mankind. They have consequently given advice which has been relevant, important, and moving. Unfortunately they overstate their advice in capsule propositional form. In that form it crystallizes in the traditions of academic debate, and thereafter we argue about the wrong thing. Consider some examples:

Locke and Rousseau, each in his own way, proclaimed that

## CONDITIONS OF SOUND ADVICE

man is naturally good. When you study what they have to say in full and in the contexts of the problems with which they were faced, it is clear enough that they were saying something which within limits is sound and important. Essentially they were recommending that social institutions should be thought of as instruments through which men can achieve what they want. Machiavelli said that men are selfish and acquisitive; Hobbes said that they are governed by the instinct of self-preservation; the Puritans said bluntly that men are depraved. Again, if you study what they have to say in full and in the contexts of the problems with which they were concerned, it is clear enough that these men too were saying something which within limits is sound and important. Essentially they were recommending that social institutions must be so set up that individuals cannot use authority to satisfy their own interests at the expense of the general interest.

Surely, abstract debate concerning whether *the* nature of man is good or depraved is a way of sidestepping rather than solving the fundamental question, which is: Under what conditions do you advise men to assert their interests and desires, and under what conditions do you advise men to suppress those interests and desires? Machiavelli rightly saw that greed was rampant in sixteenth-century Italy, and within limits he gave intelligent advice to the petty potentates of that day. It is important to ask under what conditions advice of that sort is sound and under what conditions not; but it is a waste of time to discuss the absurd thesis that greed is somehow a unique clue to human nature. The Puritans rightly saw that men's actions did not conform to the religious principles they mouthed. In *that* sense men *were* depraved. It was important to alert social theory to the need for checks and balances upon individuals inclined to act less nobly than they speak; but it is a waste of time to discuss the absurd thesis that men cannot do good. Human nature is no more naturally good than bad; it is complex enough to be both. The important question is: When should we base our action on the assumption that we and others are likely to express what is good in us, and when should we base our action on the assumption that we are more likely to express what is bad? This is a question of the conditions under which certain kinds of advice are sound; it is not a question of defending absurd generalizations about *the* nature of man.

Marx proclaimed that man is the expression of material economic forces; the Christian idealist tradition has proclaimed that man is an expression of spiritual forces. What is the important issue here? Marx rightly saw that whatever men may *say*, they are often in fact motivated by economic interests; but the Christian tradition rightly sees that men can be and often are motivated by spiritual ideals. It is absolutely essential that we discuss the issue: Under what conditions should one advise a man to consider those with whom he deals as motivated by economic interests, and under what conditions should one advise a man to consider those with whom he deals as persons with spiritual dignity? It is a waste of time to discuss the absurd thesis that all motivation is economic or the unmanageable thesis that all men have eternal destinies elsewhere.

I cannot too often stress the point that I am not attacking these theories about man's nature as "unempirical." If we were discussing empirical hypotheses, negative instances would be worth their weight in gold. In political theory we simply are not dealing with empirical hypotheses. How easy it would be if we were! By pointing to one case where a man was motivated by considerations contrary to his economic interests, by pointing to one case where the value of something is not a function of the labor involved in its production, by pointing to one case where something has not generated its opposite, I would at a blow dispose of three of the cardinal doctrines of Marxism. By pointing to one unselfish act I would dispose of Machiavelli and Hobbes. By pointing to one case where power has not corrupted and one case where the majority has been dead wrong I would dispose of two of the classic principles most often reiterated in the democratic tradition. Why is it not that easy? Because these theories or principles are not empirical generalizations and were never so intended. They are not telling you what is or was or will be the

## CONDITIONS OF SOUND ADVICE

case. And it does not follow from this that they are "merely definitional." They are none of this. They are ways of advising you what you ought to do. You will never silence a Marxian *or* a Christian with negative instances; and you will never decide to be one or the other on the basis of evidence alone.

There are many truths about man, no one of which is *the* truth. There are many ways of interpreting what we do, what we hope, and what we want; no one of them is *the* interpretation. Political proposals rest upon emphasizing certain truths rather than others, certain ways of interpreting rather than others. The important question to ask of a proposal is: when, if ever, is it appropriate?

*Merely* to say this is, however, not enough. The honesty of submitting our proposals to the constant demand that the conditions of their appropriateness be specified, may on occasion be superseded by the wisdom of recognizing the limits of such a demand. Can we honestly contend that all of our proposals are always conditional and hypothetical? Is it in the very nature of a proposal that it sometimes constitutes good advice, sometimes bad advice? Surely there is something wrong-headed—something excessively unrealistic if you will—about such an attitude. Unless there is something for which we stand *in any case*, we stand, in the last analysis, for nothing. The very demand for an attitude of self-criticism, the very refusal to be dogmatic and doctrinaire, itself suggests that there are points at which we must commit ourselves unconditionally. *Some* advice we take to be always good advice; which is to say that we take it to be both general and binding. This, and nothing short of it, is the problem to be faced by political philosophy. How do we justify those general and binding commitments on which all our further attempts to justify our proposals as to action depend?

I am well aware that many will be repelled by this appeal to a kind of advice which is conceived as always binding. It is fashionable to associate appeal to the categorical and unconditional with the root of all evil. It will be said that no piece of advice is unconditionally binding, and that in political philosophy in particular the entire of our task is to ascertain with respect to any special bit of advice the conditions under which it is (or would be) binding. Saying this, or something very like it, is the basis on which many will take their stand that the major role of political philosophy is to recommend, to foster, and to develop a more adequate social science. Study of the conditions under which rules hold and of the conditions under which they do not hold is essentially empirical and scientific in character. Men in action must no doubt take a stand; but the role of philosophy is reflective, and reflection makes a difference. On reflection, nothing is categorical; and what is needed in political philosophy is an antidote to the intransigency required by effective action. A Secretary of State cannot be wholly wise; but a philosopher can. And a philosopher in his wisdom will always recommend careful piecemeal studies of the conditions under which advising in one way is sound and advising in another way is unsound.

Within limits, the foregoing paragraph correctly states a vast and urgent need. Nothing that I can say against it should be read as a belittling of the need for social science. We need all the piecemeal empirical studies we can get; there cannot be too many of them. My point is simply this: To argue that such studies, or the recommendation of their proliferation, is the only significant role of political philosophy, is to misconstrue what is most important even in the demand for the piecemeal scientific approach itself. You may proliferate the special projects of social science to your heart's content; but you will not escape the fact that *embedded in* all that you are doing there will lie commitments as to modes of advice which you assume as binding under any conditions. Because this is so, it will always constitute a defeat of your own intentions to truncate political philosophy, and to deny it the right to speculate upon the unconditional.

I here wield a sword with two cutting edges. One edge cuts at those who naïvely suppose that science can be pursued with none but "hypothetical" decisions and commitments. The other edge cuts at those who perhaps more naïvely suppose that concern for "categorical" decisions and commitments is independent of

## CONDITIONS OF SOUND ADVICE

the concerns of science. The disastrous myth that science concerns itself only with ascertaining means to ends provisionally entertained generates and is generated by the companion myth that morals and ethics, in raising questions about ends which ought unprovisionally to be endorsed, are raising questions with which science as such has nothing whatsoever to do. Both myths, or perhaps one should say—this single myth is one of the most blinding products of the pigeonholing tendency. Moral philosophy has no monopoly of categorical decisions. A scientist *as a scientist* must make decisions which are every bit as categorical as those he must make as a father.

The view that scientific reasoning is one kind of thing, and that moral reasoning is another kind of thing, is bound to leave political philosophy hopelessly straddled on the fence between. It is high time the fence be torn down. The philosophy of science is concerned with isolating those basic commitments apart from which the undertaking of science makes no sense; the philosophy of morals is concerned with isolating those basic commitments apart from which our whole conception of living rightly makes no sense; and political philosophy is concerned with isolating those basic commitments apart from which our ways of behaving as a group and our common purposes in action make no sense.

Here then is "the problem of political philosophy." And enough has been said to make it evident that it is not a self-contained or isolated problem. It is part of the problem of philosophy as a whole. Political philosophy has grown up from the tendency on the part of human beings to reply, when asked for justification of their actions, with elaborate theories. What *is* the relation between an action and a theory, such that when we are asked to justify the former we offer the latter? This question need only be formulated to be recognized as of general moral purport; and it need only be reflected on to be recognized as fundamental far beyond the scope of what we usually conceive as the limited subject matter of moral philosophy.

# CHAPTER THREE: THE PROBLEM IN MORAL PHILOSOPHY

## I. *The Categorical*

IN MANY ways the discussion of political philosophy in the preceding chapter has led us into problems traditionally associated with the larger problems of ethics and of moral philosophy. How, indeed, could it be otherwise? It would be the height of folly to draw an arbitrary line of demarcation between political and moral problems. They defy any absolute separation; and in taking a stand in political philosophy one is *eo ipso* committing oneself on basic moral issues.

But there are two aspects of our previous discussion which have involved us in questions normally associated with moral philosophy, and which we must consider in far greater detail if our position is to be made clear. One of these aspects I shall reserve for later discussion; the other will be our major concern in the present chapter.

I reserve for later discussion the justification of my attack on solving problems of action by reference to general theories about *the* nature of man. I have no doubt that my remarks in that connection, whether welcomed or deplored, were taken as revelatory of a larger perspective in moral philosophy as a whole. It is certainly right that they should be. In many quarters the guiding motif of moral philosophy is believed to be that of formulating a general conception of *the* nature of man as a standard of reference against which human activity is to be judged. It will doubtless occur to some that in excising the guiding motif I have destroyed the symphony at one blow. Of anyone who so reacts I can only request patience. I might hint that to reject generalizations about *the* nature of man may lead to fuller understanding of the complexities of men than might otherwise be obtained; but hints are likely to be coy, and in any event the whole question is far more than a merely *moral* one. I am unwilling to tackle it in detail except in the context of a larger philosophical perspective; and, at the moment, must proceed with a plea of *pace* to those who may be unfavorably disposed.

I have already remarked that my persistence in focusing attention on the "unconditional" in advice and in decision will be met with disfavor. And this is the second sense in which what I have already said has involved me in a problem traditionally associated with moral philosophy. "Categorical" is one of the key words of philosophical ethics. In a sense, the sum and substance of the preceding chapter is that political philosophy requires some way of justifying advice which is categorical. And it will be pointed out that saying this is to skate on the very thin ice of a problem that has cracked under the weight of many a previous philosopher who has sallied forth upon it.

One might claim that "categorical" is a perfectly good English word, defined in dictionaries by use of the innocuous phrase "without qualifications." It might be said that on the face of it the meaning intended by the word has little to do with most of the thorny problems with which it has come to be associated in technical philosophical debate. I want, as a matter of fact, to say something very like this; but it will be a long and difficult job to say it well.

The recent history of the word in technical philosophy stems back to the philosophy of Immanuel Kant. Kant it was who placed at the center of moral philosophy the question whether there is any imperative on which we base our action which is categorical in nature. Indeed, if one hacks one's way through all the technical jargon in which Kant phrases his moral theory, one may read his primary intent in a way not unlike what I have been saying. Unless one stand for *something* without qualification—with no ifs, buts, or maybes about it—one stands in the last analysis for nothing. A sense of duty with an "if" attached to it is no sense of duty at all; and unless there is something that is good "without qualification" there can be no content to which the sincerest of intentions can attach itself.

Kant certainly, however, said much more than this. You cannot slough off the technical jargon and remain faithful to his purpose. For at every point he associates his plea for a categorical imperative with his broader philosophical insistence that there are, that there must be, synthetic a priori propositions. You cannot divorce Kant's *Critique of Practical Reason* from his *Critique of Pure Reason*. His treatment of moral philosophy parallels at every point his treatment of the philosophy of science and of sense perception.

Kant literally did think of the categorical imperative as a synthetic a priori proposition. It seems not to have occurred to him that an imperative is not a proposition at all. This was more than a strange "quirk" in a brilliant mind; and in order to understand it we must look squarely for a moment at the association of the word "categorical" with the doctrine of the synthetic a priori in the *Critique of Pure Reason*.

Consider, first, the kind of thing one might say if one were moved to use the word "categorical" with reference to deductive systems. It surely makes sense to say that, given certain definitions and axioms, deduction is a matter of deriving theorems which follow without *further* qualifications. There is a logical sense of the word "must"; and where the word "must" is appropriate it is futile to dictate that the use of the word "categorical" is taboo. It would thus violate no rule of grammar to associate the words "categorical" and "analytic." The analytic is that which is tautologous (i.e., cannot not be true) given certain definitions and postulates. *Within* a system of discourse, analytical steps are categorical. This is merely to say that certain steps in reasoning require no further justification, no further qualifications or reason-giving, provided that the definitions and axioms of a system are accepted as given.

We may find ourselves toying with the idea of the *wholly* categorical by abstraction from this kind of situation. Especially if we conceive of all proper reasoning as deductive, we will be inclined to envisage a kind of reasoning which is wholly categorical if we are willing to conceive of the initial definitions and axioms from which it proceeds as themselves without qualification. That is to say, we would be concerned with something wholly without qualification if we thought we were deducing from definitions and axioms which had no ifs or buts or maybes about *them*. If what we had before led us to associate the words "categorical" and "analytic," what we had now would lead us to associate the words "categorical" and "a priori." Still we would be violating no rules of grammar.

What Kant tried to do in the *Critique of Pure Reason* was to fuse this full sense of the word "categorical" with talk about empirical reports and descriptions. All of the above remarks about the coercions involved in deduction could be made on the assumption that the definitions and postulates in question are all of them formal and empirically empty. Kant undertook, however, to defend the view that certain full-blooded remarks about the empirical world confront us in the character of "not being qualified." There are (so he thought) no ifs or buts about the predictions that anything I see tomorrow at 10:40 a.m. will be seen as temporal, three-dimensionally spatial, causally related to its antecedents, and so forth. Rightly or wrongly, he phrased his whole problem on analogy with distinctions appropriate to deductive systems. His search for a "synthetic a priori" was a search for unqualified axioms (no ifs) which are *also* empirically descriptive.

When Kant turned to ethics and moral philosophy all of this language, and the thought-model it entailed, continued to preoccupy him. He was unwilling *merely* to discuss the need in ethics for commitments and a kind of advice which stand up under analysis as binding always and unconditionally. He had *also* to persist in finding *propositions* which would function as unqualified axioms in a kind of moral reasoning viewed on the pattern of deduction. He accordingly slips from the terminology of categorical imperatives into the terminology of synthetic a priori propositions. As a result, most of the talk about what functions as categorical in moral reasoning has concerned itself since Kant with the problem of the synthetic a priori.

One of the most important questions we must ask ourselves

is the following: Can we say what we want to say in political philosophy and in ethics about commitments which are unconditional, about those elements in our advisings and recommendings which function in an unqualified way, without reference to thorny debate as to whether there are propositions which are synthetic a priori? Let there be no mistake about the fact that propositions and propositions only are properly spoken of as being either synthetic or analytic. And part of what we have said in discussing political philosophy is that important parts of our advisings are often in the nature of proposals, recommendations, and performatives which are misconstrued when stated in propositional form. In moral philosophy as a whole it may be a mistake to confuse the notion of advice which is binding with the notion of propositions which are in some sense unqualifiedly "true." Kant had sufficient insight into moral philosophy to recognize that its primary concern is with "imperatives" which are unqualifiedly binding; but his preoccupation with the dubious assumption that the canons of proper reasoning derive from the canons of deduction led him to obscure that insight in the cloudy discussions of synthetic a priori propositions.

One may be tempted to go too far here, and the temptation must be avoided. One may be tempted to say that the problem of the categorical had been wholly mistreated and is not concerned with propositions at all. Unfortunately the matter is not that simple. We have hitherto been assuming that there is a reasonably clear distinction between propositions on the one hand and recommendations or advice on the other. It is now time to direct attention to the fact that even this distinction may be misleading if we think of it as sharper and more rigorous than it is. The dichotomy "proposition or non-proposition" may be as dangerous a weapon as any other dichotomy. One cannot deny that what functions in an unqualified way in advice is sometimes simply analytic propositions; nor can one deny out of hand that it is sometimes empirical descriptions which are advanced as beyond reasonable doubt and questioning. The

## THE CATEGORICAL

difficult truth of the matter is that we cannot talk, in these days of the vogue of talk about rules and recommendations and advice, as though our expressions must be *either* propositions *or* non-propositions. The pigeonholing tendency is never more dangerous than when it is applied to forms of expression.

I have several times been tempted to use the word "performatives" in reference to the language of advice in political and moral theory; and I believe that the word is often enough encountered in recent literature to call for comment. The word "performatives" is associated with the work of Professor J. L. Austin, who himself now uses the expanded phrase "explicit performatives" in its stead. Austin, who is ever sensitive to range and an archfoe of the dichotomizing tendency, is aware that whenever a person makes *any* utterance he performs *some* act. In the general sense which we occasionally read into the word, any utterance may be viewed as a performative. When he first used the word, and when he now uses the phrase "explicit performative," Austin has had a very limited set of cases in mind: namely, those in which a person by saying something performs the very act which would be named by the gerund form of the key verb in what he says. Thus, to say "I promise" is to perform the act of promising.

But the loose and imprecise sense of "performative" need not be discarded. Thus, to say "I will come" may also perform the act of promising; and to say "This room is hot" may on one occasion perform the act of proposing the room as a place to inhabit and may on another occasion perform the act of commanding a timid servant to open the window. Notice that one and the same string of words may be said on different occasions as a means of performing quite different acts. Now, so far as I am aware, no one has ever denied that there are many *kinds* of important and reasonable acts which can be performed by the making of utterances—such acts as admonishing, warning, encouraging, defying, assuring, instructing, correcting. But there are certain writers who either insist or assume that only two among such a swarm of possible acts are such that an utterance by virtue of performing them may lay claim to being "cognitively meaningful" or "rational." These two acts are the act of enunciating an empirically testable hypothesis and the act of enunciating a logical truth; and it will be noticed that these are the two acts which, together with the criteria for determining whether they have been performed, are so widely accepted as delimiting the range of those utterances which are properly and in the strict sense to be called propositional.

One may concede this strict use of the phrase "propositional utterance" (as I have done in the preceding chapter) and still resist the tendency to stigmatize all other linguistic performances as non-cognitive or irrational. And we must also be suspicious of the notion that a string of words as such is simply *either* propositional *or* non-propositional, for it may well be both. As for the first point, we may applaud the work that has been done by way of specifying, with varying degree of precision, the criteria which make the question "Is it true or false?" sensible and relevant in connection with such utterances as I may make. As we increase our precision there is no need to object to an increasingly precise use of the word "propositions." But it does not follow that where the "Is it true or false?" question is irrelevant or inappropriate other and equally important questions cannot be formulated.[1] Where one or two versions of the request for justification are out of place a whole range of others may well be in order. This is the point upon which my argument has hitherto hinged.

But we must now emphasize the second point; for whenever we are inclined to speak of a distinction between propositions and non-propositions we should remind ourselves that there are some strings of words in connection with which we may find it extraordinarily difficult to say whether the "Is it true or false?" question is appropriate or wrong-headed. Consider the following two utterances:

[1] I quote with great pleasure Professor J. L. Austin's footnote on p. 11 of his Presidential Address to the Aristotelian Society, *A Plea for Excuses*, 29 October 1956: "And forget, for once and for a while, that other curious question 'Is it true?' May we?"

## THE CATEGORICAL

(a) "I will be there at 2 p.m. Saturday" said by me on Wednesday.

(b) "All hands will remain aboard today" said by a ship's captain.

In the first case let us suppose that, having fallen ill on Friday, I telephone my apologies and am *not* there on Saturday. In the second case let us suppose that seaman Jones jumps ship before nightfall. Do we want to say either of my Wednesday utterance or of the captain's order that it is false? Try this question on a group of professional philosophers and you will guarantee heated discussion. Some will say that it is a mistake to call either utterance false. But surely it is not a *mistake*. One can surely understand the impulse to interpret either (a) or (b) as a prediction, and understood as a prediction each has turned out to be false. But while not a mistake, such as reading would be at the very least odd; and at least in case (b) the captain would certainly suspect intent to insult if you told him he had said something false in the morning. The puzzle is generated by selecting among several uses to which a string of words may be put a use which is not the one chiefly relevant. In the one case it would be more to the point to say that I was unable to keep my promise than to say that I uttered an untruth. In the other case it would be more to the point to say that the captain's order was disobeyed by Jones than to say that the captain said something false. The line between propositions and non-propositions is not as rigid as we sometimes take it to be.

Such matters are seldom attended to when discussions of the "categorical" are under way. If we reflect upon them, however, we may gradually learn to avoid basing our conception of the "categorical" upon analysis which is directed exclusively toward the special properties of true and false propositions. True and false propositions (whether analytically so or empirically so) are esoteric things in human discourse. Most of what we say is strictly neither; and too much philosophy rests upon the misleading assumption that only propositional utterances are deserving of serious attention. At the same time it would be wise to avoid so far as possible a classification of types of utterance which suggests that everything we say can be pigeonholed neatly as one sort of thing rather than another. The problem is not a neat one. Intelligent discussion must achieve a neatness of a sort; but it must never be a neatness which distorts by oversimplification. What we say with reference to the word "categorical" must be said with reference to many different ways of talking and believing and committing ourselves. There are various kinds of utterance, for example, in connection with which it may be inappropriate or wrong-headed to request a "reason"; and this may be an important sense in which we wish to use the word "categorical." The request for reasons is sometimes out of order when what we say is not propositional; but there may also be conditions under which it is out of order when we offer empirical reports or stipulate definitions and axioms. A careful consideration of the concept "categorical" must strive for sufficient flexibility. It should be *sensitive* to such special uses of propositional utterances as it will find; but it should not *confine itself* to the properties of propositional utterances alone.

Perhaps the best way to start is by dropping the *word* "categorical" altogether. Suppose we shake off our preconceptions (insofar as anyone can!) and begin by examining the various ways in which moral philosophers have made the claim that ethical reasoning involves steps which are unqualified or unconditional. It is surely a proper beginning to notice that these ways *are* various.

First of all, there is the long dispute concerning the alleged irreducibility of "ought" to "is." This dispute in itself has taken many forms. In some forms it forces us at once into talk about "propositions." Indeed, the problem is sometimes stated in the following way: Are *propositions* containing the word "ought" translatable without remainder into *propositions* containing only various forms of the verb "to be"? Sometimes the word "propositions" is avoided; and we are asked: Can the sense of an expression which contains value words be wholly translated into expressions which contain solely descriptive terms? Anyone

## THE CATEGORICAL

acquainted with the copious literature on this subject will recognize, however, that the dichotomy between "value terms" and "descriptive terms" carries with it the rumblings of an elaborate machinery of so-called propositional analysis.[2] In still another form the question is asked: Can we derive "ought" conclusions from "is" premises? Here the whole syllogistic apparatus of deriving theorems from premises is at work; and what a syllogism would be which is not concerned with *propositions* is a dubious and puzzling query.

But all this debate about the reducibility of "ought" to "is" is only one of the wings from which the unconditionally binding makes its appearance upon the stage of moral philosophy. Sometimes its entrance is a grand sweep down center stage in the flowing garb of intuitionism.

Now, "intuition" is a versatile actor. And there are at least two entirely different ways in which it sweeps on stage. Each in its turn involves appeal to something unconditionally binding, and each in its turn has traditionally led us to talk about propositions. One form that intuition takes may be called the "rationalist" form; the other may be called the "empiricist" form. Rationalists are prone to talk about intuiting the truth of first principles from which all further argument proceeds deductively. Empiricists are prone to talk about intuiting immediate data from which all further argument proceeds by way of reflection and induction.

Both forms of intuitionism have had long and distinguished careers in ethics. One takes its stand on general principles which are universally "true." The other takes its stand on clear-eyed "looking." If the former stakes its case on general propositions which cannot not be true; the latter stakes its case on particular propositions which cannot not be true.

[2] For example: a "value term" is sometimes *defined* as a term which adds nothing to the descriptive import of the expression in which it occurs. Thus, the concern for the propositional character of an expression takes precedence in our attempt to localize value terms. One often encounters a curious circularity in this connection. At the same time that value words are defined with reference to their function in expressions, value expressions may simply be defined as those in which value words occur.

One cannot say with any assurance how many problems here face us, any one of which may call to our attention some way in which an ethical decision will force us to commit ourselves unconditionally. *Can* we eliminate such words as "ought" from a theoretically perfect language? And if, as I believe, there is no good reason to suppose that we can, does this have anything to do with pigeonholing types of propositions? If we use the word "ought" in an unconditional way, can we in any sense offer a justification of what we in so doing say?

Can we really conceive of ethical reasoning as deduction from clear and self-evident truths? And if, as I believe, we cannot, does this make a complete shambles of what rational intuitionists have been trying to say? Or can one find in what they say some core of good sense?

Can we on the other hand conceive of ethical reasoning as induction from uncontrovertible immediate awareness? Is there a point in ethical reasoning where one must simply plead with one's audience to look and see? And if, as I believe, this is the case, does it have anything to do with the usual claims of empiricism in moral theory?

One kind of language seems to me appropriate to use in all these connections. It is vague language; but on occasion vagueness is a virtue. It seems to me that in all these ways the moral philosopher is driven to a single overriding question: "Are there limits beyond which the request for reasons makes no further sense?" We learn as children that as a matter of sheer animal response the question "Why?" can be reiterated ad infinitum. As mature and rational beings, however, we learn, not in isolated matters, but in all matters, that whatever our concern there comes a point at which a further request for reasons shows nothing so much as that what has been said has been misunderstood. Unconditional oughts, clear and self-evident axioms, reports of immediate experience, simple and direct performatives, covert ways of distributing emphasis: in how many ways do we express ourselves in a manner calculated to render why-questions childish? And most important of all, if a request for further

## II. *Ought and Is*

The controversy as to whether "oughts" are reducible to "ises" has been extensive; but, for all that has been written, the central issues are nowhere more evident than in the contrast between the writings of John Stuart Mill and Immanuel Kant.

Few passages Mill wrote have been more often quoted than the following:

> The only proof capable of being given that an object is visible is that people actually see it. The only proof that a sound is audible is that people hear it; and so of the other sources of our experience. In like manner, I apprehend, the sole evidence it is possible to produce that anything is desirable is that people do actually desire it. . . . No reason can be given why the general happiness is desirable, except that each person, so far as he believes it to be attainable, desires his own happiness. This, however, being a fact, we have not only all the proof which the case admits of, but all which it is possible to require, that happiness is a good. . . .[8]

Now, it is common practice in textbooks on the history of ethics to accuse Mill of an argument which commits the fallacy of four terms. Mill has failed, so it is said, to note the ambiguity of the term "desirable." In one of its senses it means "is capable of being desired"; in another sense it means "is such that it ought to be desired." Mill thus fails to note that the word "desirable" (which has two senses) is not parallel to the word "visible" (which has only one). His argument is paraphrased as follows:

> That which is desired is desirable (capable of being desired)
> Happiness is desired
> Therefore, Happiness is desirable (such that it ought to be desired).

[8] John Stuart Mill, *Utilitarianism* (New York: The Liberal Arts Press, 1949), p. 37.

Whenever I encounter this standard "refutation" of Mill's argument, I marvel that so many people have been satisfied to accept such a paraphrase of what Mill actually says. The paraphrase is a syllogism, albeit fallacious; and I do not see that Mill's argument is a syllogism at all. What Mill *says* is that the word "desirable" *is* parallel to the word "visible." His thesis is that there is *not* a difference in meaning between saying "is such that it ought to be desired" and saying "is capable of being desired." He may be very mistaken in this; but you can only say that he commits the fallacy of four terms if you *assume* that he is mistaken. The whole question is whether "desirable" in its ought-sense is reducible to "desirable" in its is-sense. The argument that this is the case is not a syllogistic argument; and you cannot show that the argument is wrong by pointing out that *if* it were wrong the quite different argument of the paraphrase would commit the fallacy of four terms. Indeed, if Mill were right this different argument would not commit that fallacy.

The real significance of one sentence in the passage reproduced above is too often ignored. Mill says that no reason can be given why the general happiness is desirable except that each person desires his own happiness. Now, on the face of it, this sentence has not been ignored. It has been discussed at length insofar as it raises a very difficult (and a very strange) inductive problem. From the fact that each man desires his own happiness can we infer the conclusion that the "general happiness" is in any sense desired? That is a thorny problem; but there is an even more subtle one *behind* it; and one which should not be ignored. It will be noticed that Mill's complex sentence means that you *can* "give a reason" why the general happiness is desirable. In short, he is claiming that the final, the basic, the overriding end of human action (which according to his view is the general happiness) is such that you *can* give a reason for it. What kind of a reason? Simply the facts—what men do desire—the way the world *is*.

This is the key to Mill's ethical reasoning. Not a syllogism; not a problematic induction; but a basic commitment as to the kind of reason which can be provided as a justification for our most basic and most unqualified commitment in action. Where does the question "Why?" cease to make sense? At that point where we simply exhibit the way the world is.

While we are in the frame of mind produced by these comments, let us turn to Kant. If some of Mill's critics have tried to sidestep his major point, Mill I think tends to sidestep Kant's. I apologize for the following rather lengthy quotation from Mill:

> I might go much further and say that to all those *a priori* moralists who deem it necessary to argue at all, utilitarian arguments are indispensable. It is not my present purpose to criticize these thinkers; but I cannot help referring, for illustration, to a systematic treatise by one of the most illustrious of them, the *Metaphysics of Ethics* by Kant. This remarkable man, whose system of thought will long remain one of the landmarks in the history of philosophical speculation, does, in the treatise in question, lay down a universal first principle as the origin and ground of moral obligation; it is this: "So act that the rule on which thou actest would admit of being adopted as a law by all rational beings." But when he begins to deduce from this precept any of the actual duties of morality, he fails, almost grotesquely, to show that there would be any contradiction, any logical (not to say physical) impossibility, in the adoption by all rational beings of the most outrageously immoral rules of conduct. All he shows is that the *consequences* of their universal adoption would be such as no one would choose to incur.[4]

Surely Mill here misses Kant's point. Kant never once says that in reaching moral decisions you will not *consider* consequences. What he says is that you will never justify your basic standpoint of reference by *induction from* any empirical considerations, including those involving prediction of probable consequences. Once again, Kant's moral theory can only be understood by placing it in the context of his larger theory con-

[4] *Ibid.*, p. 4.

cerning the nature of human knowledge. Some readers of the *Critique of Pure Reason* have been puzzled by a question which might be formulated as follows: If, as Kant holds, so much of what we know in physics is a priori, why do we need laboratories in which we constantly conduct experiments? The answer is that according to Kant what is a priori in physics are purely formal principles. An actual science of physics develops only as we succeed through constant experiment in filling out these formal principles with the concrete matter of experience. One must experiment to find out that friction in particular causes heat in particular. This is consistent, Kant maintains, with the doctrine that we know before experiment that whatever we see will be seen causally related to something else. Similarly, though we know before experiment (according to Kant) that anything seen tomorrow morning at 10:40 will be spatial, one must wait and *look* to find out whether it will be square, round, or triangular.

Just as the *Critique of Pure Reason* does not deny that an actual science of physics depends upon constant experiment; so Kant's moral theory does not deny that concrete moral decisions will depend upon consideration of consequences. The *Critique of Pure Reason* insists, however, that mere experiment and induction do not constitute a science. Behind experiment there must be general principles independently justified. Similarly, no amount of induction, no amount of predicting consequences with a high degree of probability, will constitute a fundamental ethical decision. Beneath the level of induction, the possibility of a reasoned ethics depends upon our success in justifying those decisions on which will rest our very selection of the material on which we focus our empirical attention.

It should be remarked in passing that Kant and Mill have both been misunderstood by mistaking the form of their argument. The misunderstanding of Mill rests on the assumption that his argument is deductive in form; Mill's own misunderstanding of Kant rests on the assumption that because Kant concerns himself with consequences his form of argument is inductive. The tendency to assume that there are two and only two models of sound argument, either strict deduction or strict induction, is here at work. It is a factor of additional interest that the great empiricist Mill should have his remarks thrust into a deductive mold, while Kant, of all people, should have his thrust into an inductive mold. This suggests that it is he who attacks who prescribes the model to be adopted as standard. It may also warn us that any such prescription is dangerous. If Mill's argument is improperly read as a deduction and Kant's as an induction, it does not follow that a reverse reading would be proper in either case. Both Mill and Kant are forcing us to take a stand on matters which will determine where all subsequent deduction and induction in moral theory will start out. We are as it were "back behind" those thought processes which such neat models seek to map.

Now, we have seen that Mill places a limit on the question "Why?" at that point where one simply exhibits the way the world is. It would not be difficult to show that Kant proceeds in a remarkably similar fashion. Consider, for example, the concluding paragraph of the Second Section of the *Fundamental Principles of the Metaphysic of Morals*.[5] Kant there points out that he has not yet "proved" how the categorical imperative is possible—i.e., he has not yet justified it. He has merely shown that the categorical imperative is in its turn the "foundation" of "the universally received notion of morality." Incidentally, this paragraph is an exceptionally clear instance of Kant's peculiar notion that the categorical imperative is a true proposition, synthetic a priori. But the point with which we are now concerned is that, having confessed his failure to justify the imperative ("This section, like the first, was merely analytical."), he proposes in the Third Section to justify it "so far as is sufficient for our purpose."

Thus, the Third Section of the *Fundamental Principles* is all-important. It is there that Kant as it were pushes the question "Why?" to its limits. Hitherto we have been answering all moral

[5] Immanuel Kant, *Fundamental Principles of the Metaphysic of Morals* (New York: The Liberal Arts Press, 1949), pp. 61-62.

why-questions by "analysis" of the categorial imperative; now we apply the why-question to that imperative itself. What happens? Kant launches into an account of his "two-layered" metaphysic. When, toward the end of the section, he finally introduces the heading *"How Is a Categorical Imperative Possible?"* his first sentences are:

> Every rational being reckons himself *qua* intelligence as belonging to the world of understanding.... On the other side, he is also conscious of himself as a part of the world of sense....[6]

Surely, Kant like Mill is placing a limit on the question "Why?" in morals at that point where we simply exhibit the way the world is. As it stands, the whole difference between the moral theories of Kant and Mill stems back to a difference between two ways of looking at how the world is. If I may so express it, the world *is* for Mill one-layered; it *is* for Kant two-layered. So long as you call a halt to moral why-questions at that point where you accept the world as it is, and so long as you disagree as to the way the world is, just so long will your disagreements on moral matters be ineradicable.

There are two directions in which analysis can proceed at this point. The tendency to rest one's moral case on "just seeing the way the world is" leads directly to all of the issues involved in the notion of intuition. When "we just see the way the world is" are we somehow "grasping the truth of general principles" (as the followers of Kant have tended to assume), or are we somehow "inspecting the data of experience" (as the followers of Mill have tended to assume)? One job that analysis can perform will be to examine the notion of justification by "just seeing" in either sense, and to raise the question whether such justification procedures are in any strict sense relevant to fundamental moral decisions. With justification by "just seeing" the following section will be concerned.

There is, however, a prior job which analysis must perform if

[6] *Ibid.*, p. 70.

## OUGHT AND IS

confusion is to be avoided. "Reductionism" is a recent word. When we speak of the "reduction" of ought to is we are generally, I think, speaking with a linguistic reference. We are discussing whether *expressions* of the form "you ought to do so and so" can be translated without remainder into *expressions* of the form "such and such is the case." We understand Mill to be saying that in some sense they can be, Kant to be saying that in some sense they cannot. It is, however, a fact that the kind of expressions which have most interested philosophers has been expressions which assert propositions. Both Mill and Kant are typical in this regard. And it is further a fact that philosophers have until very recent times held the view (often unconsciously) that it is in the nature of a true proposition to record what is the case. Again both Mill and Kant are typical.

Now, if ought-expressions are held to be propositions, and if propositions are held to record what is the case, *one* version of the ought-is problem is prejudged from the start. An ought-proposition which is true will accurately report what is the case, just as, presumably, an ought-proposition which is false will inaccurately report what is the case. Mill clearly thought in this way. A man can say truly that he ought to desire the general happiness if it is the case that most men desire happiness. Evidently if any man said that he ought not to desire happiness he would be incorrectly recording the facts.

Kant's case is simply more complicated. It is of the utmost significance that he persists in treating the categorical imperative as a true proposition. Since Kant defends a two-layered view of the world, it is obvious that he must accommodate two senses of the word "is." There is the "is" of man's phenomenal nature and the "is" of his noumenal nature. There is in fact a kind of super-is such that Kant can insist that man's nature *is* twofold. And in the last analysis, Kant's insistence that the categorical imperative is a true proposition amounts to his insistence that it somehow accurately records this super-fact.

There is a sense in which taking an ought-expression as a proposition *consists* in interpreting an ought as an is. In this sense ought-expressions *are* is-expressions according to both Kant and Mill. But does this mean that there is no crucial difference between Kant and Mill on the issue *ordinarily* discussed when we discuss the supposed reduction of ought to is? Obviously not. For we are contemporary; and when *we* discuss is-expressions we have in mind propositions as we now conceive of them. We think of is-expressions as being either tautologies or confirmable empirical hypotheses. And when we argue as to whether ought-expressions can be translated without remainder into is-expressions we are arguing as to whether the purport of an ought-expression can be fully transcribed in a series of tautologies and testable hypotheses. Kant, for all his insistence that the categorical imperative is a true proposition most clearly did not hold that it was either a tautology or a testable hypothesis.

Kant held that you cannot justify an ought-expression either analytically (his own word, by the way) or by empirical induction. It is at this point that he disagrees with Mill, who believed that you can justify an ought-expression both analytically and by empirical induction. Many of us nowadays would try to paraphrase Kant's thesis as a denial that ought-expressions are properly treated as propositions. But, then, Kant's own insistence that ought-expressions *are* propositions rises to stare us in the face.

It may occur to us to say something like the following: "Come, come. There is no serious difficulty here. Kant did not use the word 'proposition' in our highly technical sense; and he must be allowed a corresponding latitude in his use of the word 'true.' His categorical imperative is simply not a proposition, and he has misled both himself and us by repeatedly insisting that it is." This is easy to say, and may give us a moment in which to relax. But the moment is a brief one. For it surely must lead us to ask: What was in Kant's mind when he insisted that (presumably in some other sense) this imperative *is* a proposition? And to this question we have already provided an answer. What was in his mind was his conviction that the only way in which that imperative can be justified as binding is that it alone will take account

OUGHT AND IS

in morals of the way the world is (for Kant, the "super-is" which records the two-layered character of the world).

What are we to say about this? We surely do not dispose of Kant's point of view by remarking that his use of the word "proposition" differs from ours. On the other hand, a lack of uniformity in the use of the word "proposition" is part of the trouble, and consciousness of the fact may help us to clarify what puzzles us.

We remarked a moment ago that until very recent times philosophers have held it to be in the nature of a true proposition that it records what is the case. They have done more than this. For they have also tended to suppose that our conception of "the way the world is" is coterminous with what can be expressed in true propositions. And this latter supposition has persisted even among those who have tightened up the word "proposition" so that it now has a very strict and limited technical use. There is a very long tradition of assuming that our conception of "the way the world is" (and if you are repelled by the arrogant singularity of that phrase, you may substitute the phrase "how the world is" with no loss of the sense intended) can be recorded by compiling all those expressions and only those expressions which we take to be true propositions. This tradition persisted in the face of the most rigorous specifications with regard to the proper use of the word "propositions"; with the result that our conception of "how the world is" has lately been supposed to be coterminous with what can be expressed solely in tautologies and testable hypotheses.

This latter view was formally and precisely stated by Ludwig Wittgenstein in *Tractatus Logico-Philosophicus* in 1922. Like all great philosophers, Wittgenstein was stating clearly a belief that had long been held unclearly. Subsequent to the *Tractatus*, he became profoundly dissatisfied with it and rejected it. With Wittgenstein's later views we shall be concerned when we discuss the range of analysis in philosophy.

For the moment, as we are concerned with formulating a problem rather than solving it, a warning is sufficient. It may well be that as we make the word "proposition" *more* precise, we render *less* convincing the claim that propositions and propositions only record our conception of "how the world is." I do not mean by this merely that a man's view of the world is tinged with emotion. It is no doubt true that one gains considerable insight into a man's way of viewing the world by studying his "Oh's" and "Ah's" and his grunts of disapproval. These are the data of novelists. But there is something more important here than emotions. For you will also never understand a man's way of viewing the world unless you focus your attention on his habits of decision, the peculiarity of his ways of formulating questions, and, in general, his manner of distributing emphasis. All of these reactions can in sundry ways be expressed linguistically; but few of them are happily or faithfully expressed in strict propositional form. As we increase our precision in the use of the word "proposition" we must be prepared to recognize that *expressions which are not propositions may be par excellence our linguistic tools for conveying our conception of how the world is.*

This tentative suggestion may be read as a defense of Kant's frame of mind, if not of his language. It is a suggestion which, if heeded, may make us less eager to formulate *any* completely general answer to the question about the relation of "ought" and "is." The present growing concern about the puzzling distinction between propositions and performatives,[7] the increasing attention that is being paid to the range of sensible discourse which spreads between fact-stating and theorem-deriving, will produce a more healthy temper in which to approach those problems which have long been lumped under the general heading of "the relation between ought and is." Everything points, as elsewhere, in the direction of the inappropriateness of overly-precise

[7] Once again, and this time in connection with the light it throws on a variety of ethical matters, I heartily recommend Professor Austin's Presidential Address to the Aristotelian Society, October 1956. Professor Austin's sensitivity to the range of reasons which we either do or do not accept as justification for our commissions and omissions sheds more light on the concept of moral responsibility than any amount of generalizing about "ought" *versus* "is." See also my earlier remarks about the word "performatives," pp. 65-67.

boundaries. Just as expressions in propositional form sometimes assume the role of unconditional demands, just so our demands, our recommendations, and our performatives may on occasion assume the role of communicating our conception of the world. There is, in fact, a growing tendency, and a healthy one, to translate our beliefs as to how the world is into decisions as to how language ought to be used. If we reflect on these matters, and if we keep constantly before us the principle that stereotyped dichotomies be used sparingly and with care, we will be well on the way to understanding the limits of the two neat models of justification procedure which have so long preoccupied us. Nowhere more than in ethics and in moral philosophy must we keep our preconceptions as to the requirements of rational justification flexible.

Section IV will be in direct continuation of this line of argument. But before proceeding we must fulfill our promise to examine the practice in moral philosophy of justification by "just seeing." We will find ourselves led once more to a point where these general concerns become of paramount importance.

### III. *Intuitionism*

I return, then, to the two senses in which we have been said to justify our moral notions by "just seeing." First, there is the sense in which we may be said to "just see" the truth of general principles. In such case, we are likely to be told that justification in morals is a matter of deriving theorems in syllogistic arguments wherein such principles function as major premises. Secondly, there is the sense in which we may be said to "just see" the immediate data of moral experience, which particular propositions might truly report. In such case, we are likely to be told that justification in morals is a matter of basing our further hypotheses upon these "rock-bottom" facts as data for induction.

The argument of the present section will be complex. It will therefore be helpful to begin with a summary of the points to be made. They are as follows:

A. The rational intuitionists have been correct in insisting that there are important occasions in moral reasoning when we justify both our doings and our sayings by appeal to general principles. What is more important, they have also been correct in insisting that on some of these occasions it would make no sense to request a further reason once the principle has been clearly stated. Such a request for further reasons might indicate either that the principle in question is rejected by the listener, or, more significantly, it might indicate that the principle in question has not been understood. All of this directs our attention to something basically sound which intuitionists of a certain kind have been trying to say. But we will call attention to the following points:

1. That intuitionism in this connection usually rests upon the covert assumption that in such contexts what we mean by a "principle" is a general proposition somehow immediately known to be true. This assumption is the Achilles' heel of rational intuitionism; for it involves a conception of the nature of moral principles which will not withstand scrutiny. It is important in this connection that we *do* use the word "proposition" in a strict sense, and make clear the fact that normally a principle which functions in moral reasoning in an unconditional way is not a proposition at all.

2. That when we recognize this fact we will be less certain than we have been that the deductive thought-model provides an appropriate model for moral reasoning in such contexts. The rules which govern reasoning from an accepted general principle to a specific and immediate commitment may be very unlike those which govern syllogisms.

3. That the appeal to unconditional principles is by no means peculiar to moral reasoning. If we dig deep enough in any chain of reasoning we will find a similar appeal to principle. There may be special moral principles of this sort, but they are found to function in a sporadic and occasional way. More often than not the unconditional principles of moral reasoning are not (unless we are using the word "moral" in an exceptionally broad sense) uniquely moral.

4. It is not *only* general principles which function in moral

## INTUITIONISM

reasoning in an unconditional way. The highly specific and concrete can function just as unconditionally. And this, of course, leads us to intuitionism in its second sense.

B. The empirical intuitionists have also been trying to direct our attention to something of importance. There certainly is a sense in which all our giving of reasons in morals can be brought to a terminus of "just seeing" matters in one way rather than another. There is such a thing as a moral blindness which has nothing directly to do with understanding general principles. In short, there certainly are specific matters of fact in our ethical experience, which we can do no more than simply *record*, and without which moral reasoning would have no content. But with respect to all this we shall call attention to the following points:

1. That once again it is of the utmost importance to recognize that we are indicating nothing unique or peculiar about moral reasoning. *Any* kind of reasoning faces similar limits. No matter what subject matter one is concerned with, one must start with singular categoricals. Our conception of careful justification procedure in moral theory must take account of this fact; but it is no reason for pigeonholing moral reasoning as peculiar or "incomplete."

2. That the need in moral reasoning of accepting something specific in an unconditional way has nothing to do with the usual claims of empiricism. In particular, it in no way justifies the claim that moral decisions should be treated as testable hypotheses. And it has no more tendency to show that induction is a proper model for moral reasoning than did the need of unconditional principles to show that deduction is a proper model.

3. That neither "subjective" nor "objective" is a word which helps us to characterize any general content of all the specific categoricals which occur essentially in moral reasoning. All versions of Humean "subjectivism" rest both upon oversimplification and confusion. ("Here is a matter of fact; but it is the object of feeling, not of reason. It lies in yourself, not in the object."[3])

---

[3] David Hume, *A Treatise of Human Nature* (London: J. M. Dent and Sons Ltd., 1939), II, 177.

"Objectivism" in its turn is generally either overstated or, except as a cathartic against "subjectivism," pointless.

4. That the tendency now associated with the name of G. E. Moore, to consider such basic and unqualified reports as reports of the presence of "qualities," is without justification. Moore's insistence upon the indefinability of "good" (in its intrinsic sense) points in the direction of an important fact about moral reasoning. But our understanding of that fact must be disentangled from its association with the doctrine that "good" is the name of a unique property.

It would be impossible to compress all of these points into the brief compass of a single section, were it not that much of the groundwork has already been done by others. One does not write in a vacuum; one may profit by the labors of others. It should be added that all of these points will be mentioned only as subordinate to a single theme.

To begin with the problem of general principles, we call attention to R. M. Hare's excellent little book *The Language of Morals* and to a remarkably perceptive essay by P. R. Foot entitled "When Is a Principle a Moral Principle?"

Hare has made it abundantly clear that moral reasoning can not be conceived on either of the strict models which have operated in the past:

> The upshot of all this is rather alarming. I gave in the preceding chapter reasons for holding that no moral system whose principles were regarded as purely factual could fulfil its function of regulating our conduct. In this chapter I have shown that no moral system which claims to be based on principles which are self-evident can fulfill this function either. These two contentions between them, if they are accepted, dispose of nearly all of what Hume calls 'the vulgar systems of morality.' Most ethical writers who have seemed plausible to those who studied them superficially, can be shown to suffer from one or other of these defects. A few great writers, such as Aristotle, Hume, and Kant, though it is not difficult to find

## INTUITIONISM

here and there in their works traces of these defects, can yet, if studied in the right way, be seen to avoid them in their main doctrines. But it is not surprising that the first effect of modern logical researches was to make some philosophers despair of morals as a rational activity.[9]

Hare, however, feels that such despair is premature. He first turns to the proposal of S. E. Toulmin that moral reasoning is a kind of "looser" inductive inference. This view Hare disposes of at once. He sees it as an attempt to save ethics from the attacks of the verificationist school of philosophers; but he finds that it will not do. He offers two sets of reasons. The burden of the first set will be clear in the following remarks:

> Now this programme is from the start misconceived. A statement, however loosely it is bound to the facts, cannot answer a question of the form 'What shall I do?'; only a command can do this. Therefore, if we insist that moral judgements are nothing but loose statements of fact, we preclude them from fulfilling their main function; for their main function is to regulate conduct, and they can do this only if they are interpreted in such a way as to have imperative or prescriptive force. . . . I am going to give reasons for holding that by no form of inference, however loose, can we get an answer to the question 'What shall I do?' out of a set of premises which do not contain, at any rate implicitly, an imperative.[10]

The burden of his second set of reasons is an attack on the conception of moral reasoning as "loose." He distinguishes two senses in which rules of any sort may be considered "valid in general" though not universally. One sense is the sense in which our commitment to a rule will not be shaken by the occasional occurrence of exceptions; all that is required is that exceptions be "not too numerous in proportion to the number of examples." In this sense, a rule *is* "loose." The other sense is one in which a rule

[9] R. M. Hare, *The Language of Morals* (Oxford: Clarendon Press, 1952), pp. 44-45.
[10] *Ibid.*, p. 46.

does not hold for "certain *classes* of cases." In such cases a rule is not "loose." It may be "provisional," but can always be made more precise as the "classes" of exception are more clearly defined. Hare adds, puzzlingly, that "this process is, of course, never completed"; and we may wonder whether *this* fact suggests another sense of the word "loose." But in any event, he concludes by saying:

> Thus I see no reason [to reject the notion that] principles of conduct entail particular commands. The entailment is rigorous. What we have to investigate is, not some looseness in the entailment, but the way in which we form and modify our principles, and the relation between this process and the particular decisions that we make in the course of it.[11]

The above is the final paragraph of Chapter 3. Chapter 4 opens by setting up a syllogistic model for moral reasoning, in which moral principles are assigned the role of major premises.

Hare, who has been on the verge of recognizing that neither of the classic models will quite do in ethics, thus ends by returning to one of them. In the end, he clearly rejects only the model of inducing testable hypotheses; the model of deduction, albeit with perceptive and instructive *caveats*, he retains.

Mrs. Foot's remarkable little essay takes Hare to task on precisely this point. Mrs. Foot is acutely sensitive to the complexity of what *actually* transpires when we engage in moral reasoning. The burden of her remarks is that on many, if not most, occasions it is a complete distortion to conceive of moral principles on the model of major premises of syllogisms. When one does so, one borrows a very precise notion from traditional logic and forces it upon an imprecise situation wherein it is often misleading. Many of Mrs. Foot's remarks might be reproduced with profit; but the following must suffice:

> It *is* true, as he [Hare] says, that if we make a particular moral judgment we can always be asked to support it, and we might

[11] *Ibid.*, p. 55.

## INTUITIONISM

call this "giving reasons," but on what grounds does he go on to assert that "the reasons consist in the general principles under which the moral judgment is to be subsumed"? The "reasons" in fact consist in all sorts of statements about the case concerned, and even when we are asked, e.g., why two cases are treated differently we do not always try to find a rule under which those which are similar can be subsumed. In the sense in which it is right to say that there must be a *principle* behind every particular moral judgment, a principle is not a maxim or general rule of conduct; it would be right to speak of grasping or understanding it, but not necessarily of its *formulation*. The notion of a principle as a general rule does not belong here, and seems to have been imported from other contexts, e.g., those in which a man is asked whether he subscribes to this or that moral principle. This borrowing has led not only to the invention of a hidden generalisation where there is no actual generalisation to be found, but also to a misrepresentation of the course of moral arguments.[12]

Much of what Hare says about our use of principles in moral reasoning is unquestionably sound; and Chapter 4 on "Decisions of Principle," in spite of its initial appeal to an inappropriate model, is unsurpassed in recent moral philosophy. But Mrs. Foot renders an important service when she notes the inappropriateness of that model. A careful study of both Hare's book and Mrs. Foot's essay will suggest two conclusions: First, that when we speak of general principles in moral reasoning we should avoid the idea that we are speaking of propositions known to be true. Hare sees that such principles are in no sense the self-evident truths of traditional rationalism (p. 44); he sees that they are not inductively testable hypotheses (pp. 44-54); he does, however, flirt with the analogy of major premises in Aristotelian practical syllogisms. It remains for Mrs. Foot to throw suspicion on *this*. The result is that we should avoid the notion that princi-

[12] Mrs. P. R. Foot, "When Is a Principle a Moral Principle?" *Aristotelian Society, Supplementary Volume XXVIII* (London: Harrison and Sons Ltd., 1954), p. 101.

ples in such contexts are properly conceived as propositions *at all*. Hare himself treats them as announcements of basic "decisions"; and that is precisely what they are—no more, no less. Secondly, we should be constantly on our guard lest the model of deducing theorems from axioms and premises mislead us in our description of moral reasoning and in our search for the canons of justification on which such reasoning depends. "Appeal to principle" is not synonymous with "deducing."

These will be recognized as the first two points we proposed to make about rational intuitionism. The third point is simply this: Both Hare and Mrs. Foot—indeed most writers who discuss these matters—tend to write as though what they are discussing is somehow unique in moral reasoning. If that be stated as a thesis, it is certainly false. Any scientist, or historian, or literary critic, must appeal to principles in exactly the same sense. I do not mean by this that any scientist, or historian, or literary critic, is *also* a moral agent. Though that is certainly true, it is not what I am saying. I am saying that the canons of justifications *in* science, *in* historical studies, and *in* literary criticism, will always be concerned with commitment to basic principles which are not properly conceived as propositions. The principle of empiricism itself is not a proposition. So long as it was thought to be so, and so long as we believed that there are two and only two standard models of justification procedure, our speculation about the "justification of induction" was a shambles.

This fact is becoming more and more widely recognized. Unfortunately it has led to a great deal of woolly thinking in connection with the use of such ism-words as "pragmatism" and "irrationalism"; but that is a problem which I shall treat in detail at a later stage. For the present, I record the fact and draw no morals. I am seeking in this chapter to formulate a problem, not yet to solve it.

Our fourth point was that not *only* general principles function in moral reasoning in an unconditional way. This, by the way, is part of what Mrs. Foot was trying to say in criticism of Hare. But, in any event, this point will be made sufficiently clear in our discussion of intuitionism in its second sense. To this discussion I now turn.

I begin by calling attention to an article by Isaiah Berlin, published in 1950, entitled "Empirical Propositions and Hypothetical Statements." This article does not concern itself with moral philosophy. Berlin's subject matter is phenomenalism and general epistemology. At no point in the article do any matters of moral philosophy arise. Nonetheless, it will be noticed (as we proceed) that everything Berlin says applies *mutatis mutandis* in moral matters. This being so, it follows that the basic need in moral reasoning for singular reports of a categorical kind is a need which is by no means unique in moral reasoning. I shall quote at length from Berlin's article—and in so doing I request the reader to keep his mind on *moral* matters. Berlin is concerned with an attack on the ends-in-view of philosophical phenomenalism. His thesis is:

> that no direct translation from categoricals into hypotheticals is, as a general rule, and as our language is to-day ordinarily used, a correct analysis of, or substitute for them.[13]

Now, a certain counterpart of the phenomenalist thesis is very widespread in moral theory; and certain forms of intuitionism have been principally motivated by the desire to reject that thesis. Consider the following summary of Berlin's argument; and notice its applicability *in toto* to moral matters. When Berlin speaks of a "categorical existential sentence" he has in mind sentences like "There *is* a desk in my office." When he speaks of "hypothetical sentences" he has in mind the usual phenomenalist equivalents in the form "If one performs such and such operations one will have such and such experiences." For parallels in the moral domain one may consider such a contrast as "This *is* a worthy act" or "Jones *did* insult my wife" *versus* the obvious hypotheticals which various moral theories have suggested.

[13] Isaiah Berlin, "Empirical Propositions and Hypothetical Statements," *Mind*, LIX (July 1950), p. 300.

Berlin begins:

> But what precisely, it may be asked, is it that such categorical existential sentences do that hypothetical ones fail to do? Certainly I wish to avoid saying that the former describe the facts while the latter do not, since the unhappy term "fact" has been used in too many different senses to be illuminating in this connexion. Nor do I wish to assert that hypotheticals and categoricals are never interchangeable and are mutually exclusive. . . . But I do suggest that systematic differences in verbal form are often pointers to differences in meaning which it is important not to obscure. Hence, as a tentative way of putting it, I submit that those categorical propositions which we seem to be unable to "reduce" to other logical forms without apparent violence to normal usage, tend to direct attention to—invite us to look for—things and events in a way in which other kinds of expressions do not.[14]

Several pages later he continues:

> I should not dream of maintaining that verbal or grammatical form is an infallible guide to logical form, *i.e.*, kinds of ways in which sentences mean. Indeed, that is the whole point of exposing the dispositional character of expressions which *prima facie* appear non-dispositional. But because some or many categoricals are in this sense concealed hypotheticals (*i.e.* their meaning is made clearer, or certain errors are prevented, by the substitution of hypotheticals) because language is flexible and the frontiers shifting and vague, it cannot follow that the distinction does not exist at all, that the frontiers are invisible—for if that were so, such words as "dispositional" and "hypothetical," (there being nothing with which to contrast them) would not signify anything at all. And this is not what phenomenalists or defenders of the theory of logical constructions, if their own words are to mean anything, want to say.[15]

Notice that Berlin is insisting that the phenomenalist himself must

[14] *Ibid.*, p. 302.   [15] *Ibid.*, p. 305.

## INTUITIONISM

have recourse to categoricals. He immediately takes cognizance of the fact that certain phenomenalists have conceded this. But he remarks about this:

> We are there at last: this really is what phenomenalism boils down to: that the only irreducibly categorical propositions, by contrast with which alone hypotheticals are what they are, are statements about immediate experience, capable of direct, strong, "knock-down" verification. These are basic. All else is theory and speculation. . . .[16]

And he immediately remarks:

> . . . even if we do not press for cash in the form of basic sentences against phenomenalist cheques (as being unfair and against the spirit of the conventions in use of language) the argument still remains fallacious. For what this view comes to is that material object sentences—including existential ones—are so many general propositions or hypotheses or theories about the behaviour of sense data. And this is precisely what common sense finds so repugnant.[17]

Berlin agrees with common sense. He agrees, in short, with Dr. Johnson's long-neglected refutation of Berkeley's phenomenalism.

> . . . the essence of hypothetical or conditional sentences is to be in a peculiar way non-commital. . . . Existential categoricals on the other hand, commit us.[18]

It may be objected that I cannot, as I have done, suggest a genuine parallel between what Berlin is talking about and basic singular commitments in ethics. The sentences "There is a desk in my office" or "There is an ashtray on that desk" may be said to assert empirical propositions, whereas singular moral commitments do not assert propositions but announce decisions. But surely there is no such clear-cut distinction. When we say of the sentence "There is an ashtray on that desk" that it expresses an empirical proposition, we mean that it asserts some-

[16] *Ibid.*, p. 306.   [17] *Ibid.*, p. 306.   [18] *Ibid.*, p. 307.

thing which experience may falsify. If one replies to the systematic doubting of a phenomenalist (as in effect Berlin rightly does) "Look here, this *is* an ashtray dammitall" one is *not* saying something which he considers falsifiable in the usual sense. There is an important difference here which we generally express either by our tone of voice or by the use of italics: the difference between saying "This is an ashtray" and saying "This *is* an ashtray." We may be told that the latter expression merely announces a decision as to how the word "ashtray" is to be used. No doubt it *may* fulfill such a function; but it is absurd to say that this is "mere." The fascinating thing about such expressions is that we want them to function *both* as announcements of our decisions as to the use of language *and* as empirical descriptions. The either-or alternatives of pigeonhole philosophy break down.

Singular categoricals of this sort arise in many different contexts. Philosophers as different as Kant and Russell may both be said in a sense to base most of what they say on the singular categorical "Physics *is* knowledge." We are always tempted *both* to interpret such a pronouncement as an empirical assertion that physics does in fact yield successful predictions, *and* to interpret it as a prescription that "knowledge" means "the sort of thing physics is." The interesting thing is that both interpretations are attractive; and the same is true when we insist of something that it *is* an ashtray. We are tempted both to say that we are announcing a fact and that we are prescribing how a word is to be used. And surely the same temptations arise when we encounter such expressions as "This *is* a worthy act" or "Jones *did* insult my wife."

All of this raises puzzling problems for general philosophical analysis. We shall try to meet such problems head-on in Chapter Five. For the moment, we need make only two points: First, that the need for singular categoricals in moral reasoning raises a general philosophical problem and not one which is confined to moral philosophy. We are far too prone to throw up our hands in moral philosophy when we run up against thorny problems which we fail to recognize as completely general in all contexts of justification. If misery loves company, this may be some comfort to moral philosophers. Secondly, that the need for singular categoricals in moral reasoning is in no way a support of the usual empiricist thesis that moral decisions are testable hypotheses. The point we are making—that singular categoricals are necessary in *any* train of reasoning—does not rest on the highly dubious claim that such categoricals must be *either* tautologies *or* protocol propositions. They may be either or neither. The only legitimate inference we can draw concerning the claims of empiricism is of a different character. For in the last analysis the question *whether* we interpret a given expression as a testable hypothesis will depend upon prior decisions of a categorical and singular kind. This is another point to which we shall return later.

I have now made all of the points on which my argument will hinge. It remains only to guard my flank against certain misconceptions which are likely to arise in any discussion of moral philosophy. The first is this: Someone will certainly appear who, while admitting the need for singular categoricals in moral reasoning, will insist that the only expressions which so function are reports of our feelings and attitudes. *This* is the difference between moral reasoning and other kinds of reasoning. The singular categoricals of morals are peculiarly "subjective."

I have already published two articles in which I have tried to show how unjustified such a generalized thesis is. The argument is complex and cannot be reproduced here. I shall, however, indicate its guiding theme. In an article entitled "The British Moralists and the Fallacy of Psychologism"[19] I attacked David Hume, whose writings have set much of the tone of this kind of thinking. I tried to show that Hume metamorphosed a perfectly sound generalization about the tendency of moral judgments to *express* feelings and attitudes into a grossly misleading generalization to the effect that moral judgments always *indicate* (are propositions rendered true or false by) such feelings and

[19] James Ward Smith, "The British Moralists and the Fallacy of Psychologism," *Journal of the History of Ideas*, XI (April 1950), 159-178.

attitudes. If one examines the texts one finds that Hume's argument depends upon tacit assumption of the unexamined (and misleading) notion that all moral judgments must somehow indicate (be rendered true or false by) a single unique kind of fact. This assumption, plus the discovery that the only "generic" feature about all our moral judgments is their tendency to express feelings and attitudes, generates the thesis that all our moral judgments indicate feelings and attitudes.

Now, the fact that all our moral judgments *express* feelings and attitudes does not make them in the slightest degree peculiar. Every judgment we make *expresses* feelings and attitudes—be they feelings of belief, conviction, doubt, amazement, boredom, or what-not. If subjectivism is saying that moral judgments express our feelings and attitudes, it is saying nothing which marks off moral judgments as a special class. If, on the other hand, it is saying that moral judgments always indicate (and presumably indicate nothing but) our feelings and attitudes, it is simply mistaken.

In an article entitled "Senses of Subjectivism in Value Theory"[20] I considered this question systematically rather than historically. I there distinguished three versions of subjectivism:

- a) that moral judgments are rendered true or false only by the occurrence of attitudes or feeling states.
- b) that moral judgments are not true or false at all.
- c) that moral judgments always express attitudes or feelings *of a certain peculiar type*.

The first version, which is Hume's,[21] is misleading for the reasons already given. The third version is suspect for two reasons. First, it is evident upon reflection that any attitude or feeling could have moral significance under appropriate circumstances; and

[20] James Ward Smith, "Senses of Subjectivism in Value Theory," *The Journal of Philosophy*, XLV (July 15, 1948), 393-405.

[21] Hume, as my article explains, sometimes speaks as though "x is good" indicates my feeling of approval, sometimes speaks as though it indicates the fact that x *causes* my feeling of approval. For reasons discussed in the article, the former view must be accepted as his real meaning.

it is doubtful that any restricted "generic" description of a moral attitude or feeling will satisfy all who reflect. But secondly, even if such a generic description were agreed upon, it would almost certainly not enable you to make any progress in moral philosophy. For your generic description would have to be so broad that you could surely not contend that *only* moral philosophy is concerned with judgments which express *that* kind of attitude. Your success would be solely at the level of psychological description, and would not help you to do what you have to do as a moral philosopher—namely, to define the canons of justification procedure in moral reasoning. This leaves the second version of subjectivism, which contends that moral judgments are never true or false. And I can only say in this abbreviated summary that such a contention seems to me to be absurd. No doubt many of our moral judgments are not properly spoken of as true or false—are not propositions at all. But this is equally true of much that we say as scientists and as historians; and there is no good reason whatsoever for legislating out of hand that our moral judgments are *never* properly spoken of as propositions.

The real difficulty with "subjectivism" is that it tries to offer a completely general (a "generic") description of the character of moral judgments. In this it must fail. Our moral expressions are sometimes analytic, sometimes testable hypotheses. More often than not, they are neither. A. J. Ayer, and the early positivists, performed an important service in calling our attention to the latter fact; though he, and some of them, drew grossly mistaken inferences from it. If, then, "subjectivism" errs in offering a generic description of moral judgments, "objectivism" may fulfill a legitimate role in insisting upon exceptions. We may, as "objectivists" insist that some of our moral judgments are true or false propositions; or we may also insist that where they are not there are sound canons of justification procedure for handling them.[22] Unfortunately, however, "objectivists" have been as tempted as the "subjectivists" to offer generic theories about

[22] See, e.g., William Kneale, "Objectivity in Morals," *Philosophy*, XXV (April 1950), 149-166.

the way in which moral judgments *always* function. And they have been just as guilty of the practice of pigeonholing moral judgments as sharply divisible from scientific ones, just as prone to separate the canons of responsible reasoning in morals from those in science, and just as subservient to the tradition of two and only two models of rational justification procedure. These are the habits of thought we are here attacking; and the words "subjectivism" and "objectivism" are far too impure to be of any help to us. I trust that I have said enough to prevent their arising to muddy the waters of further discussion.

My final comment, and the second flank I wish to guard, concerns the tendency associated with the name of G. E. Moore to regard singular categoricals in moral reasoning as reports of the presence of properties—indeed, of the presence of a single unique property. There has been a great deal of discussion of Moore's thesis, and there are certain points on which I believe we can record increasing agreement. To begin with, there is increasing agreement that the language of Moore's argument is misleading. Moore's assumption that the adjective "good" functions as the name of a property, rests upon incomplete analysis of the function of adjectives in discourse.[23] In the second place, Moore confuses the fact of our inability to define a generic sense of the word "good" (in its intrinsic sense) with the theory that "good" is somehow simple and unanalyzable. The final result of all the controversy over Moore's version of the so-called "naturalistic fallacy" *is the lesson that we should regard with suspicion any attempt to provide one and only one definition of "good" even in its "intrinsic" sense.* In an excellent little essay entitled "The Place of Definition in Ethics" G. C. Field proposes that we should start with all of the vagueness and lack of precision in what ordinary people say, and *find out* to what extent we can

---

[23] On this point consult P. H. Nowell-Smith, *Ethics* (London: Penguin Books, 1954), especially Chapter 5. See also R. M. Hare, *op.cit.*; and Morton White, *Toward Reunion in Philosophy* (Cambridge: Harvard University Press, 1956), passim.

## INTUITIONISM

clarify usage by sharpening up a whole range of possible "definitions" or "analyses."[24]

But while Moore's language, together with what one might call his metaphysical apparatus, is unsatisfactory, all of the writers to whom I have just referred agree that Moore was trying to say something sound and important. The burden of his argument was that limits must be prescribed to the possibility of *description* in moral philosophy. His thesis was that we can only properly be said to describe those *things* which we find good (in the intrinsic sense), never their goodness as such. If we translate this thesis out of the language of a metaphysical Platonism with regard to properties into a language which concerns itself with the rules governing the proper use of expressions, it comes simply to this: That our ethical and moral reasoning cannot be exhaustively analyzed into definitions on the one hand and descriptions subject to empirical test on the other. There are more than two kinds of expression which function in moral discourse; and in particular there must be expressions of a singular and categorical type which are neither analytic nor testable general hypotheses. This provides no ground for adopting a platonic conception of the independent existence of qualities or properties; but it *does* provide ground, as Moore rightly saw, for rejecting as unsatisfactory a good many of the moral philosophies of the past.

This completes our remarks on the claims of "intuitionism." It will be noticed that we have seldom used the word. Like all ism-words, it implies too much. If used at all, it should be used sparingly. On the other hand, those who have been labeled "intuitionists" in moral philosophy have not been devoid of insight. They have not been fulminating in a vacuum. There are

[24] G. C. Field, "The Place of Definition in Ethics," reprinted in Sellars and Hospers, *Readings in Ethical Theory* (New York: Appleton-Century-Crofts, Inc., 1952), pp. 92-102. For a discussion of Moore's conception of simplicity see Morton White, *op.cit.*, especially Chapter X, section 6.

## MORAL PHILOSOPHY

several points to which they have rightly been seeking to call attention. The most important is that there *are* points at which the request for further reasons in moral disputation has no place. The plural is important. It is sometimes inappropriate to ask for reasons when what we are saying is general; it is sometimes inappropriate to ask for reasons when what we are saying is specific and singular.

We have omitted mention of two of the most competent philosophers who have defended "intuitionism" in recent times: H. A. Prichard and W. D. Ross. Careful consideration of their writings would be out of place in the brief compass which is essential if we are to keep our focus of attention upon our own systematic line of argument. A word may suffice. Both Prichard and Ross say much which is, in the opinion of the present writer, sound; but each, in rather similar ways, is prone to overstate his case. Both are concerned at bottom with the limits of justification procedure in moral reasoning, and on this general point both may be read with profit. But the first way in which each overstates his case involves the tendency to speak of "having knowledge" in those cases where we find that giving reasons for what we say is inappropriate. Ross, for example, suggests that in certain cases where we say "we think" in morals we do not merely "think" but "know."[25] And Prichard, whose guiding theme is that moral philosophy is "a mistake" when it persists in requesting reasons where the request for reasons is inappropriate, is prone to speak of "reason-giving" and "proof" as synonymous.[26] This is why he inclines to consider an opinion for which reasons need not be given as something "known"; that is to say, as something

---

[25] "I would maintain, in fact, that what we are apt to describe as 'what we think' about moral questions contains a considerable amount of what we do not think but know, and that this forms the standard by reference to which the truth of any moral theory has to be tested, instead of having itself to be tested by reference to any theory." W. D. Ross, *The Right and The Good* (Oxford: Clarendon Press, 1930), p. 40.

[26] E.g., ". . . even if the nature of the act is completely stated, it is still necessary to give a reason, or, in other words, to supply a proof." H. A. Prichard, "Does Moral Philosophy Rest on a Mistake," in *Moral Obligation* (Oxford: Clarendon Press, 1949), p. 8.

already sufficiently "proved." But surely to say that the request for giving reasons is inappropriate and to say that we know something are two very different things. The word "knowledge," for all its vagueness, is in this connection a device for overstatement.[27]

Behind this tendency lies a second way in which both of these writers tend to overstate their case. For both are under the influence of the Platonism of G. E. Moore. Each, like Moore, is prone to assume that a singular categorical (for which reasons ought not to be asked) must in some sense designate the presence of a "property." And this, as we have seen, is certainly an overstatement. Thus, for all their valuable insight into the character of moral reasoning, both Prichard and Ross must be accused of distortion. They rest their case for an ism upon overstatements.

In the end, then, our discussion of the claims of intuitionism has brought us full circle to the conclusion we had already reached. For we have in the present section said nothing about moral reasoning which could not also be said about reasoning in science or in history or in any other rational undertaking. The limits of justification procedure in moral reasoning are tokens neither of disgrace nor of extraordinary powers. They are shared by the justification procedures of science. We are far too prone to accept an oversimplified account of the justification procedures of science. If we do so, and then find that a similar account will not be sufficient in the case of moral reasoning, we too hastily conclude that moral reasoning is "queer" or "less rigorous" or even "irrational." The antidote to this poison is a fuller awareness that there are parallel limits of the justification procedures used in science.

## IV. *The General Problem and the Moral Problem*

The formulation of our problem in moral philosophy is forcing us at every turn to recognize the existence of a more general problem. This more general problem involves what I have several

[27] I shall make my own peace with the word "knowledge" at a later stage of the argument.

times referred to as "the dichotomizing tendency." For purposes of analysis dichotomies are often useful. Consider, for example, the following list:

(i) describing *versus* not describing
(ii) describing *versus* deciding
(iii) expressions of which it is appropriate to ask whether they are true of false *versus* expressions of which it is inappropriate to ask whether they are true or false
(iv) analytic *versus* synthetic
(v) deducing *versus* inducing.

All of these dichotomies are useful for certain purposes, though they are not always useful for the same purposes. And yet, in whatever direction we turn we invariably discover that philosophical questions force us into a twilight zone in between the paired terms.

In recent literature, the most widely discussed of the above paired terms is perhaps the pair analytic-synthetic. It would surely be a mistake to say that you cannot draw the distinction between analytic and synthetic in any precise way. You may be as precise as you choose. The difficulty is that the more precise you are, the more clearly it emerges that most of your important problems concern expressions which fall in between the paired terms. Unhappily, the moment one points this out one is accused of trying to revive the synthetic a priori; and there are in fact those who want to do precisely that. There is, however, an alternative course: to concede that if you make your terms sufficiently precise the phrase "synthetic a priori" has outlived its capacity to clarify your problem, but to insist that a problem remains. For, your concession in no way disposes of those important expressions which are neither analytic nor (in your precise sense) synthetic.

Is it necessary to repeat that the same problem arises with regard to our use of the paired terms "induce" and "deduce"? Here again you can define the terms as sharply as you choose. But the more sharply you define them the more clear it becomes

## THE GENERAL PROBLEM

that our methods of reasoning seldom fall in either category. Again, the twilight zone in between, where we are misled by the assumption that two and only two respectable alternatives confront us.

It has become almost a matter of common practice among philosophers to distinguish between the concerns of science and the concerns of "moral philosophy" or "value theory" by appeal to such paired terms as the others in the above list. Science is concerned with describing; moral philosophy is not. Or more specifically science is said to concern description; moral philosophy is said to concern decision. Or again, science is said to concern expressions appropriately designated as true or false; moral philosophy is not.

Recent periodicals have been filled with articles expressing puzzlement as to our use of the word "describing." The word is certainly used in a wide variety of ways. It may be argued that it has no single meaning; and it may be pointed out with some justice that the word is often far from an antonym of such a word as "deciding." Is not the selection of one description rather than another a case of decision? And yet it would be foolhardy to deny that a dichotomy such as "describing versus deciding" can be sharpened up in any way one likes. The real difficulty is that the more you sharpen it up the more clear it becomes that most of our philosophical problems concern the doing of something that falls in between.

It may be said that the justification of all such dichotomies is precisely their tendency to lead us in this direction. There is truth in this. What we ordinarily do by way of thought, reasoning, and using language, is as a rule vague, vacillating, elusive—in a word, sloppy. Philosophy's task is to sharpen things up. We will be naïve if we suppose that one dichotomy will solve all our problems of cataloguing; but the constant application of many of them will gradually lead us to the only kind of clarity we can achieve. And yet, while there is truth in this, there is danger. Call the danger, if you will, the danger of negativism. So long as we are preoccupied with dichotomies, the discovery that important matters lie between the reference of the paired terms is only negative. It remains to consider in a positive way the canons of responsibility in between.

Suppose you start with some clearly drawn distinction between describing and deciding; and suppose you start with the assumption that science concerns the former, morals the latter. You then discover that the descriptions of science do rest on important cases of deciding, and that the decisions of morals do rest on important cases of describing. What you are likely to do is to conclude that part of what scientists do is of concern to moral philosophy and that part of what moral philosophers do is of concern to scientists. But such a conclusion fails to note that what you have *discovered* casts doubt on the assumption with which you *started*. When you drew your clear contrast between describing and deciding it simply was *not* correct to assume that science concerns only the former, morals the latter. The whole point of the basic philosophical problems in moral theory is that they fall somewhere between describing and deciding. And the same is true of the basic philosophical problems in science.

The difficulty may be expressed in another way. If you are a man whose concern is with ethics or political theory, or more generally with moral philosophy as a whole, you have to *ask* the question whether and to what extent the important things you want to say are descriptive or prescriptive. You cannot prejudge the answer to such a question by *defining* your subject as concerned solely with prescription or decision. And the same is true if your concern is with science. You have to *ask* whether what you want to say is either descriptive or prescriptive. You cannot *define* your concern as solely descriptive.

The dichotomy is thus still misleading. It leads you to discuss the relation between two disciplines which you assume to have different rules of procedure, whereas in fact those differences are not as precise as you have assumed them to be. It is a dangerous distortion to say that part of what scientists do is the concern of moral philosophy and that part of what moral agents do is the concern of science. Everything that constitutes part of the

## THE GENERAL PROBLEM

actual procedures of science is the concern of the philosopher of science; and everything men do as moral agents is the concern of moral philosophy. If part of what men do *as scientists* is to commit themselves to principles of procedure, to decide that questions ought to be asked in one way rather than another, to interpret by distributing their emphasis before any deductive or inductive enterprises can gain a foothold—then science as such is concerned with commitment to principles, with decisions, and with the rock-bottom question of justifying one's distribution of emphasis. If part of what men do *as moral agents* is to offer descriptions of the facts which constitute the world—then moral philosophy is concerned with describing. There are no sharp boundary lines between justification procedures in science and justification procedures in moral reasoning. This is the negative conclusion we reach when we understand the limited range of applicability of all these dichotomies.

But what can we say positively about that twilight zone where in the end we always find ourselves? We can say at once that we do not have in mind just a third pigeonhole. We end up not in a pigeonhole but in a vast uncharted range. If I may use a rather bad analogy, it is as though we have all along been faced with the problem of examining and analyzing a vast series of subtly modified gray patches. We have hitherto allowed ourselves only two clearly defined terms, "white" and "black," and have doggedly persisted in describing all the grays as mixtures of white and black. A little bit of this and a little bit of that. In an essay purporting to survey the results of contemporary analysis, an essay filled with either-or distinctions, Herbert Feigl describes a rule as "a tautology with added directive appeal." What an absurd description of the character of a rule![28] We need not only to recognize the limited usefulness of the terms "black" and "white"; we need more careful and more sensitive analysis of the gray patches as gray.

The paramount need both in the philosophy of science and in

[28] I shall consider Feigl's treatment of rules at length in Chapter Five. For reference and full discussion see below pp. 142 and 165.

moral philosophy is a more straightforward discussion of the canons of justification to which we can appeal when we are dealing with practices in the twilight zone. When one discovers that all his reasoning about a given matter rests upon his acceptance of a principle which is certainly not a tautology and certainly not an empirical hypothesis, how can he go about justifying what he is doing? When we discover that we are accepting certain specific reports as beyond reasonable questioning, how can we go about justifying what we are doing? Or, to return to one of the most puzzling problems I have raised: if my "view of the world" rests in the final analysis upon my acceptance of nonpropositional utterances, how can I go about justifying *my* view of the world as opposed to some other?

These questions are the questions which will arise if we accept the burden of treating grays as gray. And they are completely general philosophical problems; they do not concern moral philosophy alone. The final problem of moral philosophy *is* the problem of justifying your distribution of emphasis, but this is the final problem which we reach in any rational undertaking. Instead of black and white, instead of pigeonholes, instead of facile dichotomies, one faces a range of questions with gradually expanding scope of reference. The final problem in political theory is the justification of one's distribution of emphasis in deciding questions of public policy and group action. The final problem in moral philosophy is the justification of one's distribution of emphasis in all decisions as to human responsibility and purpose. The final problem in science is the justification of one's distribution of emphasis in all decisions concerning the canons of procedure one accepts as a scientist. And philosophy itself is concerned with nothing short of the total problem of justifying one's distribution of emphasis in any theoretical or avowedly rational undertaking.

I have plunged *in medias res* and localized this problem, first in political theory, and then in moral philosophy generally. In both cases, the justification of one's distribution of emphasis requires some attempt at formulating canons of responsibility to which

## THE GENERAL PROBLEM

we can appeal at various points where what we say or what we do, we say and do unconditionally. Merely to formulate this problem, as we briefly noted at the conclusion of Chapter One and as we now note again, suggests an inescapable circularity in all justification procedure. An unconditional commitment is one in connection with which a why-question is somehow inappropriate; and yet the persistent demand of rationality is that we seek some mode of justifying even this. We must somehow justify our very fiats as to what we will accept as a justification.

My plan of procedure is as follows. In the next chapter I shall confine myself to outlining a solution to the problem as it arises in political philosophy and in moral philosophy. I shall argue that it *is* possible to formulate rational canons for justifying our basic distribution of emphasis; and I shall argue that the key to this solution lies in the very circularity which we find inescapable. But this solution in political and moral philosophy will point beyond the limited range of problems to which we apply it. Our whole conception of the nature of philosophical method will be affected. I shall therefore turn in later chapters to the broader philosophical scene. And I hope that what I have to say will throw considerable light on the progress of philosophy in recent decades.

One final word about the problem before turning to solutions. There are few principles more respected among philosophers than the principle of fallibilism. It is a principle to which I have myself appealed in the course of my argument. And yet I fancy that I hear a chorus of objection from those who adhere to the principle of fallibilism. It will be said that my repeated recourse to commitments which are unconditional and unqualified is nothing short of a constantly reiterated recommendation that we abandon the principle. Fallibilism requires that we never block the road to inquiry by assuming that we cannot be wrong. It will be said that a commitment which is unconditional is precisely what *will* block the road to inquiry. This is a complete misunderstanding, and I am anxious to clarify the matter.

No one has more clearly formulated, or been more staunchly

devoted to, the principle of fallibilism than Charles Sanders Peirce. It did not prevent his using the word "must"—and meaning it. What confuses us? What is the relation between accepting the principle of fallibilism and use of the word "must"? In answer, two points should be made. In the first place, the "musts" which the principle of fallibilism repudiates are "musts" concerning the way the world is. Peirce rightly saw that the crucial habit repudiated by that principle is the habit of assuming that our latest and best hypotheses *are*, or adequately represent, the truth.[29] While the principle rejects all "musts" as to the way the world is, however, it *constitutes* a "must" as to our methods and canons of reasoning. In this sense, the principle of fallibilism if seriously accepted is itself an unconditional commitment.

In the second place—and I think that Peirce rightly saw this too—it is hazardous to draw too clear a division between our commitments as to the requirements of sound reasoning and our conception of the way the world is. As Peirce put it, what our metaphysics becomes is merely the making explicit of all of the asumptions on which our methods of reasoning are based. It follows that the principle of fallibilism, insofar as it constitutes a "must" governing our intellectual life, is an important clue to sound metaphysical speculation. There is nothing in all this to block the road to further inquiry. Indeed, the road to inquiry has on occasion been most blocked by those who refuse out of hand to treat the word "must" as respectable.

At heart, the remainder of this book is concerned with the word "must." And perhaps the most important "must" with which it will be concerned is that which is entailed in acceptance of the principle of fallibilism itself.

[29] Few of Peirce's doctrines have been more persistently misunderstood by later pragmatists than this one. For fuller discussion see below pp. 186-188.

# CHAPTER FOUR: OUTLINE OF A SOLUTION FOR POLITICAL AND MORAL PHILOSOPHY

## I. *Towards a Solution*

IT SOMETIMES happens that after long struggle with a problem a slight shift in the focus of our consciousness makes us aware that in the very seeing of the problem as a problem we have had in our grasp, though all unknowingly, the elusive essentials of a solution. In one of the subtlest and most masterfully conceived of all short stories, "The Beast in the Jungle," Henry James envisions a sensitive and thoughtful man whose life is haunted by the anticipation of some rare and strange event, some prodigious and terrible truth, which one day will spring upon him and give to his life such fullness as it is to have. In the end, too late, he realizes that this great and awful truth has been his constant companion throughout his years of search. He has been unaware that what he sought was in his hands; and his failure is a failure to accept what he *had*. His life is empty because he fails to appreciate the fullness that is *in* it.

The history of political and moral philosophy is a history of anticipation and search. We seek answers; we long to find the magic key which will unlock the doors to political and moral truth. Then, in that apocalyptic day, we would with key in hand nobly and confidently produce nothing but sound decisions in matters political and ethical. But as matters stand we are discouraged, depressed—almost debilitated. In times of candor we despair of agreement; and we know that whatever we say on political or ethical matters someone will find ground from which to attack us. The burden of the preceding chapters is to reject all panaceas and to cast suspicion on the favorite thought-models of the past. We cannot solve men's political or moral problems on the deductive model of mathematics. Neither can we endorse with honesty the vision of an age of political and moral engineering. We are driven by the haunting sense that somewhere, somehow, there must be a way of justifying as rationally responsible

## OUTLINE OF A SOLUTION

men our commitments in action. But wherever we look, the canons of such responsibility escape us. We come up again and again upon what we can *not* do with any honest hope of success. We seek the beast which when it springs will make us full. It does not spring, and we are empty.

Can we, with but a slight shift in the focus of our consciousness, discover that our very awareness of the conditions of the problem we face contains within it the germ of a solution? Are all of the "cannots" against which we stumble merely negative? They are of the essence; they define the problem. Take from them not despair but enlightenment. Precisely in those "cannots," and nowhere distant or unattainable, lie the keys to sound political and moral philosophy. You cannot divorce the whole question of the canons of responsible reasoning in political philosophy and in morals from the history of our past failures. We hold in our very hands, precisely *in* the clear perception of what is amiss in the eager excessiveness of the empiricists, precisely *in* the clear understanding of where deductive methods lead us astray, precisely *in* a growing consciousness of the failure of rigid models and the insidious distortion of the dichotomizing tendency—we hold in our very hands the key to responsible reasoning about our decisions in action. Look not to some far off yonder; scrutinize and *understand* the mess that is in your hands.

We have formulated the need. It is a need for the categorical, the unconditional—the need for a base on which to take one's stand. Very well; cannots are unconditional and they may be basis enough. The principle of fallibilism itself levies an unconditional demand; it prescribes a cannot from which there is no escape. From this theme which we have in hand, my thesis will grow.

When we tackle the kind of question with which political theory is concerned, nothing is more categorical than the demand that we face our own limitations. I mean by this that our plans and our proposals at the level of political action are *not* the sort of thing that can be conceived as justifiable either by deduction or by strict induction. The imperative, the performative utterance if you will, that in matters of political theory we are limited as to the kind and the degree of justification we can use, is a rock-bottom categorical. I shall argue that this imperative is the very basis from which we *can* justify the democratic approach. The binding reasons for the democratic approach to political problems rest upon first recognizing the limits within which we can expect to provide reasons at all. In short, the justification of democracy is methodological. Part of what I shall try to show is that this involves us in frankly using a way of interpreting (as we surely must) while we are in the very process of justifying it. The importance of this must never be underestimated. It leads to no shallow relativism; it leads rather to the uncompromising insistence that *all political philosophies which talk as though anything else is possible are wrong.*

I want first to make this clear as a matter of political philosophy. I shall then turn to the outline of a similar solution of the central problems of ethics.

## II. *Political Philosophy*

Fallibilism in political theory requires explicit recognition of the limits of the possibility of proof. There are three ways in which we can conceive of the major disagreements in political philosophy. Two of those ways are traditional; and both rest upon a misunderstanding.

We sometimes conceive of disagreement as a conflict between deductive systems which operate in terms of different, even contradictory, axiomatic sets. We are often told that the major conflict of the present age is the conflict between Communism and Christianity—the conflict, if you will, between the Kremlin and the Vatican. It is certainly a fact that much of the political speculation of the age is concerned with this conflict; and it is also a fact that some writers have viewed the conflict as a clash between axiomatic systems. It is evident that if a Communist proposes to "justify" his political recommendations by "deduction" from a dialectical materialist metaphysic, and if a Christian proposes to "justify" his political recommendations by "deduction" from a two-layered spiritualist metaphysic, there is an important difference between them. We have seen that deduction is a questionable model in terms of which to conceive of what either Marxists or Thomists actually accomplish. But so long as the model persists there will remain one kind of dispute in political theory.

Surely, however, this is not the only kind of conflict which characterizes the present age. We may even doubt that it is in any sense the "major" conflict. There are, as we have seen, many who despise the model of deduction in political philosophy, while continuing to read the arguments of their opponents on that model. In any event, there is a widespread tendency to conceive of conflict in political theory in a different way—as conflict between the model of deduction and the model of induction. So viewed, we may think of the major conflict of the age as one in which the Kremlin and the Vatican are ranged on the same side. Their opponents are the John Deweys and the Karl Poppers who plead for social engineering.

Now, both of these forms of disagreement rest on a common assumption. For they both rest upon the idea that proof of some special sort is possible in political theory. Disagreement of the first sort rests on the assumption that demonstrative deductive proofs are in order; disagreement of the second sort rests on the assumption that *either* deductive proofs *or* inductive statistical proofs are in order. This suggests a third form of disagreement which is in fact far more fundamental than either: the disagreement between those who believe that justification in political theory must be on one or other of the two models described—anything else being "irrational," and those who think that rational justification in political theory should not be tied down to either model. In short, there is a disagreement between those who conceive of rational justification as one or other of two special kinds of proof and those who seek to divorce the whole idea of rational justification from the idea of proof.

My thesis will be that the "foundation" of democratic political philosophy *consists in* the rejection of the concept of justification by proof. Such a thesis can be defended only by concrete reference to the actual principles of procedure which we are trying to justify when we try to justify what we call "the democratic approach." I cannot, in a limited compass, discuss all such principles; but I intend to discuss a selected list of some of the more important ones. They are:

(i) The much-discussed principle of the separation of church and state.
(ii) The less often discussed principle of the separation of science and state.
(iii) The principle of checks and balances.
(iv) The principle of the poll.
(v) The principle of equality and freedom.

One cannot discuss the justification of democracy in any other way then by explicit reference to just such principles as these.

It is not an accident that the democratic tradition has repeatedly expressed itself in the demand for separation of church and state. Nor is it accident that the separation demanded is between *church* and state rather than between *religion* and state. The church is an expression of the need for religion as a social force to crystallize into a specific creed. If what I have said in Chapter Two is sound, there is no logical or philosophical reason why a religious metaphysic may not be adapted to any political proposal one wishes to make. With ingenuity almost anything is possible—even the adaptation of a broadly conceived Christian metaphysic to specific economic and political proposals of Communism. There have been Christian democrats, Christian socialists, Christian fascists, and Christian communists. But the church as a concrete institution is not merely a body of philosophical theories; it is an institution too often based on the principle of justification by deduction. The church as a social and political force has repeatedly sought to fulfill the role of possessor of the truth from which judgment follows and on which justification is based. The Roman Catholic Church is of course the supreme expression of this idea; but the history of Protestant social thought is pervaded by the same fundamental idea. The history of Protestantism is a history of repeated revolt against the recurrent crystallization of dogma; but every successful Protestant revolt has itself eventuated in the crystallization of a new dogma.

Both Catholic and Protestant may insist that the doctrine of the church prescribes only the general ends of social life, not specific detail. Interestingly enough, the more rigorous the central dogma of the church, the more flexible it seems as to specific details. A study of the specific programs of political action supported by the Roman Catholic Church in Italy, Spain, France, England, and the United States will attest to this flexibility. But from the standpoint of political philosophy it is precisely the prescription of general ends which raises the important problems. These, Protestant and Catholic alike, insofar as each thinks as representative of an organized church, will justify as entailed by a body of religious doctrine.

The democratic demand for separation of church and state expresses the rejection of the idea that even the general ends of social action can be justified by deduction. The democratic tradition springs from suspicion of the idea that any one of us or any group of us has hold of the truth by the tail. If we did, there would be no point in democracy. If any group of us possessed the truth, and if justification in action were a matter of deduction from the truth, political policy *ought* to be dictated by those favored few. The general principle of fallibilism, which warns us against anyone who poses as possessor of the truth; the more specific methodological insight into the inapplicability of the deductive model as a model for justification of proposals in action; *these* are foundations of the principle of separation of church and state.

The Kremlin and the Vatican may symbolize the same failure to comprehend the democratic spirit in this respect. Both Marxists and Thomists too often ignore one of the most important of all the "cannots" of political theory. You cannot justify your political proposals by deduction from the truth. To assume that you can is precisely *not* rational, for it rests on misunderstanding of the kind of justification procedure which is appropriate to the type of thing you are doing when you make a political proposal.

## POLITICAL PHILOSOPHY

Now, there ought to be a principle standing on a par with the principle of separation of church and state. Call this principle the principle of separation of science and state. Suppose the "social engineers" were right. Suppose that political programs could be justified by statistical induction from the facts. What would be the point of democracy? Surely in such a case we should fill the legislative benches with social scientists. We may not have a convenient label for the principle involved, but the democratic tradition is notoriously suspicious of any such practice. Why? Because the social engineers are as guilty as the church in conceiving of justification as a matter of "proving the truth." The only difference is that instead of deducing from a priori axioms they induce from statistical evidence. The word "prove" has simply shifted from one technical sense to another. Once again, the whole nature of justification in political theory is misconceived. You can no more prove a political proposal true by induction than you can prove it true by deduction. Political proposals are not the sort of thing you "prove true" in either strict sense. The democratic tradition in its suspicion of control either by the church or by science has been the expression of a dim awareness of this fact. And that suspicion *can* be rationally justified.

I know that I will be severely rebuked by many who will read more into these paragraphs than I have put into them. I am not attacking social science; I am attacking those who claim that social science of a certain sort can solve man's political problems. I am not attacking any religious conception of the world; I am attacking the record of the church as a dictator of political goals. And in both, I am defending the essence of the democratic tradition. Social science properly conceived is one of our most urgent needs; and properly conceived can be a vitalizing force in the democratic tradition. Religion properly conceived is one of man's most living rational needs; and it too can be an expression of the democratic spirit. But this must not deter us from uncompromising rejection of habits of thought which if allowed to dominate would crush the democratic spirit.

## OUTLINE OF A SOLUTION

The basic categoricals on which the justification of democracy rests are methodological "cannots" which are internal to the record of past mistakes. "Cannots" are disillusioning only so long as we cling to the misguided goals whose attainment they prohibit. Cling to the ideal of deducing your political proposals from large metaphysical generalizations, and it will be disillusioning to learn that you cannot accomplish the universal justification you envisage in those terms. Cling to the ideal of establishing your political proposals as confirmed or confirmable hypotheses, and it will be disillusioning to learn that you cannot. If, however, you will assimilate what you have learned, and drop the misguided goals, you will find that those very "cannots" provide positive grounds for adopting one method of approach to political problems rather than another. The mistake of supposing that our policies can be justified by deduction from a Christian metaphysic (a mistake which has nothing to do with the soundness of that metaphysic) is no worse, nor better, than the mistake of supposing that our policies can be justified as hypotheses verified by social science (a mistake which has nothing to do with the soundness of social science). And the lesson involved in learning that each mistake is a mistake is fundamental in justifying the democratic policy.

Clearly, the principle of checks and balances rests upon the same internal lesson of fallibility. If separation of state from church and science rests on suspicion of any group which poses as possessor and teacher of the truth, separation of powers within the state rests on suspicion of any individual who poses in the same light. Historically, the system of checks and balances in the United States grew out of the Puritan (ultimately Augustinian) doctrine of sin and of man's depravity. You cannot trust man in the singular for he is depraved; your system must provide checks and balances to limit his capacity for harm. The doctrine of man's depravity was of course part of an elaborate metaphysical system of ideas; but I need hardly say again that a political practice of checks and balances is not "proved true" by any such theory. The doctrine of man's depravity is subject to all of the remarks which

## POLITICAL PHILOSOPHY

in an earlier chapter I made about the theory that "All men are created equal." There are no doubt numerous ways in which it could be so interpreted as to make limited empirical sense. Men are too prone to assume that they are right and others wrong; they are apt to mouth principles on which they fail to act; they find it difficult not to be corrupted by power. Any such failing *might* be called "depravity"; and the statement that man is depraved might simply state a limited empirical prediction about the way individuals will probably behave. But such limited predictions provide no binding reasons for a practice of checks and balances. As a matter of empirical fact, power does not always corrupt and men sometimes do adhere to the principles they mouth. Marxists, Thomists, and Hegelians can always take refuge in the empirical exception.

Like "All men are created equal," the doctrine of depravity *may* be interpreted as a tautology. The most interesting statement of the doctrine with which I am acquainted is Jonathan Edwards'. And Edwards' method is to provide a system of definitions such that the doctrine becomes a tautology. True Virtue is defined as disinterested. Conscious action is defined as chosen; and choice is defined as interested. It follows that all conscious action is interested and hence, by definition, not truly virtuous. This is what Edwards *means* by the doctrine of depravity: that all consciously chosen acts are consciously chosen.[1] From this you could deduce any political proposal you liked.

The system of checks and balances is not "proved." It can, however, be justified on the basis of the same methodological

[1] In *The Nature of True Virtue*, Edwards insists upon this in the following manner: To say that an action is "depraved" is not to say that it is "morally bad." He describes a "scale" of moral good at the level of depraved action. To say that an action is depraved means that it is done from "self love" (which means for Edwards the same as "is chosen"); and *either* morally good *or* morally bad deeds may be done from self-love (i.e., by choice). He then goes so far as to concede that, at the higher end of the scale of morally good (though still depraved) acts, we may choose actions which are in all overt respects indistinguishable from truly virtuous ones. The *only* difference is that in one case we choose, in the other we do not. — See selections in *Jonathan Edwards*, edited by Faust and Johnson (New York: American Book Company, 1935), pp. 349-371, and esp. pp. 367-371.

"cannots" which justify separation of church and state or science and state. You cannot operate on the assumption that power is in the hands of those who can prove themselves right. This gets us *behind* the facts that power tends to corrupt, that a man tends to assume himself right and others wrong. The source of those depravities is the very thing we are discussing: the assumption that you could prove yourself right though you may never have tried.

Consider next the principle of the poll. Few of the principles of democracy are more confusing and yet more central. One reason for confusion is that there are two entirely different senses in which we may conceive of a poll: as a survey or as a vote. In one sense, a poll is a device for estimating the facts, especially with reference to the state of public opinion. So conceived, the poll is part of social science. It is an empirical, inductive experiment. It also has nothing to do with the claims of democracy. A communist or fascist totalitarian state might conduct polls of this sort morning, noon, and night; and it might claim that in so doing it was proceeding democratically. Admittedly, it would be salutary to base your estimate of what the people want upon a statistical poll rather than upon an a priori theory as to what they "really" want. It would be a step in the right direction. But it would not yet be what democracy demands. For democracy demands a poll not as evidence to support an hypothesis but as a device for decision. The vote decides what policy is to be; there is no higher appeal. You do not justify democracy by justifying statistical methods. What requires justification is the principle of *decision* by the poll.

You will find that the justification of this principle is usually associated with the proclamation that all men are created equal. We therefore return again to our remarks about that proclamation. If, as I have pointed out, we are proclaiming no more than a tautology—that men are men as mountains are mountains—we are justifying nothing. More accurately, we can deduce anything we like; therefore we justify nothing in particular. On the other hand, if we proclaim an empirical hypothesis we proclaim truths so limited that the principle of decision by vote will derive little or no support therefrom. In what sense is the vote of an unintelligent hothead "equal" to the vote of a learned and deliberative man? Must my defense of the poll rest upon an absurd denial of inequalities? Is not the opposite the case? Does not the whole force of the principle of decision by vote rest on men's actual *inequalities*? It is precisely the fact that farmers, mechanics, and bankers are disparate in their opinions, their hopes, their aversions, and their desires which gives force to the conception of a poll.

The principle of the poll cannot be justified by appeal to a tautology, and if it entails blinding ourselves to actual empirical inequality it cannot have any binding force. My thesis is of course that it entails nothing of the sort. It entails in fact precisely the rejection of the notion of *proof*, either by axioms or by statistics. The foundation of our commitment to the poll is simply this: that without the dogmatism fostered by the idea of proof, without the presumption of those who have thought that the validity of their own solutions can be demonstrated, you have no rational ground for ignoring what people want. To state the matter otherwise: you are never justified in denying to ordinary people (with all their inequalities) the right to make their own errors in their own way, on the pompous grounds that you are yourself a privileged person incapable of error. The principle of the poll rests not on the absurd empirical hypothesis that every vote carries the same weight of intelligence or wisdom; it rests upon the mandatory concession that every man's opinion is fallible. No man can presume to demonstrate that his political opinions are gospel. A rational man will listen to the opinions of others, and will agree to regulate his action by the decisions of others, not on the ground that majorities are incapable of error, not even on the dubious ground that majorities are more likely to be right than single individuals, but simply on the ground that he realizes that his own opinion may be wrong. We never know beforehand whence a just opinion or a valid insight may come. Our commitment to decision by the poll rests not on the principle that everyone has something valid to say; it rests on the principle that where everyone is given the right to be heard, a reasonable man is given the broadest possible scope for checking his own opinion against others.

It may be argued that I overlook the one equality which the doctrine of equality justly proclaims: equality of opportunity and the freedom precisely to participate in decision. Far from overlooking this sense of the doctrine, it is the one sense I unqualifiedly proclaim. The democratic principles of equality and of freedom are not something *other than* the principles we have hitherto been discussing. They *are* those principles rightly interpreted. When one proclaims the right of all men to be heard and to freely participate in corporate decisions, one is not proclaiming a truth one is proclaiming a recommendation. One does not justify by proof, one can only justify by showing in a methodological way that any other recommendation misconstrues the very nature of justification in political theory. The principle of freedom of expression can be justified only in a peculiarly internal way. We can justify it only by showing that all attempts to violate it rest on a misconception of the limits of justification itself.

If I am right, the "willingness to learn" which Karl Popper rightly describes as the essence of rationality is also the essence of the democratic spirit. But willingness to learn is not synonymous with confining oneself to testable hypotheses. Understanding of what is required by the attempt to be rational involves understanding of what we *cannot* do. This is why "cannots" are such important grist for the philosopher's mill. They provide us with the key to a rational point of view. So far as political theory is concerned, there seem to be two ways in which this might be expressed; and the interesting thing is that it matters little which way you select. The "foundations" of democracy are, or ought to be, principles which lie behind the principles we usually state. You may say on the one hand that these "basic" principles are

## POLITICAL PHILOSOPHY

commitments as to method. In order to justify democracy (allowing people freedom to express their opinions, insuring checks and balances between separate trustees of social power, and separating political control from domination by any special clique) you need not wrangle about such questions as whether men have immortal souls, whether they are incapable of good, whether they are always motivated in some special way. It is enough to achieve a clear understanding of what it means to provide rational justification for proposals such as those on which we act. This is one way of putting it. But there is another way of saying the same thing: namely, that these commitments as to method are not "mere." They themselves provide the conception of man on which democracy is based—the conception of a creature complex enough never to be described quite accurately by any sweeping generalization. Words falter when we try to state these matters sharply; but it is as though the only adequate conception of man's nature is one based on the premise that no attempt at describing *the* nature of man can succeed.

As adherents of the democratic tradition, our basic commitments are commitments as to method; and they are often commitments which we ourselves hardly understand. As in all things, what we do and what we believe, what we ask and hope and accept and despise, commits us in ways of which we are unaware. And this means that occasional confusion is inevitable. We misconceive of the very things for which we stand. We are sometimes like the scientist who verbalizes principles inconsistent with those entailed in doing the sort of thing he does. The principles we so often discuss, the platitudes of political oratory, are too often (like the conventions which we discuss when we sit down to the bridge table) peripheral and optional. Our basic commitments as to method we do not discuss; only, unlike the basic and undiscussed rules of bridge, they are neither arbitrary nor simple. The game analogy is a poor one; but if we persist in it we can only say that we are playing a game which we do not fully understand.

This is why a thinking man finds disillusion so easy. When we look not at the principles we mouth but at the entailments of what we do the result is too often disheartening. In this frame of mind, one of the most important questions we can ask is the following: *What are we willing as a nation to recognize as a problem serious enough to act upon?* For years one of our own senators in the United States acts in ways which consistently violate and openly repudiate every one of the principles which, if I am right, are the central ones in the democratic faith. In particular, freedom of expression of opinion and respect for the principle of checks and balances between legislature, executive, and judiciary are openly despised and ridiculed. Thinking men were long tortured by the failure of the American people to react; public opinion seemed incapable of recognizing the seriousness of the problem. The less misanthropic will argue that in time the problem came to a head; but the more misanthropic will regret the fact that what brought the problem to a head was not its essential character. A nation may pride itself too hastily if it fails to ask the question: What were we willing as a nation to recognize as a problem serious enough to act upon?

But however easy disillusion may be, it is not inevitable. It is dangerous to judge a nation by the news that reaches print. Newspapers may make misanthropes of thoughtful men. We may forget that most of what is important in American life does not make headlines. Who are these men in the headlines that we should judge American standards in terms of them? Aunt Sally, and the gardener down the street, are in most things more representative of what America stands for. The tabloids scream of murders, rape, and theft; but the street on which I live is a quiet, law-abiding, happy place. My street is typical; that is why it has never, so far as I am aware, been in the news.

The "foundations" of democracy are the foundations of that street and of the life that is led upon it. If what we have said is sound, there is one commitment which is more important than any others to what goes on there. It is commitment to the principle that the rights of others be respected. This principle is essentially methodological. I cannot concede that it is "irrational." It is itself the very lifeblood of rationality.

## III. *Moral Philosophy*

It would be a mistake to suppose that we are not already committing ourselves on fundamental moral and ethical issues. Such an approach to political problems is essentially a way of approaching moral issues. Democracy is a moral matter; and everything I have been saying about political decision is part of the answer to our moral dilemma—part only, but an important part.

The first key to sound moral philosophy is recognition of the limits within which we can rationally require justification by proof. Both metaphysical mathematicians and scientific engineers must once again be put in their proper places. We cannot justify our moral maxims by demonstration. The most we can do is to show that our method of approach to moral questions is rational; and the only rational approach is one which defines its own limitations. Just as the central commitment of sane political theory must be a recognition that we cannot base our institutions on the premise that our answers are final, so the central commitment of sane moral philosophy must be a recognition of the right of all men to search for what is good in their own way. There is nothing negative about this; and it does not imply that anything is good which people see as good. It prescribes a positive conception of moral wrong and of moral right. Just as in political matters the sin of sins is the denial of the right of free decision—subject to all the dangers entailed in continuous interchange of opinion—so in ethical matters the sin of sins is refusal to be sympathetic to ways of seeking good other than your own. A sincere man will always try to persuade others to see the good as he sees it; but a sensitive man will always also try to see the good as others see it.

The key to ethics is the key to all sound teaching, sound fathering, and sound preaching. That key is breadth of sympathy—a sense of breadth and variety, a sense that there are many ways in which to find the good in life, a sense which can never flourish where we are dominated by the urge to rigorously prove. Good teachers, good fathers, and good preachers do not force men into stereotyped molds. They do not force their own methods of justification into stereotyped molds. This is one reason why a good teacher learns from his students and a good father learns from his sons. Moral philosophy is barren unless it incorporate a generous sympathy for the desires, the hopes, the shortcomings, the capacities, the purposes, the problems, and the sufferings which are other than one's own.

Now all of this constitutes a thesis *in* moral philosophy, whereas my job is to talk *about* moral philosophy and to defend a conception of the justification procedures on which it rests. It is impossible to do the latter without the former. The prescription of methodological categoricals for moral philosophy determines both a justification procedure and a conception of moral right. When as moral philosophers we provide advice as to the proper methodological approach to moral problems we cannot avoid at one and the same time providing concrete moral advice. We often try to fool ourselves in this connection. It is time that we repudiate the repeatedly announced claim on the part of philosophers that the job of philosophical ethics has nothing to do with the giving of concrete advice. It has in fact everything to do with it. What is usually said is that philosophical ethics has nothing to do with "casuistry"; but "casuistry" is simply a pejorative term. What is usually meant is that a philosopher needs to stand outside of concrete advice-giving and to examine the rules on which the concrete ought to proceed. This ignores what I have called the internality of the very concept of justification which is required. The soundest concrete advice will be that which is based on clear-headed understanding of what is and is not possible by way of moral justification procedure; and, on the other side of the picture, a philosopher's recommendations as to what are acceptable justification procedures in morals constitutes pregnant moral advice.

As is so often the case, we are wielding a double-edged sword. One edge cuts at those philosophers who, jealous of their status as aloof commentators, discuss the criteria of ethical and moral justification without ever once addressing themselves to the pressing problems of men and of nations. Ethical philosophy too often takes on the appearance of a clever but pointless game. It is rightly criticized if what it says provides no leverage for adjudicating important moral disputes. But our sword has a second cutting edge. For it cuts also at all those who too easily conclude that the results of recent analysis do *not* provide keys to sound moral advice. There may not be as much divorce as sometimes appears between the results of competent methodological analysis in philosophy and the criteria of sound moral advice.

This latter point, that the basic categoricals of sound moral advice emerge precisely from sound methodological analysis, is my major theme. I want in the present section to expand the theme in two ways. First, I want to concretize some of the lessons we can learn *as moral agents* from the results of sound methodological analysis. Secondly, I want to return, as will now be appropriate, to my earlier claim that our conception of the world is most importantly expressed in our non-propositional utterances —in our questions, our recommendations, our performatives, and our demands. In short, our moral decisions express our view of the world fully as much as does our science. All of this will bring me at long last to the problem which at the opening of Chapter Three I promised in due time to face: the problem of formulating a conception of the nature of man on which to base both our moral and our political philosophy.

One concrete lesson we can learn from competent analysis is the inappropriateness of the thought-models proposed both by the metaphysical mathematicians and by the scientific engineers. Of this lesson we have said enough, and it alone may make us wiser moral agents. But analysis has taught us more than this. The second lesson we can learn might be called "the danger of overgeneralization."

The fact of the matter is that most of what has passed as philosophical ethics in recent years has been a quagmire of overgeneralization. This charge can be levied against much of the work produced by the analysts themselves; and there may seem a strange perversity in *criticizing* analysis in the very process of commending it as teacher. Therein lies a still deeper lesson. Competent analysis begins with what men do both as philosophers and as moral agents. The very mistakes that competent analysis makes are sometimes the most vivid way in which we can throw light on what is wrong in our habits of thought both as philosophers and as ordinary men. Since the time of the early writings of G. E. Moore philosophical ethics has been struggling with the methodological problems involved in all attempts to define either the adjective "good" or the substantive "the good." Moore, as we have noted, held it to be a fallacy to believe that you have defined "good" merely by describing some characteristic which is shared by all the grammatical subjects of which that adjective is truly predicated. His contention was that "good" is itself indefinable. Others have argued that Moore commits *petitio principii*; that the fallacy he describes is a fallacy if and only if "good" is known to be indefinable on independent grounds; that if it *is* definable, defining it will be a case of specifying a characteristic common to all those things of which it is truly predicated. The argument has spread, and the participants have often written as though what hangs in the balance is the very fate of philosophical ethics. The presumption persists that philosophical ethics must *either* attempt to offer a general definition of the predicate "good" (or alternatively to agree with Moore that "good" stands for an indefinable quality) *or* attempt to offer some general characterization of "the good."

The real lesson of all of the analysis, even when it sometimes involves this presumption, is that the fate of philosophical ethics is independent of any such presumption. If ethics *is* conceived as standing or falling according as success is or is not achieved in either or both of these perverse enterprises, ethics *will* fall. There is no generic sense of the adjective "good" which will satisfactorily cover all its uses, not even the sense of naming an indefinable property. And no attempt at a general characterization of "the good" will ever satisfy a reasonable man sensitive to

## MORAL PHILOSOPHY

the complexity of live ethical and moral problems. The controversy initiated by Moore must have a therapeutic effect. It has fastened on a habit of thinking deeply embedded in our moral reasoning; it has made us aware, as nothing else could, of the perversities of the habit; it now remains for us to discard the habit and to recognize that the job of philosophical ethics is *not* the job of providing generic definitions either of "good" or of "the good." Nor is this a lesson for philosophical ethics alone. It is a lesson we must learn in our moral life.

Consider, first, the adjective "good." We need to face the fact that it has an extraordinarily wide range of different and confusingly related uses. This is evident in our everyday use of the term; it is equally evident in the wide range of theories concerning its "proper" meaning which have mushroomed in academic philosophy. Anyone so moved may select some special meaning of the word, he may even invent one, and on the basis of that initial move play whatever game he likes. But playing such a game is not, or should not be, the prototype of philosophical ethics. And it is dangerous as a source of bias and of distortion in practical moral reasoning. It is always important to ask ourselves: "Given one particular definition of 'good' rather than another, what is properly called 'good' in this sense?" It is simply wrongheaded *to* ask: "What is *the* proper definition of 'good'?" Where there are many possible meanings of a word-in-use it is profitless to argue about whether there ought to be only one. An intelligent man will prefer to be as clear as he can about the different meanings of the word, and about the things which it helps him to say in each of those meanings. The adjective "good" is rather like the adjective "true." The word "true" has a wide range of more or less haphazard and different meanings in popular usage, most of which are of little or no interest in philosophy. If, however, we slough off sloppy uses *as* sloppy, it does not follow that we are left with only *one* correct sense of "true." There are, as Leibniz saw, at least two different correct uses of the term in technical parlance, and we wreak havoc when we ignore the difference. "True" may mean "logically true" or "empirically true"; it is important, once we have made this clear, to find out what can properly be called logically true, what factually true; it is wrongheaded to continue to ask "Ah! yes, but what does 'true' mean?" "Good," as I say, is like "true" in this respect; the fundamental difference being that where "true" has two clearly designated technical meanings, "good" seems to me to have many.

Consider secondly the substantive "the good." Comparison of the adjectives "good" and "true" suggests that we might compare the substantives "The Good" and "The Truth." So far as I can see, and ignoring for the moment the ambiguity of the adjective "true," there may be two different things we may mean by "The Truth." On the one hand, we may simply wish to designate as "The Truth" the set of all true statements. Why talk *about* this? Surely what is important is to determine what statements are true and in what sense. There are no doubt complicated relations of implication and subordination between various true statements; but we have, I think, pretty well escaped from the once popular notion that all true propositions fall into a hierarchized set which either can be or ought to be squeezed into a single map. It is time we escaped from the comparable myth that all good things form a neatly ordered hierarchized set. The world is far too rich (far too "good," if you will) for that. "The Good" may be an innocuous enough phrase if it means simply all those things, events, hopes, thoughts, persons, and what-not which are appropriately designated "good"—either in some special sense or in any sense; but unless the phrase means something more than this I can see no profit which will ensue upon further discussion of it.

It may be said, however, that the phrase "The Truth" refers to something more specific than the set of all true statements. It may mean one or a few true statements which are somehow more general, or perhaps just more important, than all others. And it may be said that the phrase "The Good" has a comparable use. "The Good" is not properly translated as "the set of all good things"; it is properly translated only by such phrases as "the final end of human action," or "the summum bonum." This means that when we talk about "The Good" we are not talking about the set of all good things; we are talking about one or a few good things which are somehow more inclusive or more important than all others. Now, I do not for a moment decry the attempt to discuss the ends of human action. I am highly suspicious, however, of the unargued assumption that there is, or must be, *one* end which occupies a special position of pre-eminence. What we take as an end in action depends upon how we are interpreting, upon what we are considering more basic and in what sense. We come back, in short, to the theme which has been preoccupying us throughout. It seems to me that arguments about *the* end of human action rest upon failure to appreciate the complexity and richness of human life. It will profit us more to seek what clarity we can achieve concerning the wide range of ways in which we can interpret the world and find good in it.

There is a kernel of insight hidden away in every ethical system. It would be remarkable if thinking men would specify as *the* meaning of "good" something which nobody including themselves ever meant by the word. It would be remarkable if thinking men would describe as *the* final end of human action an end which nobody including themselves had ever sought. Unfortunately the kernel of truth is embedded in a mass of overgeneralization. Some who have recognized the existence of many kernels of truth have suggested that we discuss either "good" or "the good" in a still more generic sense.[2] This, however, is like trying to correct a fault by committing it in a more excessive way. When one man tells us that the final end of human action is happiness, another that it is security, another that it is understanding through suffering, another that it is knowledge, another that it is love of God; and when we convince ourselves that there is something important which each of them is trying to say; are we to conclude that the final end of human action is somehow all of these things? Surely it would be more reasonable to recognize that each of these men, while trying to say something important, has been misguided in referring to what he has in mind as *the* end of

[2] See, e.g., E. A. Burtt, "Generic Definition of Philosophic Terms," *The Philosophical Review*, LXII (January 1953).

human action. When one man tells you that man's nature is depraved and another tells you it is naturally good; and when you convince yourself that each is trying to say something significant concerning human problems; you may be tempted to conclude that the nature of man is somehow both depraved and good. But it would be more to the point to recognize the misleading character of all talk about *the* nature of man. Human beings are like horses. You do not *understand* them by concentrating on generic definitions which apply to all of them. The same can be said about understanding what is good in life. When you say that one meaning of "good" is *the* meaning, or that one good is *the* good, you reveal a lack of self-consciousness. You are not sufficiently aware of what you yourself are doing. You are yourself interpreting; but you are forgetting that fact in the very process. Your use of the word "the" suggests that you are blind to the possibility of alternative interpretations; and your blindness has caused you to shift the focus of your attention from an important question to a wrong-headed one.

What is the important question? What is the task of philosophical ethics? It is nothing more nor less than to advise men as to how they should approach moral questions. And we advise men *badly* if we advise them to approach those questions in a spirit of overgeneralization. We must advise them to act and to think as fallible men in the midst of confusion, not as potential calculators in a well-defined game.

We must fight the notion that philosophical ethics requires us to substitute neat propositional calculi for all of the welter of nonpropositional puzzlement and decision of which our moral life consists. One of our most potent weapons in this fight will be clear-headed analysis of the limits of propositional calculi as models for the rules governing our proper use of language as reasonable men. I thus return to the theme that philosophy's most crucial problems—in any of its branches—arise at that point where what we need to say is not in any strict sense propositional.

Few points I wish to make are more difficult to express clearly than the one I here confront. I want to say that the foundation of a rational moral life must involve conscious concern for an important difference: the difference between the sense in which one's moral decisions do and the sense in which they do not express one's conception of the nature of the world. Confusion on this crucial matter has misled us and will continue to mislead us in our attempts to justify what we do as moral agents. I shall try to make my point succinctly by starting with something familiar enough to common sense, familiar too in recent philosophical literature, and by then revealing the inadequacy of the familiar.

The familiar start has perhaps been best stated by C. L. Stevenson in a book entitled *Ethics and Language*. We often want to say that in some sense our beliefs about the world are determined by our attitudes. Stevenson repeatedly uses the peculiar phrase "rest upon" in this connection. Very well; in some sense our beliefs do rest upon our attitudes, just as our attitudes rest upon our beliefs. This is plain common sense. What follows? Stevenson rightly sees that, whatever else may follow, it is important to determine in cases of ethical disagreement whether we are disagreeing primarily about beliefs or about attitudes. He then finds himself led, however, to the following conclusion:

> *If* any ethical dispute *is* rooted in disagreement in belief, it may be settled by reasoning and inquiry to whatever extent the beliefs may be so settled. But if any ethical dispute is *not* rooted in disagreement in belief, then no *reasoned* solution of any sort is possible.[3]

This remark is followed by a chapter entitled "Persuasion." The thesis is that insofar as disagreement is rooted in attitudes, only persuasive techniques are appropriate, and the implication of the passage cited is that conclusions arrived at by even the best of persuasive techniques are not "reasoned."

Now, we have admitted something at the level of "plain common sense" from which all this purports to follow. Does it really?

[3] C. L. Stevenson, *Ethics and Language* (New Haven: Yale University Press, 1944), p. 138. Italics are Stevenson's.

Let us go back to what we admitted; and let us in particular pay closer attention to these words "beliefs" and "attitudes."

These are very vague words; and we must be careful if we are using them as a paired dichotomy. In ordinary parlance we speak of "an attitude of belief." This is not a serious difficulty, and, as in all matters of this sort, vague words may be sharpened up. Stevenson, who represents a well-known strand of contemporary analysis, is certainly using the word "belief" as a label for any of our opinions which can properly be expressed in propositional form, either as a tautology or as a testable hypothesis. Other forms of expression express our "attitudes." The question then is this: When we conceded that our ethical disagreements, and indeed our beliefs themselves, often or always "rest upon" our attitudes, what were we conceding? The answer is enormously complex. Our ethical disagreements, and indeed most of the propositions we utter, "rest upon" a great many non-propositional things. They rest upon our choice of the questions we ask; they rest upon our decisions as to the criteria we will use for accepting one answer and rejecting another; they rest upon a whole gamut of decisions, recommendations, interests; they rest, in short, upon all of the ways in which we distribute emphasis. The point at which we opened the door to confusion was the point at which we lumped all of this under the single label: "attitudes." That was the blind which obscured our further vision.

What we conceded to common sense was that our "view of the world," even if we limit our use of that phrase to that which we can express in propositional form, rests upon all of these other ways in which we distribute our emphasis. The limiting condition is in fact arbitrary. We might as well concede at the start that our "view of the world" is *expressed in* all of those non-propositional utterances (and behind these all those non-linguistic acts) which variously commit us to our distribution of emphasis. There would be few better antidotes to the disastrous conclusion that only our so-called disagreements in belief can be reasonably adjudicated.

The essence of the moral problem is the search for rational justification of our distribution of emphasis. I cannot too often repeat that moral philosophy is not alone in its concern for this; but it *is* concerned. The distinction between rational and irrational lies far back of the models Stevenson accepts for "reasoned solutions." *And in recognition of this very fact lies an important key to distributing our emphasis reasonably in moral matters.* It is this last point which is so difficult to state clearly. Once again, the key to a proper approach—the key, if you will, to a proper "attitude"—is thorough understanding of the conditions of the problem itself.

Our way of formulating a problem constantly misleads us. We persist in arguing, as we have seen, about the problem of reducing "ought" to "is." So long as the problem is formulated in that way it has no general answer. There are two crucial matters which require attention. First, that much of what we try to say with the help of words like "ought" is misconstrued when stated in propositional form. Secondly, that much of what we can only say in non-propositional form expresses our conception of the world. Recognition of the first point may lead us to say that "ought" is not reducible to "is." Recognition of the second point may lead us to say that "oughts" are "ises." In point of fact, the generalized "ought-is" terminology is confusing and misleading. All we need to say is better expressed without it.

Everything I have been saying, all of it methodological, *provides* an answer to the moral problem. The first sound categorical of moral theory is methodological. It *consists* in recognition of the fact that you cannot prove that you alone are right, and it *demands* an ethic of sympathy and of toleration which will categorically repudiate all those habits of thought on which lack of sympathy and lack of toleration rest. The core of a reasoned ethic is intolerance of intolerance.

## IV. *The Nature of Man*

Kant distinguished the "form" of the categorical imperative from its "matter." I have been claiming that the basic requirement of a rational approach to political and moral problems is "methodological." My "methodological" principles of fallibilism and tolerance differ markedly from Kant's formal requirement of "universality"; though I suspect that the difference is more apparent than real. But someone is certain to ask whence these methodological principles I have proposed derive any content. What is their "matter"?

Now, in one sense the distinction between method and matter is misleading. The "matter" of political and moral philosophy is after all precisely people's "methods" of going at their problems in action. We call sex a moral problem; but what is sex? Mere acts are not moral problems; moral problems arise when acts are done in a certain way and for certain reasons. There is a disgraceful tradition which associates the word "sin" with the physical as opposed to the mental or spiritual. In point of fact all sin is spiritual (if such words must be used), for all sins concern acts of commitment and methods of approach. The cardinal sin of all is lack of sympathy for one's fellow men; from this all others flow. The "matter" of ethics *is* "method." And so of politics. When we condemn fascism we condemn a method, a practice of thought, a way of approach—not an "object" or a "thing."

But words creak and strain; for there *is* a sense in which "method" and "matter" may be profitably distinguished. I long ago conceded that the distinction between propositions and non-propositions is by no means clear-cut. And I have repeatedly tried to make clear that my attack on "social engineering" as a governing principle of political and moral philosophy is not an attack on social science as such. There is most assuredly a sense in which biology, psychology, medicine, and social science can provide us with "matter" as concerns the whole question of sex. And there is most assuredly a sense in which history and studies in government and economics can provide us with "matter" as concerns the whole question of democracy.

The crux of the problem is simply this: There is much that we want to say, much that we need to say, which *is* properly expressed in propositional form. And there are many contexts in which the rigid models of deduction and induction *are* appropriate to the demands of reason. In fact, everything I have been

## THE NATURE OF MAN

saying hinges on this fact. The demand of reason is that we provide such justification *as is appropriate*. Where what we are saying is propositional, rigid models of justification procedure are appropriate.

Now, I think that the proper use of the word "matter" or of the word "content" with reference to political and moral questions may sometimes have reference to just this fact. If (as an arbitrary fiat) we use the word "know" with reference to those propositions which *have* sufficiently satisfied the canons of those two rigorous models, we can say that there is much that we "know" both about sex and about democracy. And we may if we like refer to this as the "matter" with which we are concerned. I almost said "the matter with which we *start*," but this will not do; we do not start with such knowledge, we end up with it after considerable prior distribution of our emphasis. Nonetheless we *have* it; and it would be fatuous to deny it.

If we use the word "matter" carefully enough in some such way as this I suspect that there is a perfectly good sense in which we can say that the "matter" of sound ethical and political thinking consists in all that we "know" about "the nature of man." Let us not be frightened of a mere phrase. There are after all competent and richly instructive sciences of biology, psychology, and medicine. And there are many products of human intellectual effort (philosophers should read more of the great literature of the world than many of them do) which do in fact provide us with propositions about human beings, propositions which can weather the most rigorous tests. These may or may not fall short of the criteria specified by "science," but they are fully as much a part of what we know as is any proposition ever uttered by Freud or Watson.

Now, any phrase may be made innocuous; and the phrase "the nature of man" is innocuous enough if we use it as a label for all those true propositions concerning human beings which, within the limits prescribed by fallibilism, we may be said to "know." Why then have I repeatedly attacked the phrase and the overgeneralizations which have been spawned by its misuse?

I happen to be sitting at the moment in a room which contains more than a thousand books. And there is nothing whatsoever wrong with the mere phrase "the contents of those books." Anyone who had read all of them might, if he were willing to spend a very long time about it, start recording in some systematic way all of the matter that is contained in those books. He would face many problems. I, for example, have often rearranged those books in an attempt to maximize the order of their arrangement in accordance with their contents. Anyone who has ever done this knows that one always reaches a point where one throws up one's hands in despair. Many books belong in two or three places; and some are always left over, belonging to no convenient niche in one's system of ordering.

There is nothing wrong with the phrase "the contents of those books" provided one recognizes that one is referring to something too complex to summarize in a nutshell. We achieve nutshell summaries only at the risk of saying nothing. It would not be very helpful to describe the contents of those books as "the opinions, the results of research, and the flights of fancy of all of the authors represented" or even as "part of the outpouring of the man's intellectual activity." Or we may, of course, just say something ridiculous. We may say of the contents of those books that "it is all nonsense" or that "it overwhelms us." Such remarks will not help us to understand the contents of those books.

Men are more complicated than books. The phrase "the nature of man" is innocuous only so long as you do not attempt to fill it out with anything short of a vast set of more specific statements. You have never run through the gamut of such a set; you never could; it is ideal only. Every piecemeal attempt will be rough at the edges. Every system of ordering you try will leave you with overlaps and gaps.

One further fact about the books: The way in which I arrange those books is in part determined by my interests, my point of view, my distribution of emphasis. Another person with the same books might arrange them very differently. Just so with the nature of man. The way in which you organize all your bits and pieces

## THE NATURE OF MAN

of information about men depends in large part upon what you are interested in and how you distribute your emphasis. In short, your method will in large part determine your conclusions.

I was once present at a lecture given by an eminent and unusually competent scientific psychologist. The title of the lecture was, remarkably enough, "The Nature of Man." At the conclusion of the lecture, the first question asked came from a young priest in clerical garb who arose in the rear of the room. "Sir," the question ran, "do you or do you not believe that man has a soul?" The psychologist, of marked behavioristic leanings, paused but an instant and replied: "I do not know whether men have souls or not; but one thing I do know: that if men do have souls, they form no part of the subject matter of the science of psychology." In view of the etymology of the word "psychology" such an answer is delightful. It expresses in a moment the degree to which any advanced discipline, and especially a developed science, allows its conception of proper method to govern its conception of subject matter.

Your method of approach to any problem determines in large part where you come out in the end. The way in which you fill out the content of a phrase like "the nature of man" will have its origins in the methodological categoricals and the distribution of emphasis to which you commit yourself as you go along. Thus, in recommending basic methodological categoricals, as I have been doing, one is never neutral so far as the "matter" or the "content" of conclusions is concerned. In particular, the methodological categoricals of fallibilism and of the rejection of two and only two rigid models for justification procedure will lead to at least one conclusion concerning the nature of man: namely, that we are never justified in summarizing man's nature in a nutshell and overgeneralizing in the rigid ways we have found so attractive.

There is a momentous philosophical principle involved in all this, which, if I am right, is at least part of what Ludwig Wittgenstein was trying to say in his later works. Too often in the past, philosophy has conceived of the kind of understanding it sought as a kind of generalizing. And, of course, there *is* a kind of understanding which rests on generalizing. Nothing can be understood except in context; and the very notion of a context rests on generalization. But the generalizing tendency must be closely watched. One understands in this sense at a price; and generalizations produce puzzles and perplexities which one avoids or surmounts only by delicate sensitivity to difference. One is never certain that one fully grasps Wittgenstein's intentions, but of one thing I am sure. Wittgenstein was convinced that the kind of understanding sought by philosophy is found much more in sensitivity to difference than in the urge to generalize. To the uninitiate all wines taste alike; and the novice's proud recognition that the glass of liquid in front of him is wine is certainly not a mistake. Chateau Yquem 1937 *is* wine and not milk. But to the connoisseur every wine is different. There is a sense of "understanding" in which understanding wines requires discrimination. Just so, in understanding horses or college undergraduates. It is no doubt true that a horse is a horse; and intelligence requires ability correctly to apply a general label. It is no doubt true that college undergraduates fall into recognizable patterns. But he is a very poor teacher who sees all undergraduates as the same. "Understanding" your students requires the most subtle sense of difference. In most affairs of living, to see everything in a certain group as the same, to emphasize similarities at the expense of ignoring differences, is the sign of meagre understanding. It is the mark of the novice.

Few principles are more important in ethics and in morals. Few principles are more important in formulating one's conception of the nature of philosophical activity. With this I shall be concerned in the following chapter. It is enough at the moment to make the point in ethics and morals. Our conception of man's nature must be undogmatic enough to accommodate the richness of our concern. Only thus will we achieve that frame of mind in which all of us seeking understanding in our own way may gradually learn to live in harmony with each other.

# CHAPTER FIVE: THE PRESENT STATE OF PHILOSOPHY: ANALYSIS

## I. *Self-Correctiveness and the Analysis of Analysis*

THE history of philosophy is in large degree a record of blunders and mistakes. There is a small kernel of truth in the familiar claim that philosophy "gets nowhere." There is always something wrong with philosophical "solutions." The greatest philosopher, of any age, always ends up dissected and bleeding at the hands of competent though lesser men. Those of us who spend our lives teaching philosophy know that there is nothing easier than to attack the classics we assign to our students. What is hard is to communicate the sense of greatness.

These facts are most often stressed in connection with metaphysics and all grandiose attempts to provide world-views. Indeed, one sometimes receives the impression that disagreement and lack of concord are being offered as the distinguishing marks of metaphysics. But the same facts may with equal cogency be stressed in connection with philosophical "solutions" of a more analytic character. The great philosophers have as often posed analytic methods as cure-alls as they have posed *Weltanschauungen* in a more obvious sense. And in neither case has agreement been achieved. In either case, competent though lesser men gnaw away at the great. After every enthusiasm we seem left with mangled bits and pieces far less exciting and provocative than the original savory roast.

Many have reached the point of disillusion, not only with so-called metaphysics but also with careful analysis itself. But once again, the difference between disillusion and insight may lie in a slight shift of the focus of consciousness. There will always be those who seek from philosophers apocalyptic answers—be they metaphysical or methodological. We long for solutions; we would *know*. Again and again the enthusiasm for the final answer metamorphoses into the disillusionment which accompanies the gradual dissipation of a vogue—be the vogue metaphysical or methodological. This has happened so often that we may become suspicious of vogues; and such suspicion may itself achieve the status of a vogue. We so despise isms that we revel in anti-ism-ism. This inevitably produces those who will condemn philosophy for ceasing to fulfill, for ceasing even to care about, its primary role. It gives no answers, it shuns the great questions, it withdraws into a safe retreat of "mere analysis."

Shift ever so slightly the focus of consciousness. The very facts which disillusion us may be a key to insight. At a very minimum, it is certainly progress of a sort to recognize mistakes as mistakes. If a competent instructor can clearly understand the mistakes committed by Plato or Hume or Kant, we are making progress of a sort. Still more so, if he can clearly understand the mistakes of Russell or Carnap or Quine. It has more than once been remarked that the history of man's thought has been in all fields a history of constant error. Error is precisely what the history is a history of. Note then that it is of the utmost importance that the errors be made. We learn what we do learn by making attempts and finding out that we are wrong. Disillusion is the product of misdirected hopes; and there is no safe retreat from the fact that shattered hopes are the very essence of what we must seek as philosophers to understand. The canons of responsible philosophizing are to be found, if anywhere, *in* the whole complicated history of philosophizing. And it may well be that there is no more important knowledge of the world than our increasing knowledge of what we can and cannot do in our theories. Understanding the world is not something *other than* understanding the way in which our theories function in it.

Ever since the vogue of the thesis that there are two and only two proper ways of talking good sense, metaphysics has been the whipping boy of philosophy. Most utterances by means of which metaphysical theories have been promulgated were recognized from the start as being neither tautologies nor testable hypotheses. Metaphysical theories cannot be "proved" either by deduction or by induction; and they were summarily classified as poetry. The classification was originally intended as pejorative; but before long there were those who welcomed the classification as flattering. Indeed, in any literal sense, it is as false as most flattery. Not all good metaphysics is poetic; though some of it may well be. But if all that is intended is the classification of metaphysics under the general heading of imaginative, recommendatory uses of language, who would wisely complain? Whether poetic or not, such uses of language may have their rational justification.

Now, one of the lessons we have learned, as a result of all the whippings to which metaphysics has been subjected, is that metaphysics goes wrong at that point where it poses as *the* apocalyptic solution. This point has been admirably expressed by G. J. Warnock in an essay entitled "Analysis and Imagination." Warnock's title leads me to issue a warning before citing, with approval, from the essay. Warnock is distinguishing analysis from metaphysics, and his remarks are intended with reference to metaphysics only. I intend to turn the tables, and to say about philosophical analysis something very like what Warnock says about metaphysics. The "he" of the passage cited in Berkeley, whose views have been under discussion:

> He saw the same world that the rest of us see, but saw it from a rather different angle. It ought, of course, to be remembered that this is not all that Berkeley himself would have claimed. He did not think of himself as inventing simply a *new* way of looking at the world, but rather as expounding the *right* way, the only way in which one sees things as they really are. But this, I think, is only to say that he, like other metaphysicians, had his illusions. The builders of such imaginative systems have always been prone to claim, not that they were inventing something new, but that they were discovering something real, penetrating the disguises of Reality. But such claims are fatal as well as unfounded. For it was precisely by making these claims, by presenting themselves as super-scientists, discoverers *par excellence*, that metaphysicians drew on their own heads the formidable bludgeon of Logical Positivism. Of course there was much misunderstanding here. It was often and justly urged

that the Positivists had mistaken, or disregarded, the actual character of their adversary; but this was due in large measure to the fact that their adversary, the metaphysician, had habitually presented himself in false colours. A metaphysical system, an invented conceptual apparatus, may have many virtues, such as elegance, simplicity, originality, comprehensiveness, depth, or the power to give psychological satisfaction; but the claim that any such system is exclusively true, or uniquely faithful to Reality, is a claim which sets metaphysics on quite the wrong ground, ground from which it is liable to be destructively expelled.[1]

Understanding just this kind of fact about the status of metaphysics and the proper context in which to discuss the justification procedures available to it, has been the result of careful analysis. But analysis too seldom turns inward upon itself and realizes that its ultimate insight might lie in self-appraisal in similar terms. Every version of philosophical analysis is in the same boat with metaphysics. They will sink under the same conditions. An analytic movement in philosophy is not promulgated by means solely of expressions which are *logically* analytic, nor by means solely of testable hypotheses, nor by both alone. Analytic philosophy must itself be classified under imaginative, recommendatory uses of language. This should teach it to modify its conception of "proof" and to relinquish its own apocalyptic claims. Analytic philosophy faces the same problems of internal self-justification faced by metaphysical philosophy. In fact, the supposition that there is a clear-cut dichotomy between two ways of doing philosophy, one of which is analytic while the other is not, is a dangerous and misleading supposition.

In moral philosophy we are gradually learning how important it is to achieve sensitivity to the wide range of use of such key words as "good"; and we are gradually learning that our understanding of moral matters will depend upon our detailed sense

---

[1] G. J. Warnock, "Analysis and Imagination," being the final essay in *The Revolution in Philosophy*, by Warnock *et al.* (London: Macmillan and Co. Ltd., 1956), pp. 122-123.

## SELF-CORRECTIVENESS

of the dangers of overgeneralization. We have gradually learned the same kind of lesson with regard to many traditional philosophical problems which we have been accustomed to call "metaphysical." The word "cause," for example, has an enormous range of uses; and we are learning to avoid the overgeneralization consequent upon any attempt to legislate that one such use is the only proper use. Similar remarks could be made about many of the key words in philosophical debate: words such as "event," "objective," "real," "ultimate," "substance," "illusion," "sin," "art," and the rest—words both technical and ordinary. Attention to ranges of use is often thought of as "analysis"; and it is a strange phenomenon that many who are most sensitive to the dangers of legislating "proper" uses in such cases, many who consider themselves as advocates of analysis, fail to recognize that "analysis" is a term with just such a wide range of use. Those who oppose the practice of legislating single use where sensitivity to range is of the essence, sometimes fail to turn their searchlight inward upon themselves. "Analysis" is a word with wide range of use; and any specification of a single proper use of the word is as misleading as a specification of one proper use of "good" or one proper use of "cause."

I intend in the following sections to examine the range of the term "analysis." In so doing, I shall have three purposes in mind:

*First*, to show that each of the various versions of analysis has arisen to meet an important need in philosophy. In innumerable ways philosophy will ignore the results of analysis at its peril. But analysis serves many needs, not one.

*Second*, to show that no single version of analysis, nor all of them together, is properly conceived as "mere." None of the various ways of doing analysis hangs in mid-air. It follows that all reductionist talk (all claims to the effect that in any one sense, or in all senses combined, philosophy should be "reduced" to "mere" analysis) is wrong-headed and misleading.

*Third*, to show that there is no justification for thinking in terms of a supposed dichotomy between something called "analysis" on the one hand and something called "problem solving in the grand tradition" on the other.

We must recognize *both* the wealth of insight to be achieved through many ways of analyzing *and* the dangers of reductionism. Nothing short of this conjunction will produce in philosophy a spirit congenial to the kind of understanding it seeks.

## II. *The Range of Analysis (Part One)*

The following passage occurs in the introductory essay of a well-known volume entitled *Readings in Philosophical Analysis*. The author of the essay, Herbert Feigl, was a member of the original Vienna Circle, and is one of the more influential of present-day "analytic" philosophers.

> In the more technical enterprise of a logical reconstruction of our empirical knowledge, certain fundamental choices must be made as to the basis and the logical forms to be employed. In the great tradition of Hume, Comte, Mill, Mach, Avenarius, and Russell, this directed form of *analysis* consists in a gradual retracing of the validating steps of knowledge to the data of experience. If all psychological considerations are excluded and only logical ones admitted, this results in an *analysis* of derived terms and sentences as logical constructions erected on primitive terms and sentences which have direct experiential reference. For certain purposes, like the *analysis* of scientific constructions, it may be unnecessary to push the reduction as far as all that. In order to know the evidential basis of a physical or biological theory, for example, it is usually sufficient to pursue the *analysis* only to the level of terms designating observable things and their properties. We may therefore distinguish between experiential and physicalistic bases of reconstruction or of epistemic reduction. Carnap, utilizing the efficient and adaptable apparatus of symbolic logic, has worked out detailed sketches of such *analyses* for either reduction basis.[2]

[2] *Readings in Philosophical Analysis*, edited by Herbert Feigl and Wilfred Sellars, introductory essay by Feigl, pp. 16-17. In the next to the last sentence quoted, Feigl himself italicizes the words "experiential" and "physi-

## THE RANGE OF ANALYSIS (PART ONE)

Now, the word "analysis" has occurred five times in this passage. Consider for a moment the practices to which it refers. Its first occurrence refers to tracing knowledge to the data of experience. This, together with the particular names cited, suggests to anyone acquainted with the history of philosophy an old and familiar method. We are well acquainted with the "analysis" of experience into its constituent parts. My experience of a chair is said to be composed of color patches, tactual pressures, shapes, smells, and so on. Philosophical analysis might be, and often has been, characterized as an attempt to separate out the experiential elements or simples within experienced complexes.

The second and fourth occurrences have a different and more recent sound. These speak of analysis of terms and sentences, and suggest to the reader something currently passing under the label "linguistic analysis." One may wish to insist that analysis of experience is performed only with the help of language, and there is no doubt a sense in which, without further analysis of the language we are using, analysis of experience may be superficial and misleading. Surely, however, it is one thing to analyze experience, another to analyze language; and it is quite possible that failure to retain a consciousness of the difference may lead to serious trouble.

The third occurrence of the word refers us to the analysis of "scientific constructions." Now, Leibniz and Spinoza and Kant analyzed science as earnestly as Hume or Mill or Russell. "Analyzing" the constructions of science seems *prima facie* to be a notion independent of the traditional conception of "analyzing" experiences into their constituent parts. There may be a connection; but it is certainly a connection between two different undertakings. At the same time, it would certainly be a mistake to equate analysis of the constructions of science with analysis of language. The latter is a task far broader in scope than the former; and even where the analysis of scientific constructions is

---

calistic," but I have dropped these italics in order that the occurrences of the word "analysis" may stand out more clearly. These, in turn, I have placed in italics.

*143*

performed in a linguistic manner, one may question whether analysis of science is only, or even primarily, a mere branch of linguistics.

The fifth and final occurrence of this slippery term, occurring as it does in a sentence concerning symbolic logic, at once suggests something which none of the previous occurrences has clearly introduced, namely, the more strict notion of that which is logically analytic. There may be those who feel that the logical use of the word "analytic" (i.e., logically true or false) has little or nothing to do with the meaning of the word "analysis" as it is ordinarily used in philosophy; but Feigl's final sentence, and the performance of influential men like Carnap, must stand as a warning that our feelings about the matter stand in need of review. Perhaps the sense in which Kant *might* have accused the rationalists of "reducing" philosophy to analysis would, as an accusation, involve this sense of the word and none of the previous senses. To state the matter succinctly, then, this odd passage suggests to the reader four possible contexts within which the characteristics of analysis might be considered: the analysis of experience, the analysis of scientific theories, linguistic analysis, and the practice of confining oneself to the saying of that which is logically analytic.

There are no doubt uses of the word "analysis" not provided for in such a list. One much-used phrase which comes to mind is the phrase "analysis of meanings." What is more, some of the phrases of the list are themselves ambiguous. "Linguistic analysis," for example, is sometimes conceived as a description of actual languages, sometimes as a construction of ideal languages. And even if one felt that one's list was exhaustive it would still perhaps be difficult to straighten out a variety of traditional disputes with which the word "analysis" (used either as a term of opprobrium or as a term of praise) is associated in all sorts of confusing ways: for example, empiricist *versus* rationalist disputes, clarity *versus* profundity disputes, and epistemology *versus* metaphysics disputes. The compiling of such a list in no way implies that there are hard and fast distinctions between the

## THE RANGE OF ANALYSIS (PART ONE)

actual procedures which would constitute the performance of analysis in any two of the senses suggested. We have tended to use the general term "analysis" as though it has some *one* meaning precisely because (in part) very different procedures tend to shade off into one another and to overlap in confusing ways. But though such a list is by no means exhaustive, and though it suggests theoretical distinctions which may be blurred in practice, it serves as a convenient entering wedge for a discussion of the claim that philosophy ought to concern itself either primarily or solely with something called "analysis."

In order to introduce some neatness into our attempt to discuss a very complicated matter, I propose to divide this "analysis of analysis" into two parts. So many recent versions of analysis have in one way or another originated in the early positivist pigeonholing of proper modes of discourse, that I shall confine the present section to a consideration of the effect of that pigeonholing upon our conception of the nature of analysis. It will be important, however, to stress the fact that our reference will not be to recent movements only. I shall indicate that the pigeonholing tendency with which we are concerned has exerted influence at least from the time of David Hume. Many recent claims are part of older traditions. In any event, I shall first discuss only those versions of analysis which rest upon the view that unless we are enunciating either tautologies and derived theorems or empirically testable hypotheses we are not behaving in a rationally responsible manner. In the following section I shall turn to those senses of the word "analysis" which do not necessarily depend on this assumption.

Let us, then, assume for the moment the classification which I have hitherto been so intent upon attacking. Let us assume that there are only two "cognitively meaningful" (wretched phrase!) ways in which we can use language. Either we utter tautologies and deduce theorems from axioms and postulates, or we formulate empirically testable hypotheses. This view, as I have said, is at least as old as the time of David Hume. If you will turn to Hume's *An Inquiry Concerning Human Understanding*, you will find that the final paragraph of that inquiry, in conjunction with the opening paragraphs of Section IV, clearly suggests that there are only two "proper" ways of talking. Either we say something the denial of which would involve self-contradiction, in which case what we say is a priori; or we judge a matter of fact, in which case what we say is only problematic and experimental. The real basis of Kant's attack on Hume was his conviction that these two pigeonholes do not provide any convenient niche for some of the most important things that must be said both by physicists and by fathers; but, be that as it may, the twentieth century has tried with great energy to tighten up Hume's pigeonholes and to characterize them more completely.

Now, if you wish to recommend something called "analysis," and if you simultaneously accept the view that there are only two proper ways of talking, there are two obvious alternatives which you can take in an attempt to make "analysis" respectable. On the one hand you may claim that the utterances which constitute your analysis are themselves empirically testable hypotheses. In this event, your claim that philosophy must confine itself to analysis will be a claim that philosophy *consists in* the promulgation of testable hypotheses. On the other hand, you may argue that the utterances which constitute your analysis are themselves logically analytic. You may, in short, insist that philosophy *consists in* logical analysis, where the latter phrase is interpreted in the strictest possible sense. Both of these claims have in fact been made; and so has the obvious conjunctive claim that philosophy may be both of these things but nothing else.

One might think that no further possibility remains. But there is in fact a third possibility of great importance. To the uninitiate it may sound strange; but we must always combat our tendency to overlook a possibility merely because it is strange. If you assume that there are only two ways of talking sense, and at the same time conclude that for one reason or another philosophical analysis cannot be pursued by talking in either of those ways, you may conclude that philosophical analysis is not a way of "talking sense" at all. You may conclude that philosophy, and

## THE RANGE OF ANALYSIS (PART ONE)

this is a third sense in which you may seek to confine it to "analysis," *consists in* the exemplification of method rather than in the saying of anything "sensible." Such a claim has in fact been made.

There are thus three notions with which we shall be concerned in the present section. In each case we must distinguish the question whether philosophy can at least in part do the kind of thing the doing of which is being recommended, from the question whether philosophy can be reduced to that kind of doing.

A. Can the task of philosophy be conceived as one of providing empirically testable hypotheses; and if in any sense yes, can this be conceived as the whole of its task?

B. Can the task of philosophy be conceived as one of providing completely formal analytic systems; and if in any sense yes, can this be conceived as the whole of its task?

C. Can the task of philosophy be conceived in such a way that what it provides is a method rather than a theory; and if in any sense yes, can this be conceived as the whole of its task?

In a sense, our ultimate concern in the present section is with A, B, and C taken as a block. Our overruling question will accordingly be whether the limits of each conception of philosophy prescribe no more than the legitimate provinces of the others. We thus have four senses of "analysis" on our hands: analysis conceived as empirical description, analysis conceived as formal and logical, analysis conceived as a non-linguistic activity, and analysis conceived as a conjunction of all three.

In view of all that we have said in earlier chapters we might be tempted to terminate this section at once. "This," we might say, "is what we have been talking about all along. All that is needed is a closer look at what is involved in any attempt to justify our distribution of emphasis, and these severely truncated conceptions of the nature of philosophical enterprise would no longer tempt us. Why start now by assuming what we have been attacking all along? Get rid of the idea that there are only two ways in which we can talk sense, and *then* let's see what philosophical analysis would be like." Well, that is precisely what I intend to do in the next section; but first a good deal more needs to be said about the themes here presented. We have been discussing politics and morals and ethics; and though we have repeatedly insisted that the problems there raised are completely general philosophical problems, we have not yet squarely faced them as such. Prior discussion will make our present task easier, but it does not remove the need for it.

A. The first claim we must face, then, is the claim that philosophy's task is descriptive; and we must distinguish the claim that philosophy's task is partially descriptive from the claim that its task is solely descriptive.

I am using the word "descriptive" here in a highly technical sense suggested by much recent literature. In this sense a "description" *is* an empirically testable hypothesis. But precisely at this point our difficulties begin; for in ordinary parlance the word "descriptive" has a much wider use than this, and the claim that philosophy's task is descriptive sometimes derives its appeal from the ordinary rather than from the technical sense of the word.

In 1952, an article appeared in *Mind*[3] which announced in its opening sentence that descriptions are never true or false. This announcement was undoubtedly intended to shock. It is almost certainly an overstatement, as a subsequent note in the same journal carefully pointed out.[4] In fact, the authors of the article had made clear in the course of their argument that their real objection was to the preoccupation of philosophers with the technical use of the word "description," which they exemplified from the writings of Mach, Russell, Moore, Ogden and Richards, Ayer, Hart, and Austin. There has, however, been very good reason for this preoccupation. For traditional empiricism had long been contending, prior to the attempt of the positivists to formalize the claim, that the task of philosophy is to promulgate hypotheses

[3] S. E. Toulmin and K. Baier, "On Describing," *Mind*, LXI (1952), 13-38. The opening sentence of this article declares: "Descriptions can be as emotive as you please, and are never 'true or false.'" The second sentence refers to this as a "truism."

[4] Everett Hall, "On Describing Describing," *Mind*, LXII (1953), 375-378.

which can be subjected to empirical tests. This was precisely the sense in which many of them had insisted that philosophy be considered as descriptive.

We had better note in passing that the word "hypothesis" is marked by the same ambiguity as the word "description." In one quite ordinary sense, an "hypothesis" is just any tentative and provisionally adopted theory. *Webster's International Dictionary* lists a variety of ways in which the adoption may be provisional: e.g., without belief, without argument, without action, without examination of consequences. But traditional empiricism has meant something more precise than this in arguing that philosophy must confine itself to "hypotheses." It has meant that philosophy should confine itself to the saying of what can be subjected to empirical test. Thus the tendency to use the word "hypothesis" as a shorthand for the phrase "empirically testable hypothesis" is not a misleading trick on the part of recent philosophy. It is a device for making more clear what is involved in certain traditional claims of empiricism.

The question thus formulates itself whether philosophy can be conceived, either in whole or in part, as promulgating empirically testable hypotheses. And if that is the question, we must surely also ask: hypotheses about what? To this latter question there are three important answers that might be given. Of course, a philosopher is free to claim that he is promulgating hypotheses about anything he pleases; but our interest must be determined by what is historically important. And there are three important kinds of thing that philosophers have claimed to offer hypotheses about.

(i) about the world as a whole.
(ii) about experiences in the plural.
(iii) about the use of language.

Let us consider each of these claims.

(i) In a book entitled *Some Problems of Philosophy*, G. E. Moore has said that one of the most important and interesting things which philosophers have tried to do is "to give a general description of the whole of the Universe." In subsequent pages he continually speaks of what would be required to "prove" any such description "true."[5] This is a perfectly good statement of what many have taken to be the aim of metaphysics. Any good empiricist would have insisted that the "proof" be on the inductive model. He might in fact have argued that the word "prove" is too strong. When Charles Sanders Peirce called for a "laboratory philosophy" he was not demanding the annihilation of metaphysics (as some have supposed). He referred indeed to the "moonshine" of the metaphysicians, but by this he meant the wrong kind of metaphysics. He certainly believed that part of a sound "laboratory philosophy" would consist in the promulgation of testable hypotheses about the nature of the world as a whole. His demand was not that metaphysics be eradicated; his demand was that metaphysics confine itself to hypotheses which would make some sensible difference in experience.

In recent years, very powerful arguments have been advanced against the notion that any theory about the nature of the world as a whole is empirically testable. The difficulty is simply this: that if a theory purports to describe *everything* which has been, is, or will be, it is itself claiming that no one thing could occur which it is incapable of describing. A theory might claim the capacity to *conceive of* an occurrence or an observation which might falsify itself; but its claim would have to be that no such occurrence or observation ever has been, is, or will be. Since the empiricist claim is that what we conceive must be based on the evidence of what has been, is, or will be, no hypothesis it offers could be about more than *almost* everything. Otherwise it would be incapable of formulating a test case.

This formidable argument may fail to convince us. We may argue that the attempt to "offer a general description of the whole of the Universe" never has been intended in a logically extreme sense. At best it is concerned with "most" not "all." And what is wrong with conceiving more modest proposals as empirically testable?

[5] G. E. Moore, *Some Main Problems of Philosophy* (London: George Allen and Unwin Ltd., 1953), pp. 1-2, and p. 24.

## THE RANGE OF ANALYSIS (PART ONE)

The answer is: nothing whatsoever. If a philosopher wishes to try for a generalized description of most of the empirical facts we know, and if he is willing to specify the conditions under which what he is saying would be false, I cannot see that anyone can reasonably say him nay. He would have to be very wary of two important dangers. The first danger is that he may specify as the conditions under which what *he* is saying would be false, conditions under which what *anybody else* is saying would be false too. The defense of any theory must rest upon adjudicating between itself and others. For example, one encounters advocates of certain theories of perception who argue that their theories are empirical on the ground that they might be confuted by observing that the apparent shape of a physical object did *not* change as one changed one's vantage point of observation. Theory "X" is empirical because if the facts were otherwise theory "X" would be false. But so, unfortunately, would all known theories of perception. If a supposed observation would confute all known theories, it is evident that it is in principle irrelevant as concerns any choice between one of those theories and another. It is one thing to claim that a theory is empirical on the ground that a supposed observation would remove the subject matter of the theory; it is quite another thing to claim that a theory is empirical in the sense that specified observations would adjudicate between that theory and another.

The second danger is the danger of supposing that because what we say is *about* the occurrences and occasions of the world, what we are saying must be either true or false. The command "shut the door" is presumably "about" or "concerns" the fact of an open door. If the door were closed, the command would presumably not be uttered. It does not follow that "shut the door" is an empirical hypothesis. No amount of evidence will render it a true or a false proposition. The rules of chess are no doubt "about" such things as checkered fields and the various complicated moves which constitute the activity of playing chess. It does not follow that the rules of chess are empirical hypotheses. Just so, the fact that a philosophical theory is "about" the occurrences of the world does not signify that philosophical theories are empirical hypotheses.

Our first point, however, is that there is 'nothing intrinsically wrong about a philosopher's attempt to offer empirical descriptions of a highly generalized kind. I remarked in a previous chapter that all metaphysics runs the risk of inventing terminologies so general as to be capable of describing anything whatsoever, and that we must never confuse a mere linguistic exercise with theoretical justification. But we are at present concerned with an honest empiricism which seeks to prevent just such confusion. There is an honorable place for attempts at generalized description in philosophy.

But is this the whole story? Certainly not, and for two very good reasons. First, because so many of the problems with which we are concerned in philosophy are not problems of description. Secondly, because even where we are concerned with description we are never concerned *merely* with description. These are the two central points I wish to make; but they will best be made in the very process of examining the two other contexts of philosophical description to which I have referred.

(ii) In one sense I have already impinged upon the second context; for in confining description of the world as a whole to its more modest claims I have in effect shifted the discussion to the problem of describing experiences in the plural. In any event, if a philosopher wishes to describe experiences, be they actual or possible, I can see no good reason for denying him the privilege. At the same time, and in direct continuation of what I have just been saying, we must be on our guard against certain misconceptions.

*Any* description, be it technical or common sense, requires a theoretical context. This means, in part, that any attempt to defend one description as opposed to another may involve the defense of one theoretical set of categories rather than another. This kind of thing has happened again and again in philosophy; and the danger is that we fail to notice the difference between two kinds of argument. One kind of argument concerns whether experiences are being in some way accurately described; the other kind of argument concerns whether experiences are being described in the only correct way. The latter kind of argument, which so often arises in philosophy, has a way of misleading protagonists into believing that they are still analyzing experience when in fact they have shifted to analysis of an ideal theoretical construction.

Consider for a moment the main stream of empiricist philosophy since Locke. Empiricism has traditionally been associated with the demand that whatever is complex or grandiose or profound can be rigorously understood only if it is resolved into its component elements. Empiricist philosophy has been conceived as a kind of analytic chemistry of experience. In the hands of its practitioners, "analysis" has played the role of a microscope (the analogy is Hume's) through which have been revealed the elements in experience which unreflective consciousness overlooks or takes for granted. As the centuries pass, this microscope becomes more and more powerful. The eighteenth century focused upon such elements as "ideas," "impressions of sensation and reflection," "feelings of approval and disapproval," and the like. The more refined equipment of the twentieth century has revealed tremendous complexity in these apparent simples, and probed more deeply to find more basic elements. H. H. Price's microscope has been able to isolate sense data from sensing from sense-datum-genesis. Empiricism teeters into a fantastic quantum-analysis of experience.

Now, there are two kinds of objection you may wish to make against this main stream of empiricism. One kind of objection is well represented by William James. James attacked Hume for having overlooked something: namely, that relations are as much a part of the "given" in experience as are the items related. James's attack is not upon the basic conceptual framework of the tradition. He believes as unquestioningly as Hume that empiricist description must proceed by breaking complexes down into simples. He accepts the "bricks" which Hume used as building material; he simply insists that there is more in experience than the bricks, and concentrates attention on the relations which serve as mortar.

Recently a very different kind of argument has been going on, much of it as a result of the impact of Wittgenstein's later work. The new objection involves doubt as to whether the main stream of empiricism has been operating with a set of categories which is really properly geared to empirical description. It might have been noticed for some time that though the so-called "sense-datum school" of analysis started with the claim that experience was the object of its analysis, it usually ended by defending the elegance of a theory. There is nothing new about the question whether anyone ever "experienced" a bare or simple sense-datum; and the traditional answer given this question by the "sense-datum school" is an appeal to *logical* priority. Of course, what ordinary people "experience" is tables and trees; and it is a difficult task to introduce them as college sophomores to bare sense-data; but since they are being introduced to something "logically prior" they are simply being introduced to what they *must* have been experiencing all along.

For one thing, there is a covert shift here from analyzing experience to analyzing the requirements of a theory. But more importantly, a good many philosophers have grown suspicious of certain presuppositions of the theory. For example: one requirement of the theory turns out to be that the categorical statements of ordinary discourse be translated into hypothetical statements of the sense-datum language; and we have seen in an earlier chapter the kind of objection which can be raised against this requirement. Further detail is extraneous to our present purposes. It is sufficient to point out that recent objections to the empiricist tradition are far more radical than James's. For they are objections to the claim of the tradition to offer the only kind of description of experience which is correct. Indeed the point of the objection is that certain basic assumptions of the tradition are misleading.

Two overstatements must be carefully avoided. First: since any description involves as I have said the context of a theory, you cannot avoid constructing a theory in the process of describing experience. The danger is that you lose sight of an important difference between "analyzing" experience and "analyzing" your resultant theory. All empiricism steers a perilous course on the knife-edge of this divide. Second: on any literal interpretation there is nothing wrong with the mere phrase "sense-datum." No one, so far as I am aware, has yet offered any good grounds for rejecting the distinction between what is given in experience and interpretation of it. To doubt that there are sense-data (a favorite pastime at present) is usually a way of doubting that the *kind* of empiricism which has talked most about the "given to sense" has been offering a faithful account of the matter. The objector is conscientious only to the extent that he has himself been examining his own "given."

Well, there are a great many unsolved problems here; but there is only one point we need to make. There is nothing wrong about a philosopher's trying to offer the best description of experiences he can provide; but it will be a complete mistake if he ever supposes that this is all he is doing. No philosopher *merely* describes. He describes only in the context of simultaneously proposing a *recipe* for description. Proposing a recipe for description is a matter of defending decisions as to distribution of emphasis, and recommending one set of concepts or categories rather than another.

If anyone wishes to say that providing the recipe is *part* of the description, and that in this fuller sense it is legitimate to claim that philosophy's task is descriptive, there is little point in arguing. We have been concerned with the claim that philosophy is descriptive in the technical sense of uttering only empirically testable hypotheses. Once decisions and recommendations are admitted as *part* of the descriptive task, this technical claim has been abandoned. The word "description" has, as I have said, its broader uses. In a broad enough sense *any* way of doing philosophy might be said to be descriptive. For any way of doing philosophy, insofar as it lays down its initial assumptions, clarifies its key concepts, introduces the very words it intends to use,

## THE PRESENT STATE: ANALYSIS

is laying down its recipe for the "descriptions" it will thenceforth offer. It would not be far from the truth to admit that the choice between philosophical theories is usually a choice between recipes any one of which will in its own way provide "descriptions" of experience.

(iii) Now, it will be noticed that there is a linguistic way in which each of the above claims might be put. The first claim might be said to concern itself with the construction of a terminology general enough to describe everything or almost everything. The second claim might be said to concern itself with recipes which are after all essentially linguistic. The most persistent traditional form of the claim has been, as we have seen, a claim that ordinary categoricals of common discourse can be (or ought to be) translated into hypotheticals of a sense-datum language. When we engage in philosophy we are always skirting on the edge of "linguistic" problems; and, indeed, the present age in philosophy has on occasion been described as an age of linguistic analysis.

But what is linguistic analysis? In some of its manifestations the very heart and soul of linguistic analysis is the claim that there are only two respectable models for cognitively meaningful discourse. In other of its manifestations, its whole point is to show that these models are esoteric and misleading. Even where the two models are accepted, the character of what is recommended as linguistic analysis is misleading. Sometimes one is given the impression that linguistic analysis is an empirical science describing "use"—whether technical or ordinary. At other times one is given the impression that linguistic analysis is a purely formal discipline on a par with logic and mathematics. At still other times one is given the impression that linguistic analysis is neither descriptive nor in the narrow sense logical, but an exemplification of a method, a "therapeutic" regimen. Thus all of the ambiguities of the term "analysis" attach to the phrase "linguistic analysis," and it will be necessary to refer repeatedly to *various* claims of linguists. At present I am concerned only with the claim, sometimes made within the tradition of the "great dichotomy," that philosophy's job is to undertake an empirical descriptive science of language. I thus turn to the third kind of object about which philosophy has been said to offer empirical hypotheses. (See *supra*, p. 149.)

Now, I do not believe that the proposal to reduce philosophy to a linguistic science is ever intended quite literally. More often what is intended is the recommendation that philosophy in midtwentieth century has a unique opportunity of paving the way for a new science which is not itself philosophy. But the idea of a linguistic science is so often bruited about that, whether offered as an equivalent of philosophy or as a protégé thereof, it should be given a hearing.

Let us begin with a passage from Stuart Hampshire which is in many ways typical of what is being said:

> We no longer have any need of arm-chair programmes of science; contemporary philosophers are in effect proclaiming this fact when they denounce all metaphysical systems as useless and misleading. But speculation of a kind which may be absurd and useless at one stage in the development of our knowledge may be significant and useful at another; associated with the beginnings of experimental physics, it is natural to find philosophical speculation about the ultimate nature of Matter; associated with the beginnings of experimental psychology, it is natural to find philosophical speculation about the powers and faculties of the mind; and today, at the beginning (it is to be hoped) of a proper empirical and comparative study of the forms of language, we have philosophical speculation about the forms of Language. Experiment replaces speculation, and makes it otiose, as natural knowledge advances; but it does not follow that metaphysical speculation is in itself always useless; it follows only that speculation of a particular kind is discarded when it has finally served its purposes.[6]

This passage is, in fact, somewhat puzzling. It seems in part

[6] Stuart Hampshire, *Spinoza* (The Pelican Philosophy Series, London: Penguin Books, 1951), p. 212.

## THE PRESENT STATE: ANALYSIS

to suggest "therapeutics." That is to say, it seems to suggest that philosophical "speculation" really says nothing at all (it is eventually rendered "otiose," and even now is contrasted unfavorably with "experiment") and that its function is one of temporary stop-gap only. Some, however, may take away from the passage the impression that sensible philosophers will actually *engage in* a science of language. If the speculation is temporary only, and eventually otiose, why not by-pass it? Hampshire does not here defend either therapeutics or the idea that philosophers should themselves indulge in a linguistic science; but he does suggest the idea of an empirical science of language which is so attractive to a great many advocates of a certain kind of philosophical "analysis."

Hampshire's remarks raise certain difficulties. What, for example, is implied by the contrast between "speculation" and "science"? Does Hampshire really believe that the need for speculation (to call it "arm-chair speculation" is simply pejorative) has disappeared forever in physics and psychology? I do not find competent physicists saying such things; and although psychologists *were* saying such things twenty years ago they speak differently today. Psychology is growing up; the sign of maturity in a science is always increase rather than decrease in recognition of the need for speculation about the basic concepts in terms of which the science operates.

The remarkable thing which must be emphasized, however, is that Hampshire, in the chapter from which I quote, is *defending* philosophical speculation. The limits which he prescribes for that defense may be mistakenly narrow, but defense is defense for all that. Even as a temporary stop-gap, wrongly contrasted with science, and qualified by needlessly pejorative terms, speculation makes, according to Hampshire, some sense. If one asks what kind of sense, one seems to be left with the answer: the sense of a recommendation to a further study which is "proper" and "empirical." There are two points to be noted here. First, that Hampshire is himself a philosopher engaged in recommending or prescribing; secondly, that present speculation (about the forms of Language) must be differentiated from the proposed future "science." Indeed, much of what Hampshire wishes to say can be said without predicting the emergence of a future science. It is in fact more common among the British linguists to equate what is needed with what they are now doing, and to refer to both as a study of "the logic of expressions." In the sense in which they use the word "logic," logic is not a science in the strict sense at all. Indeed, those who are accustomed to thinking of logic as a science occasionally have serious difficulty with the British use of the word. We hear of the "logic of adjectives," "the logic of sentences," "the logic of moral words,"[7] and one American spokesman for Oxford philosophers has referred to their method as a "logical description of our employment of certain kinds of concept or expression."[8] The word "logic" is not here being used in the strict sense of Church, Quine, Tarski, Carnap, *et al.*, but in a looser and no doubt more classical sense. Nowell-Smith, for example, quotes approvingly H.W.B. Joseph's remarks about the way in which "the logician can best study the laws of men's thinking."[9]

It is true that the word "science" has more than one use. We call logic (in the Church-Quine-Tarski sense) a "science" as well as biology. It would be entirely false, however, to claim that logic in this sense is an empirical study in the way in which biology is an empirical study. Surely logic in the older (Joseph) sense is even less a science—empirical or otherwise. The phrase "logical description" uses the word "description" in a very loose and ill-defined sense. Logic, whether in the new formal and mathematical sense or in the older more classical sense, is above all *prescriptive*. Insofar as it is concerned with language, it prescribes how language ought to be used. We may find, when we subject the science of biology to a careful scrutiny, that it too

[7] All of these expressions will be found in P. H. Nowell-Smith, *Ethics* (London: Penguin Books, 1954). The first two occur in chapter headings; the third will be found on p. 22.

[8] Morris Weitz, "Oxford Philosophy," *The Philosophical Review*, LXII (1953), 190.

[9] See Nowell-Smith, *op.cit.*, p. 63.

prescribes how a technical terminology is to be used, but this is a hidden methodological feature of a discipline whose purpose is to offer an empirically accurate description of actual organisms. There is certainly no parallel in logic. Logicians are not seeking to describe how carpenters, theologians, and James Joyce do in fact use language; they are attempting to prescribe how all of us ought to use language.

Now, all of these matters must be kept in mind when we confront the claim that philosophy should concern itself with "describing" linguistic use. It would be foolhardy to deny that recent attention to linguistic use has shed a great deal of light on traditional philosophical problems. The enthusiasm of the linguistically minded is in large measure justified. But sweeping proclamations of a reductive kind are not justified in the slightest degree. No one would wish to deny that *in some sense* a philosopher's job is inescapably linguistic. Language is the tool with which a philosopher works, and like any artisan he will work better if he keeps his tool in constant good repair. Philosophers are not alone among professional people in performing their function primarily by using language. For the most part, they have always been aware of this, and few of stature have failed to comment upon the fact. The whole point of emphasizing language, when it is carefully stated without exaggeration, is not new at all. Insofar as it is defensible, the claim that philosophy's job is linguistic is neither new nor exciting nor sensibly phrased as a recommendation that philosophers confine themselves to describing linguistic use. A philosopher may learn much from describing the untidy uses of ordinary parlance; he may learn much from describing the artificially precise uses of technical disciplines. But his purpose transcends description. His job is to adjudicate disputed questions and to throw light on the puzzles which description isolates.

This concludes my remarks concerning the claim that the function of philosophy is to advance empirically testable hypotheses, i.e., descriptions in the narrow sense. On the one hand, there is no good reason for denying philosophers the right to propound testable hypotheses of a great many different kinds, and the myth

## THE RANGE OF ANALYSIS (PART ONE)

that philosophers are not concerned with empirical description has been overworked. On the other hand, there is every good reason for rejecting the reductive claim that this is all they are doing. The truth, as always, lies somewhere between opposed excessive claims. Even where philosophers seek to describe, their function is basically selective, recommendatory, and adjudicative.

B. The second question we formulated on page 147 was the following: Can the task of philosophy be conceived as one of providing completely formal analytic systems; and if in any sense yes, can this be conceived as the whole of its task? Our answer to this question will be much briefer than our answer to the first question—for two reasons. To begin with, the claim is not as ambiguous as the descriptive claim; and in addition it is, unlike the descriptive claim, almost wholly the result of the "great dichotomy" which limits sensible talk to two exclusive models. Indeed, having rejected the great dichotomy, we might be forgiven in the present case for rejecting the claim out of hand. Certain remarks, however, might profitably be made. The recent appeal of the claim is deeply involved in what we sometimes call the "cult of science-worship." I shall orient my remarks about the claim to a consideration of what is sound and what is dangerous in "science-worship."

It is a commonplace in textbooks in the history of philosophy, and it is certainly a fact, that modern philosophy in the West has been heavily dependent upon modern science. The modern era opened with two widely differing attempts to systematize the world view implied by modern science—rationalism and empiricism. Kant followed with an attempt at "synthesis" which sprang directly from his attempt to make sense of the science of physics. Philosophers who have cut loose from the apron-strings of science have (so it is said) invariably perverted the philosophical enterprise. And, after all, even Hegel could not have attempted what he did had not Kant's speculations about mathematics and physics preceded him. It is a fact, not a theory, that Western philosophy is closely tied to the apron-strings of science. Certain philosophers, profoundly impressed by this phenomenon, have concluded that philosophy's central task lies in systematic scrutiny of the vast amount of information which has resulted from the application of scientific method, together with scrutiny of the implications of the success of that method. The task of philosophy is held to be one of analysis—not of experience as such, but of the systematic results of empirical science. Feigl, in the introductory essay which I have already quoted, uses the phrase "logical analysis" in a wide variety of ways. But he remarks at one point, when discussing "scientific work in psycho-physiology" that "logical analysis, here as elsewhere, merely examines possibilities and makes explicit the basic assumptions of programs of research."[10] This suggests what may perhaps be called the "apron-strings" conception of philosophy, which confines it to "mere" analysis of the deliverances of technical science.

This conception of philosophy is sometimes said to be a version of empiricism. But it is not empiricism in the older sense of that word, and in its strict form involves a claim which runs counter to traditional empiricism. Since science itself purports to be a firsthand systematic analysis of experience, any philosophical writing which consists in the analysis of science might be held to be an analysis of experience at one remove. Even if this be granted, however (and I wish at the moment to ignore the not unreasonable claim that scientific concepts are at a level of abstraction which may distract attention away from concrete experience), there is a highly significant corollary of any attempt to equate the role of philosophy with analysis in this sense. The corollary is that it is never the role of philosophy to provide new factual information. Factual information is the province of science; science alone formulates and tests hypotheses; philosophy's province is not some mysterious area of new and strange hypotheses, but simply the analysis of the meaning of hypotheses which as hypotheses belong to the province of science.

[10] *Op. cit.*, p. 22. See also the remarkable statement, "philosophy of science is philosophy enough." W. V. Quine, "Mr. Strawson on Logical Theory," *Mind*, LXII (1953), 446. It is not entirely clear whether Quine is recommending this view or merely describing it favorably.

## THE RANGE OF ANALYSIS (PART ONE)

The usual empiricist claim is that philosophy *constitutes* empirical description, and that the deliverances of a philosophical theory are properly treated only as themselves empirical hypotheses subject to all the tests appropriate to such hypotheses. The conception of analysis with which we are now concerned differs sharply and insists that empirical description is always the task of the scientist, never of the philosopher. Philosophical "theories," it is said, are never hypotheses to which the techniques of empirical verification are applicable, but are rather attempts to elucidate the logical structure of science.

Unhappily, the phrase "logical structure" *is* an ambiguous phrase. To say, as is so often said, that one is analyzing logical structure, may mean a variety of things. In a very old and very broad sense of the phrase, a sense which is by no means obsolete, the concentration of philosophy upon analysis of the logical structure of science would signify pretty much what one would mean by saying that the central task of philosophy is epistemology or the theory of knowledge. In a more recent and far more strict sense of the phrase, to analyze logical structure means to investigate the purely formal properties of syntax. At the present time one encounters a variety of "mixed" meanings which range between these extremes.

Kant's *Critique of Pure Reason* certainly attempted to associate philosophy with analysis of the method and the results of science. Charles Sanders Peirce demanded that philosophy take its cue from science—that both logic and metaphysics be rooted in a proper analysis of scientific method. Neither Kant nor Peirce, however, had in mind what is often proposed today. Peirce believed that such "analysis" provided new hypotheses—a kind of laboratory metaphysic. Kant never held that his philosophy yielded new hypotheses (in that he is more modern than Peirce), but it has often been said to yield something else, called "necessary presuppositions." When Carnap asserts that all philosophical problems are really syntactical, that when one clears away syntactical errors philosophical problems are either solved or dissolved, he surely claims more than is obviously conveyed by the claim that philosophy is uniquely concerned with analysis of the methods and results of science. One way in which the difference may be made more precise is as follows: Strictly speaking, the logical meaning of the word "analytic" is "tautologous given appropriate definitions." An analytic statement is one which says nothing about the world, in the sense that whatever the facts may be the statement is true given stable definitions. Now, the claim that the task of philosophy is to "analyze" the results of science is very often made in such a way as *not* to be synonymous with the claim that the only proper constituents of a philosophical theory are analytic statements. On the other hand, it is sometimes made in such a way that it *is* so synonymous.

We are at present concerned with the narrower claim. It is almost wholly the product of the idea that if we are not enunciating testable hypotheses the only reputable thing we can do is utter tautologies. The most remarkable fact about those who adopt this position is that what they *say* is so often a hopelessly inadequate account of what they *do*. One example will suffice, and as I have already called attention to a paper by Feigl I shall retain this as my example. Feigl is a good example, because he is both competent and influential.

On page 7 of his paper Feigl offers the following classification under the heading "Functions of Language":

    A. Cognitive
        1. Purely formal
        2. Logico-arithmetical
        3. Factual-empirical

    B. Non-cognitive
        1. Pictorial
        2. Emotive
        3. Volitional-motivational

No definition is provided for the words "cognitive" and "non-cognitive." One is not certain whether they are intended as defined by the classification or as adding something to the classification.

## THE RANGE OF ANALYSIS (PART ONE)

In any event, on pages 10 and 11 he offers a second list which he calls "a general classification of sentences and expressions":

1. Logically true
2. Logically false
3. Factually true
4. Factually false
5. Emotive expressions

This second list shows a decided preference for group A of the first list, the whole of group B now being lumped under the label "emotive." Perhaps this was part of the intention of calling group B "non-cognitive" in the first place. But the interesting point is this: that throughout his essay Feigl discusses "syntactical-semantical rules." One wonders where these fit into the classifications. We are given only one sentence by way of clarification. On page 15 we are told that a rule of procedure "turns out to be a tautology with an added directive appeal." What *does* this mean? Presumably the following would all be classified as tautologies with added directive appeal: the rules of chess, the methodological principles of science, the rules of evidence in courts of law, canons of literary criticism, and moral standards.

Surely there is some confusion here. Rules may be very puzzling objects of analysis, but one thing they clearly are *not* is tautologies. A linguist may notice that certain rules function as recommendations that other expressions be accepted as tautologous; but even such rules are not themselves tautologies. Feigl's limited listings have misled him. He knows that rules are not empirical hypotheses; he knows that they can be perfectly respectable, and indeed that he himself cannot get along without them; having only one alternative available in his list, he has to use it. Nothing else could explain the absurd description of a rule as a tautology. The overwhelmingly obvious fact that rules are devices we use for recommending, advising, teaching, warning (indeed a perfect swarm of "ing" words) is catered to by the postscript "with added directive appeal." This simply will not do; for rules are not tautologies at all. Logicians describe tautologies as true under any and all conditions, or as true solely on the basis of the occurrence of the logical words therein. Rules are not true at all; and they are seldom appropriate in any but a limited range of circumstances.

Classifications of possible uses of discourse may at times provide a fruitful way of clarifying philosophical arguments; but woe betide the philosopher who adopts a classification which will not accommodate the most important things he is himself trying to say.

This leaves us with the broader sense of "analyzing" the results and the methods of empirical science. Now, whatever this broader sense might involve it is surely one of the most important things philosophy does. I have suggested in an earlier chapter that one of the principal lessons we can learn from an analysis of science is that science itself cannot get along with tautologies and testable hypotheses alone. Thus one of the mistakes of "reductionism" may well be the assumption that science itself is "mere." Even if we are impressed by the fact, as eminent philosophers like Russell are, that science at its worst contains most of what we know best, it does not follow that the decision to give special pre-eminence to the philosophy of science is an act of mere analysis.

The view that philosophy is the handmaiden of science has all the earmarks of the medieval view that philosophy is the handmaiden of theology. And the point I want to stress is that there is nothing wrong with either view so long as it avoids the claim that it is specifying philosophy's *only* role. A philosopher must learn to serve many masters. If science contains much of what we know best, history, art criticism, legal theory, and even theology contain a great deal of what we know at a kind of second best. Precisely because a philosopher can learn something by paying careful attention to each discipline, it is a suicidal restriction to confine his attention to any one. Most of us have come to feel that philosophy was stifled by the medieval demand; but it was stifled in the long run after a remarkably productive career. We are witnessing the productive career of scientific medievalism;

but we must be alert to the ultimate dangers of a similarly stifling demand.

The eminent theologian Carl Barth has written a masterful little book entitled *Dogmatics in Outline*. He starts by accepting the point of view of revealed religion and proceeds to an extraordinarily subtle examination of the entailments and presuppositions of that point of view. This is "analysis" of a kind remarkably like what is being recommended by many scientific philosophers. The difference is that one's starting point is supposed to be the deliverances of scientists rather than saints. Barth himself does not call what he is doing "philosophy"; he calls it "dogmatics." Theology merges into philosophy at another point, where dogmatics are freely questioned. Just so with science. The dogmatics of science is grist for the philosopher's mill; but the philosophy of science is not dogmatics.

C. Few virtues more become a philosopher than the virtue of self-correctiveness. All virtue is scarce, and so is genuine self-correction. But there are cases. One such case was Ludwig Wittgenstein.

Wittgenstein began by accepting the view of Russell and of the Vienna Circle that there are only two good ways of talking sense. He accepted the entire apparatus of this, with its fanatical distrust of the phrase "synthetic a priori," its dedication to the ideal of scientific method in philosophy, and its strict adherence to the rigid classifications suggested by logic and mathematics. But his *Tractatus Logico-Philosophicus* expertly manipulates this apparatus to a strange and perplexing conclusion. The essence of the conclusion is contained in the following string of quotations:[11]

> The object of philosophy is the logical clarification of thoughts. . . . Philosophy is not a theory but an activity. A philosophical work consists essentially of elucidations. (p. 77)
>
> My propositions are elucidatory in this way: he who understands me finally recognizes them as senseless. (p. 189)

[11] All quotations are from Ludwig Wittgenstein, *Tractatus Logico-Philosophicus* (London: Kegan Paul, Trench, Trubner and Co. Ltd., 1933).

## THE PRESENT STATE: ANALYSIS

Whereof one cannot speak, thereof one must be silent. (p. 189)

These quotations contain in germ one of the most important points I have been trying to make. *If* you accept the prescription that there are only two ways of talking sense, you must conclude that the job of philosophy is not to talk sense. The contention that philosophy is elucidatory rests upon the argument that it cannot confine itself to descriptions. Wittgenstein's associates, stressing this, sought from philosophy what they called "logical clarification," and Wittgenstein accepts the phrase. But unlike others he was aware that philosophy is not like ideal mathematics. It does not talk sense of the *other* kind either. Therefore, *if* there are only two ways of talking sense it is senseless.

Wittgenstein once remarked that all his later work was intended as showing how very wrong the *Tractatus* was. The error was not in maintaining that philosophy cannot confine itself to testable hypotheses and tautologies. The error lay in assuming that these are the only two ways of talking sense. All of Wittgenstein's later work is concerned with the mistake of supposing that language either does or ought to behave like technical calculi. The examination of "use" rather than "meaning," and the insistence upon "ranges of use" rather than upon clear-cut pigeonholes, is all part of this. There had been two forces at work in the Cambridge to which Wittgenstein came. One was the force of Russell's demand for technical analysis in the spirit of logic and quantum mechanics; the other was the force of Moore's demand for clarificatory analysis in the spirit of common sense and the appeal to ordinary discourse. Wittgenstein entered the philosophical arena as a proponent of the former force; but his ultimate effect was to set in motion an energetic movement as heir to the latter force.

The view that philosophy is an "activity" rather than a way of "talking sense" expresses a profound insight provided one is stuck with the premise that there are only two ways of talking sense. But "remaining silent" is such a queer and frustrating kind of activity that it may force one to reconsider premises. It forced Wittgenstein to reconsider; and reconsideration led him to see that there was after all much he could, with sense, say.

I thus take it that the third kind of analysis we set ourselves to examine in this section expresses the final self-correction of the premise on which the section is based. It therefore points beyond itself. It points to the question: What sort of thing is philosophical analysis seen to be if we rid ourselves of the "great dichotomy"? This will be recognized as the question to which I promised to turn in the next section.

### III. *The Range of Analysis (Part Two)*

Many words are most useful, and in a puzzling way mean most to us, when they are used most vaguely. The words "analyze," "analysis," and "analytic" are words of this sort. There are many occasions on which we want to call attention to analytic tendencies both in philosophy and in other areas of intellectual activity; but just where such words are most appealing we find it extraordinarily difficult to be precise about their meaning.

*Webster's International Dictionary*, in defining the word "analysis," remarks that "analysis clarifies rather than increases knowledge." It would be foolhardy to deny that this remark conveys any meaning; but it is evident upon the slightest reflection that it is extraordinarily loose. It is loose in two different ways, each of which is worth considering. On the one hand, it is as loose as the word "clarify" is ambiguous; and on the other hand, it is loose to whatever extent we find it impossible to draw a sharp line between "clarifying" and "increasing knowledge."

One way in which we clarify is by describing more accurately. Another way in which we clarify is by deducing consequences. Nor are these our only alternatives. You may sometimes clarify, for example, by making explicit covert distributions of emphasis. A judge may clarify a law either by describing court decisions in detail, or by deducing consequences (either from general expressions in the formulation of the law or from general expressions recorded in prior decisions), or by himself deciding the law's intent as to distribution of emphasis. Still another way of clarifying is by translation of technical theories into the terms of common sense; an undertaking which sharply contrasts with the

## THE PRESENT STATE: ANALYSIS

kind of clarification sought within a technical theory by way of escape from the vagueness of common sense. We may speak of Moore and Ryle as engaged in an attempt to clarify the concept of knowing; we may speak of Whitehead's attempt to clarify the concept of a point; and we may speak of Quine's struggle to clarify the concept of synonymy. In each case we may know well enough what we mean; but we court disaster if we think the word "clarify" has retained the same meaning throughout. The word "clarification" helps to remove none of the ambiguity of the word "analysis."

And what of the suggestion that clarification does not increase knowledge? The word "knowledge" has its own share of vagueness; but whatever sense we give to it it seems strange to suggest that we can render something clear without *eo ipso* knowing more. Even if the dictionary is covertly suggesting a rigorous confinement of knowledge to verified hypotheses, clarification may surely be achieved on occasion by just that.

Consider one of the most important senses of clarification in philosophy. One of Willard van Orman Quine's favorite phrases is the phrase "intellectual underpinnings."[12] Whatever the phrase may mean, philosophers devote a great deal of time and energy to isolating the "intellectual underpinnings" of what we say and do. And this is very often what we have in mind when we speak of "clarification" in philosophy, or of "philosophical analysis." The premise of the present section is that such an undertaking is never *merely* a matter of describing the facts on which induction rests or of formalizing the axioms from which deduction proceeds. It may be both, but it is always more. It is a task with some affinity to any attempt to isolate the basic rules of a game—an analogy to which I briefly referred in the opening chapter, and of which I intend to say more in the present chapter. In any

---

[12] The phrase "intellectual underpinning" occurs in *Mathematical Logic*, p. 121. In Quine's later review of P. F. Strawson's *Introduction to Logical Theory* the following phrases occur on the same page: "the theoretical, nongenetic underpinnings of scientific theory" and "the refashioned logical underpinnings of science." See "Mr. Strawson on Logical Theory," *Mind*, LXII (1953), 446.

## THE RANGE OF ANALYSIS (PART TWO)

event, it is surely a mistake to suppose that one can draw any sharp line of demarcation between isolating intellectual underpinnings and increasing knowledge. I have already suggested that our most important knowledge of the world may consist in our understanding of what we can and cannot do by way of theory. We cannot define our categories in such a way as to preclude the possibility of that insight.

Now, when we speak of certain rules as "basic," and when we refer to "underpinnings," the very metaphor behind our words suggests that we are focusing our attention on matters of emphasis. To emphasize is to weigh importance. And it may be objected that isolating decisions as to what is basic or important is *not* what we mean by analysis. Some self-styled analysts are suspicious of all talk about "importance." They have their reasons. We often mean by "analysis" something like the following: an open-minded review of a problem based upon refusal to be predisposed in one way or another on the basis of assumptions as to what is and what is not important. Much recent philosophy, illustrative of this spirit, is criticized by its opponents as "quibbling"; but a strong case for it can nonetheless be made. You never know beforehand whence something of importance is going to arise; and it may well be that we increase our chances of saying something important by talking less about importance.

Once again we run the risk of losing our way in a quagmire of ambiguity. There are many different *kinds* of importance. Empirical reports are "important" as a basis on which inductive inferences rest. Axioms are "important" as a basis from which deduction proceeds. Questions are "important" in that the way in which they are framed may determine the whole subsequent course of our investigation. The very structure of our language is "important" in determining what kind of theoretical moves convince us. In all of these ways, and in many others, you cannot avoid assumptions as to importance; and to refuse to talk about importance *in any sense* is to condemn yourself to silence.

The "analytic" distrust of considerations of importance too often rests on the vague assumptions of the familiar emotivist theory of value. The moment we speak of emphasis, of what is basic or important, it is assumed that we are in some pejorative sense emoting. If we allow ourselves to be swayed by such an assumption we will find ourselves burdened once again with the unsatisfactory premise of the preceding section. Isolating what is basic or important—in a word, the distribution of emphasis—is simply not an emotive and pejorative alternative to fact-stating and/or system-building. It is a general and inescapable part of all theoretical activity, be such activity called analytic or otherwise.

Every way of analyzing or of clarifying consists in one way or another of distributing emphasis. We must thus recognize, and it need be with no emotive overtones, that analysis, even if it insists to the contrary, is always committing itself as to what is and what is not important. The moral to be drawn from this fact is that the defense of any piece of analysis is ultimately the defense of a distribution of emphasis. There is no such thing as mere analysis which fails to distribute emphasis; there is only analysis which refuses to be self-critical. Self-criticism is the essence of good philosophy; and analytic philosophy, if it is to be good, must turn upon itself and justify its own distribution of emphasis.

Our thesis is that self-criticism will always involve the focusing of attention upon a range of problems which spread across a twilight zone between the two standard models of "talking sense." This is, if you will, a linguistic way of expressing the thesis; and calls for the adoption of a final stand on the philosophical purport of "linguistic analysis." The study of the rules governing proper linguistic usage not only *can* rid itself of the presupposition that there are only two proper ways of talking; it is in fact the best possible way of accomplishing that end. The study of language runs as much danger of unjustified bias as any other kind of study. But bias can be resisted. Two such biases to be resisted are those involved in assuming *either* ordinary discourse *or* technical calculi to be sacrosanct. There are many uses of language, all with their keys to insight as well as their lures to

## THE RANGE OF ANALYSIS (PART TWO)

confusion. But, as I have already said, language is the tool of all theory; and a self-critical theory must understand its tool. In one sense there is nothing new about the present emphasis upon language in philosophy. What is new is greater self-consciousness; and, whatever misconceptions may plague us in the process, that very self-consciousness is a major advance.

Linguistically, then, the central philosophical problem is to determine the rules governing the sane rational use of discourse in what I have called the twilight zone. Throughout our discussions of political and moral theory, this was the problem toward which all others pointed. Those earlier chapters sought to isolate at least one question which emerges as basic and as of central importance in those areas: How can one justify commitments as to basic methodological categoricals? I now add that the same question is basic and central in all philosophical "analysis." This is why no sound analysis is "mere"; and it also explains the fact that nothing other than sound analysis must be the core of all self-critical and rational world-view.

One must always bear in mind a distinction between a restricted and an unrestricted object of analysis. Our purposes are usually limited. General as it is, the attempt to isolate the basic categoricals of democratic political theory is an undertaking with a restricted object in view. So is the attempt to isolate the basic categoricals on which science rests. Philosophers are human beings with limited interests; and what they are after is more often than not an object which falls short of everything important. This is why the limits we assign to the reasonableness of the why-question are usually tentative and provisional. We are usually asking "what must we do *if?*" rather than "what must we do in any case?"

The unrestricted object of analysis dispenses only with conventional ifs. Even the unrestricted question "what must we do in any case?" carries with it the governing conditional "if we are to adopt a sane and rational course." Which is merely to concede that even unrestricted analysis is an undertaking predicated upon limited interests. A general purpose is narrow to whatever extent

## THE PRESENT STATE: ANALYSIS

it excludes specific purposes. And the love of wisdom itself is only one passion among others.

The thesis on which I am trying to throw light is the thesis that the road toward rational self-criticism in general philosophy is a road which runs parallel to the road toward rational self-criticism in political theory and in moral theory. All such roads involve the rejection of standard models of proof, and the cultivation of a broad sympathy based upon the most rigorous fallibilism. The disease of analytic philosophy has not been analysis but reductionism. Reductionism deadens our sympathy and our sense of fallibility; as reductionists we cease to be self-critical. The cure is not less analysis but more.

One important clue to a proper frame of mind in general philosophy can be found if we will make our peace with history. Not many years ago a philosopher of eminence was on the verge of accepting an invitation to join the staff of one of our major universities. In a final interview it was explained to him that he might be called upon from time to time to conduct classes in a large introductory course on Plato. Reddening with indignation he announced that he would not teach Plato, he would teach only the truth.

It so happens that in the same university at the same time a seminar was being offered in Plato, the thesis of which was that Plato in the dialogues of the *Republic* period expressed a view of the world which is in the main true. The fact that Plato in his later dialogues severely criticized many of his central assumptions in the *Republic* period, the fact of Plato's own intense self-criticism, was ignored. So were most of the valid findings of twentieth-century analysis. The theme of the course was that philosophy has stagnated since Hegel and Royce, and that we should return to the great insights of the past.

Here is the great divide. Must we *either* burrow in an analytic hole and refuse to learn from the wealth of insight in the grand tradition, *or* prostrate ourselves before the grand tradition and refuse to learn from the wealth of insight contained in rigorous analysis? If we will only learn that justification in philosophy, as

## THE RANGE OF ANALYSIS (PART TWO)

elsewhere, is inescapably circular; that our method as philosophers will be sound only to the extent that it emerges from self-corrective insight into what we can and cannot accomplish by way of proof; we may make our peace with history. The efforts and the mistakes of Plato, of Aristotle, of Hume, of Kant, of Russell are precisely what we need to understand. Whatever we know in philosophy we know because such men have tried and always been partly right and partly wrong. We cannot short-cut our attempt to understand the world. There is no shorter road for philosophy than that which leads through all that has been tried and failed. And there is also no shorter road than that which leads through all that the most competent analysis can do—with or without success. The key to a sound approach in moral and political matters we found in a careful methodological fallibilism based upon detailed understanding of the record of our mistakes and the limits of traditional justification models. Just so, the key to a sound approach in general philosophy will lie in self-correctiveness in relation to a less restricted object.

The very wealth of the history of ideas may baffle and mislead. The very wealth of history often lies behind the mistaken notions that we can get by in philosophy either with mere description or with mere dogmatics. So many descriptions have been offered of the world, either in whole or in part, that we are sometimes tempted to be sycophants and without ourselves describing we discuss other descriptions. Only thus could we be fooled into thinking of description as "mere." So many systems have been erected (whether by philosophers or scientists or theologians) that we are tempted to be sycophants and to "merely" elucidate logical structure. The wealth of history gives us too good a head-start; and let us confess that most run-of-the-mill philosophy is "mere." But, as we have found before, the slight shift in emphasis is all-important. If you will understand this wealth of history from inside you will understand that significant description and enlightened system-building are never "mere" in the original. No great idea has ever been mere description or mere elucidation. A great idea is always a new searchlight of emphasis. And the ultimate lesson of history lies in a multitude of searchlights. This is why that very attention to history which may make sycophants of us is essential to the fallibilistic insight.

I would conclude this plea with an explicit reference to history. The main stream of modern philosophy grew out of reflection upon the methods of science. In point of fact, that method combined both deductive and inductive aspects. Prior to Kant two traditions had grown up side by side according as one or the other of these two aspects was stressed. The rationalists isolated deduction as a standard model; the empiricists isolated induction as a standard model. Kant rightly perceived that neither standard model would do, and sought a middle ground. His entire philosophy hinges on the search for a kind of justification procedure alternative to theorem-deriving and statistical experimental testing.

He made enormous blunders. I have already conceded that his attempt to defend a "synthetic a priori" involved an unhappy and sometimes misleading terminology. He never quite succeeded in ridding himself of the deductive model. He failed to escape from the misguided ideal of a "final solution." And most importantly of all, he certainly never succeeded in clarifying the relation between expressions which convey basic recommendations and expressions which do conform to the theorem-deriving and fact-stating models. But, then, neither has anyone else; and this much can be said for Kant: that, however puzzling his solutions, he rightly insisted on *that* problem as the central concern of philosophy. He rightly insisted that the nub of the whole matter lay in the insufficiency of Hume's two neat pigeonholes.

It is remarkable how up-to-date a study of the conflict between Hume and Kant is. When one examines that conflict in the light of all that is transpiring in recent philosophy, one is tempted to conceive of the entire nineteenth century as an unfortunate and relatively unprofitable digression. Of course, even digressions are instructive. The best thing to do with a wrong-headed notion is to give it rope and see where it leads. The nineteenth century performed this service with several of the wrong-headed ideas which hampered Kant himself. But the real key to what is important in a man's thought is the questions he considers fundamental. And the central questions Kant asked are as fundamental now as they were when he asked them.

Kant saw himself as adjudicating in face of the impasse between rationalism and empiricism. Those ism words instill less passion now than then, but the habits of thought on which they rested are still with us. We face the same impasse in new guises. There are, after all, three basic questions asked by Kant. They are these:

1. What is the status of those basic recommendatory expressions for which no place is provided in Hume's neat dichotomy?

2. In any special or restricted intellectual undertaking, such as physical science (the subject of the first *Critique*) or moral theory (the subject of the second), what are the minimum presuppositions required?

3. If, as Kant rightly saw, the unrestricted attempt to formulate a way of viewing the world (metaphysics) is not properly conceived as knowledge, how can we properly conceive of it?

Now, I have said all that I intend to say about the first of these questions. It is not a question with any easy capsule answer; but it is a question the spirit of which can be defended; and in formulating it Kant has for once and for all placed in the forefront of philosophy its most important analytic concern. It remains to examine the present force of the other two questions. The second, with special reference to the presuppositions of science, will be our concern in the next section. The third will be the subject of our final chapter.

## IV. *The Musts of Science*

In Chapter Two we noted that a scientist, *as* a scientist, must make decisions which are fully as categorical as any decisions we make as moral or political agents. In Chapter Three we rejected any facile dichotomy between the realms of science and value. We there remarked: "The final problem in science is the justification of one's distribution of emphasis in all decisions concerning

## THE PRESENT STATE: ANALYSIS

the canons of procedure one accepts as a scientist." Once again our stress was on the phrase "as a scientist."

Both in Chapter Four and in the present chapter we have attacked what might be called "scientism." This is a disease of philosophy rather than of science. We reject any view which presumes to dictate *either* that all important questions can be settled, if at all, by inductive experiment, *or* that philosophy should attach itself exclusively to the apron-strings of science. We have at all points, however, sought to avoid the absurd mistake of attacking science as such. The competence of science as a method of discovery and of control is demonstrated. But the best antidote to scientism is a better understanding of science itself.

Kant's question concerning the minimum presuppositions of restricted disciplines forces us to face directly the question: What *are* the categorical decisions of science? A question as important as this should not be enshrouded in jargon. It can in fact be put very simply. J. Robert Oppenheimer, who is a competent physicist, has pointed out that physics is learnt by apprenticeship.[13] If we are interested in isolating the basic principles or the categorical decisions of physics, we should pay close attention to the kinds of advice the transmission of which is the heart of the apprenticeship relation. Of course, the "principles" which function as "basic" in such advice may not be explicitly verbalized at all; and even when verbalized they may shine forth in questions asked and instructions given as well as in propositions either singular or general. There are many ways in which advice is transmitted.

But one general way of stating the question may, I think, be instructive. When we talk, as we sometimes do, of the basic principles of science, we have something of the following sort in mind. The principles which govern the giving of advice in science, whether tacit or explicitly stated, might be expressed thus: "If you are to provide a scientific account of a given matter, proceed as follows." And when we ask which of these principles are

[13] J. Robert Oppenheimer, *Science and the Common Understanding* (New York: Simon and Schuster, 1954).

## THE MUSTS OF SCIENCE

basic, we are simply asking which of these principles are such that you can insert a "you must" before the word "proceed." Some of the principles upon which scientists act are such that, if those principles were changed, scientific procedure would be altered but science as we conceive of it would remain intact. Some of those principles, however, are presumed to be such that, if you changed them science would simply disappear. When we talk about the basic principles or the categorical decisions of science we have in mind those principles which state what you *must* do if you are to engage in science at all.

A few examples will be helpful. First, an example of a principle which does not seem to be basic in the sense in question. Philosophers of science have had a great deal to say about the principle of parsimony. Now, this does not seem to me to be a principle which is basic in the sense we are discussing. It would be a complete mistake to say that in order to give a scientific account of the stars we *must* adopt the most economical description. Economy is desirable in science, but it is less than necessary. The principle of parsimony prescribes a standard of choice between alternatives already presumed to be sufficiently "scientific." By way of contrast consider two classic examples of a very different kind of principle. Charles Sanders Peirce maintained that you cannot indulge in science without assuming that there are occurrences which are independent of your observation of them. Bertrand Russell has maintained that you cannot indulge in science without assuming that there are separable causal lines. If either Peirce or Russell is right, he is pointing to a principle which is such that science would collapse upon its serious rejection.

Two points should be noticed. First: neither Peirce nor Russell is trying to report what scientists have *said*. Each is trying to bring to the surface of verbalization principles which are operative in what scientists *do*. Peirce would not be shaken by a competent scientist who mouthed solipsism. Russell would not be bothered by the claim that he is saying something no scientist ever thought of. Each is trying to formulate a must which is imbedded in practice rather than in doctrine. Second: even if they are correct, neither Peirce nor Russell is isolating a principle which is the exclusive property of science in any narrow sense. Surely historians and literary critics are as coerced as physicists to assume occurrences independent of the methods they use; and most theologians who have worried about the forces of evil have been as committed to the assumption of separate causal lines as any engineer. But it would still be instructive to know that either Peirce or Russell was right. It would be instructive to be able to specify certain principles which you must accept if you are to indulge in science at all.

Now, the best way to test such a notion as we here confront is to give the opposition a fair hearing. Let us therefore see how forcefully we can state the case *against* any such conception of the musts of science.

Our ability to use the general noun "science" does not justify us in assuming that science is in any sense a definite object. When we use that noun we are referring to a very indefinite series of practices. We do not ordinarily have much difficulty distinguishing scientists from, for example, humanists in our university faculties; but we base our distinction upon exceedingly rough rules of thumb. If we are candid, so it may be said, we cannot distinguish between "what we must do if we are to engage in science" and "what we may or may not do if we like" *in any hard and fast way*. But to say that we cannot draw this distinction in any hard and fast way, is to say that we cannot draw the distinction *at all*. For unless the distinction is drawn in a hard and fast way the force of the "must" is entirely lost. The best that you can do is a combination of two far less ambitious things: (i) You may at any given time describe the more predominant traits shared by the hodge-podge of activities called "scientific"; these descriptions will vary from time time; and such uniformities as you discover are no more nor less than uniformities which show up in these descriptions. There is nothing in all this which will allow you to insist that there is any one thing you *must* do in order to engage in science. (ii) You may legislate by fiat either that what you have found common, or that something you personally

## THE MUSTS OF SCIENCE

choose to do, is to be taken as the defining trait (or traits) of science. In such case, of course, anyone must do that kind of thing in order to engage in what you call "science"; but the "must" is now reduced to a matter of definition. Obviously, for example, if you define "science" as (in part) a method of approach which ignores moral considerations in choosing between alternative hypotheses, then you must (in part) ignore moral considerations in choosing between alternative hypotheses if you are engaging in science; but the "must" here merely reveals that you are so defining the word "science."

Such a view considers the problem of what you must do in order to engage in science as altogether on a par with the problem of what you must do in order to play the game of bridge. There is a distinction of sorts in the game of bridge between much-discussed conventions and seldom-discussed basic rules of play. But the latter, the basic rules of bridge, force upon us no cosmic puzzles. It may be of interest to ask whether bridge still remains bridge when played, as it was for a while in the 1930's, with five suits. This is a problem on a par with the problem whether two-dimensional and three-dimensional chess are in any sense the "same" game. But there is no real difficulty in either case. We may describe as we will the common practice of bridge players, and we may prescribe as we will the use of a label. Arguments as to whether "bridge" is being played are either arguments concerning the conformity of one case to a general description or arguments as to the proper use of a label. There are no other and mysterious senses of "must" with respect to the proper playing of bridge. And just so, the present argument runs, with science.

Now, there are two fundamental oversights of such an argument; and my final defense of the need for categorical commitments *in* science will rest upon calling attention to these oversights. It will be noticed that the view at hand presents us with our old friends once more neatly dichotomized: either describe or define. As always, whether we are concerned with politics or ethics or general philosophy, categoricals tempt us to read them

## THE PRESENT STATE: ANALYSIS

either as hypotheses or as tautologies. The musts of science are no exception. But let us concentrate upon two oversights.

The first oversight in the present instance is the failure to mark a serious difference between science and any game such as bridge or chess. The reason we do not call science a game is that it is a complex of activities engaged in with significant purpose. We are willing to accept arbitrary fiats as sufficient to establish basic rules only so long as what we are *doing* is arbitrary. For this reason we are willing to concede that the basic rules of bridge or chess are arbitrary fiats. No one could deny for a moment that when we engage in science we do as a matter of fact constantly lay down arbitrary fiats; but in this case we are not satisfied. In a game, the rules are laid down; you may play it or not as you choose; it makes no important difference one way or the other. In science what is laid down is a purpose—sometimes vague, sometimes relatively clear. We want to find out all we can about something, or we want to achieve control of a situation by accurate prediction. The purpose being laid down, the whole point of science is to develop a set of rules which will be dependable. Laying down the rules is not something which is done "outside" the "game"; it is not a *fait accompli* before we start to play. We do not read up the rule books and then sit down to play. Playing here *is* an attempt to examine and re-examine the rules to find out which we can and which we cannot avoid.

A scientist is rightly suspicious of accepting any description of what others have done as binding upon himself; and his interest in the basic principles of scientific method is not an interest in labels. His interest is in determining what we must *do* in order to achieve a certain kind of understanding. And this suggests the second oversight which mars the easy escape we have considered. This second oversight consists in failure to recognize the confusion and the uncertainty which is the background out of which all genuine science emerges. How easy it would be if we knew just what the "musts" and the "mays" of science were! By listing the "musts" we would define science; and from this list we could deduce what any competent scientist would do. By listing the

## THE MUSTS OF SCIENCE

"mays" we would give a complete description of science. Our predilection for uttering nothing but tautologies and empirical hypotheses would be satisfied. The key to understanding science lies in forthright perception of the utter inappropriateness of this simple view of the matter. We do not know where to draw these lines. We have no definite set of axioms from which to deduce; and, on the other hand, no merely empirical description of what scientists do will give us leverage for deciding what can be dispensed with and what can not.

This is why philosophers, and scientists themselves, are forced to worry about what we must do if we are to engage in science. In science, as in morals and in politics, we who play the game are fallible creatures; and our only clue to rational method is to commit ourselves to basic categoricals which turn inward upon our own limitations. We face again, as always, the ultimate circularity of all rational justification procedure. We face again the imperative that, if we are to talk sense in these matters, we cannot do so by confining ourselves to tautologies and testable hypotheses. All of which does after all put musts at the heart of science itself. The overriding must is the must of fallibilism, a categorical most violated by many self-styled scientific philosophers.

It would be a complete mistake to suppose that from this central categorical of fallibilism one could "deduce" any complete set of the musts of science. We are once again operating in the midst of a subtle and perplexing range of concepts to which no sharply defined map will do justice. But, as in the case of political theory and of moral philosophy, we can focus our attention on crucial examples. I propose to cite three examples of categoricals which are entailed by the fallibilism of sound scientific method.

The first of these categoricals has been emphasized by almost every philosopher who has understood the actual procedures of science. In one way or another it is a basic premise of Kant, of Peirce, and of Russell, all of whom, however unlike they may be in other respects, are alike in possessing firsthand acquaintance with the working method of science. This is the categorical of realism; and it has a twofold bearing. On the one hand, there is the categorical of assuming the independent occurrence of events and occasions; and on the other hand there is the categorical of assuming that order is an object of discovery. You cannot realize that you may be wrong without realizing that it would mean something to be right. Realism cannot be proved; it is simply a categorical as to our distribution of emphasis if science is to proceed.

Kant's postulation of "things-in-themselves," conjoined with his insistence that we can "know" only "phenomena," greatly bothered his nineteenth-century successors. Their assumption was that you cannot talk about that of which you can know nothing. To state the matter in Royce's way: unless you can specify the "what" of which you speak, you cannot mention "that." But Royce is spellbound by a philosopher's myth. Science could not proceed without mention of "thats" in the absence of "whats." So to do is the prelude to all finding out; and where we once find out, we a thousand times do not. As always, philosophers' words creak and strain, and I hasten to add that Kant inferred much from his initial insight less coercive than that insight itself. To state the matter at its minimum, where knowing consists of demonstrated propositions (either theorems or verified hypotheses), the core of science is something else. Kant's unknowable things-in-themselves are simply a poetic device for expressing this fact.

Stripped of all unessential inferences, the first part of the realist assumption is a straightforward categorical involved in the concession that you may be mistaken. Events and occurrences, interpret them as you will, have a life of their own; and all our knowings, actual or possible, form a limited map which will always fall short of the terrain which is its object. No one has seen more clearly than Peirce (who owed much to his study of Kant) that there is no "proof" of realism short of an internal, circular, self-critical attitude. One can only remark that no amount of use of the method which rests upon that categorical can possibly lead to doubt of it.

But Peirce saw too that there is a second part of the realist assumption. He rightly perceived that a realism as to events and occurrences entails equal realism as to order and the efficacy of law. Prediction is the soul of science; and prediction assumes not only that events are occurring but also that they are occurring in an orderly way. The obverse side of fallibilism, that it would mean something to be right, entails not only that events and occurrences are discovered but also that their *ways* are discovered.

Kant distinguished the objectivity of things-in-themselves from the objectivity of the order discovered by science. The latter he accounted for in terms of an elaborate apparatus of transcendental categories embedded in the human mind. Neither Peirce nor Russell endorses this apparatus; but this difference is here secondary. Peirce defined the "real" as "that whose characters are independent of what anyone may think them to be"; and he called this a "fundamental hypothesis" of science. So far he is at one with Kant, though his use of the word "hypothesis" may be misleading. He is enunciating not a testable prediction but rather the initial categorical of realism. And though both Peirce and Russell reject Kant's apparatus, though both are willing to concede that such order as we discover is at least part of the order of things as they are in themselves, all three are agreed as to the basic imperative. Whether such order as science discovers *is* the order of things-in-themselves or is a "transcendental" order imposed upon them, that order is at any rate objective in the sense that it is independent of any special set of scientists or any special set of observations.

A problem which is secondary in one context, however, may be primary in another. There is a second categorical at the base of scientific method, which stands alongside the general categorical of realism. For in one way or another, whether it be in Kant's way or anyone else's, fallibilism commits us to a dualism between all objects of our conception and our conceptions of them. Once again, Peirce has stated the matter as clearly as it can be stated. Science demands that we resist the temptation to equate our latest and best hypothesis with the truth." This profound insight,

## THE PRESENT STATE: ANALYSIS

so persistently ignored or misunderstood by the later pragmatists, deserves restatement. It cannot be reiterated too often.

Peirce once remarked that "The opinion which is fated to be ultimately agreed to by all who investigate, is what we mean by the truth, and the object represented in this opinion is the real."[14] Now, later pragmatists have persistently taken this to mean that the latest and best hypothesis agreed upon in science *is* the truth. Peirce meant nothing of the sort. His own account of the scientific method, and his own defense of fallibilism, leads him again and again to insist that we can never justify the assumption that our latest and best hypothesis is, or adequately represents, the truth. Even if we had the truth in our hands we could never be sure of it; tomorrow inquiry *might* encounter a negative instance, for all we know. Peirce's mathematical mind was thinking of the truth as the *ideal* limit of a process. "The truth" is conceived as that opinion upon which competent observers *would* agree; this has nothing to do with identifying "the truth" with that opinion upon which we *do* agree. Peirce was aware of this. In discussing Schiller's account of pragmatism he remarks:

> I hold that truth's independence of individual opinions is due (so far as there is any 'truth') to its being the predestined result to which sufficient inquiry *would* ultimately lead. I only object that, as Mr. Schiller himself seems sometimes to say, there is not the smallest scintilla of logical justification for any assertion that a given sort of result will, as a matter of fact, either *always* or *never* come to pass; and consequently we cannot know that there *is* any truth concerning any given question; and this, I believe, agrees with the opinion of M. Henri Poincaré, except that he seems to insist upon the non-existence of any absolute truth for *all* questions, which is simply to fall into the very same error on the opposite side.[15]

Now, you may not like Kant's gaudy terminology; and you may in particular distrust the words "phenomena" and "noumena."

---

[14] *The Philosophy of Peirce, Selected Writings*, edited by Justus Buchler (New York: Harcourt, Brace and Company, 1940), p. 38.
[15] *Ibid.*, p. 288.

## THE MUSTS OF SCIENCE

But whether it will or no, all science works with the distinction between how things seem to be and how they really are. In one form or another the dualism between the objects of our conception and our conceptions of them is the starting point of all genuine inquiry. What puzzles us about Kant's distinction is the further claim that we *cannot* know anything about things as they are in themselves. But this "cannot" is ambiguous. If, as Kant's successors read it, it is taken as a true proposition, it would seem to contradict itself. It says what it announces cannot be said. Suppose, however, that it is not intended as a true proposition. As a recommendation, as a formulation of a basic commitment altogether on a par with Peirce's demand that truth be conceived as an ideal limit, it makes perfectly good sense. It does more than make sense; it expresses, as Peirce saw, a categorical which is basic if inquiry is not to be stopped. For, the moment you conceive that you *are* knowing things as they are in themselves you embrace the dogmatism that blocks further inquiry.

All of this, however, is incomplete without an additional comment. There is, as a matter of fact, a third categorical involved here. As to this, neither Kant nor Peirce has been fully explicit; though it is entailed by their practice if not openly formulated. The categorical of realism and the categorical of dualism between our conceptions and their objects are incomplete. The third categorical which is involved is the rejection of any claim to the effect that total skepticism makes sense.

There is a persistent philosophical myth that solipsism is an unassailable logical fortress. The source of this myth is the mistaken notion that ideally we should say nothing which is neither a verifiable hypothesis nor a demonstrable tautology. If skepticism meant merely that we cannot confine ourselves to these two ways of talking, it would be harmless enough. But in fact skepticism conjoins this truth with an utterly wrong-headed retention of the ideal that we *ought* to be able so to confine ourselves. That is where it goes astray; and that is what produces the absurd notion of the impregnability of solipsism.

You cannot think that you are always wrong; and you cannot

doubt everything. Santayana has argued that skepticism can only be countered by "animal faith"; but "animal faith" is as misleading a label as he could have picked for describing what he himself had in mind. What he had in mind was the necessity of unqualified categorical commitment. It is ridiculous to suppose that animals have any monopoly on this; and "faith" is a word loaded with overtones suggesting the irrational. We *must* stop thinking of skepticism as the impregnable stronghold of purified reason. Skepticism is in fact irrational; and the vaunted skeptical powers of philosophers are sheer myth.

The method of science legislates fallibilism and care; but it simultaneously and categorically repudiates skepticism. It does so simply by committing itself to the principle that there is a difference between being right and being wrong. Science as such in no way prescribes that we confine ourselves to demonstrated theorems and confirmed hypotheses; properly understood it prescribes the opposite. But it does prescribe that demonstrated theorems and confirmed hypotheses are very important ways of talking. Science insists that we cannot be *wholly* wrong. Every time a prediction is fulfilled we have a guaranty that we do not wholly misunderstand the world. Science may be fraught with mistakes and confusion, but mistaken and confused though it be it teaches no lesson more important than this: that deductive techniques, and especially mathematics, enable us to predict and to control matters of fact. A philosopher who pooh-poohs the science of engineering reveals nothing so much as his own lack of wisdom in his distribution of interpretative emphasis.

These, then, are examples of the kind of categoricals which are embedded in the fallibilist outlook of science. These are not the rules of a game; they are commitments involved in the attempt to understand in a certain kind of way. We state them as propositions; we try to "prove" them; and we always fail. Events, occasions, and their order are independent of our observations; there is a dualism between our conceptions and their objects; there is a difference between right conceptions and wrong ones. These

## THE MUSTS OF SCIENCE

are not propositions; they are rules; they are categorical commitments the rejection of which is the essence of irrationalism.

And thus we conclude our analysis of analysis. Are we analyzing "merely"? Anything but! We are gradually learning that the results of analysis, in whatever form we conceive it, merge into world-view. Within analysis itself the keys to rational metaphysics must be found. Nothing we have said is neutral; rational discourse is never neutral. It is only either self-conscious and self-critical or not.

One final task remains. If metaphysics and analysis are not dichotomized and relegated to separate pigeonholes, what emerges as a proper understanding of philosophy's "grander" and "more moving" role? What is our present standing as part of, rather than as alien to, the grand tradition?

# CHAPTER SIX: THE PRESENT STATE OF PHILOSOPHY: THE GRAND TRADITION

## I. *Metaphysics as Critique*

AMONG the most instructive pages Kant ever wrote are those which constitute the closing section of the *Prolegomena to Any Future Metaphysics,* entitled "Solution to the General Question of the Prolegomena." It is not my purpose to endorse what generally passes as "Kantianism" nor to deny that Kant's positive system contains much mistake and confusion. But I should nonetheless maintain that in its basic essentials the view Kant here expresses as to the proper role of metaphysics is a correct, and indeed the only justifiable, view.

Stripped of all unessentials, the view Kant expresses is the following: He is aware that he has been devoting most of his time to the specification of what metaphysics *cannot* do. He has now reached the point where he feels that he can recommend that slight shift in the focus of consciousness which we have ourselves shown to be so important. His thesis is based on the recommendation that we accept what has already been done, all of the analysis which supports and enlightens these "cannots," as constituting the very soul of metaphysics properly conceived. Metaphysics *is,* to use Kant's word, "critique." The subject matter of metaphysics is not something *other than* an exhibition of (to use Kant's language again) "the fundamental laws of the faculty of reason." If we may use our own oft-repeated language: metaphysics is not something *other than* the study of what we can and cannot provide by way of responsible rational justification.

One can go even further. For, in spite of his preoccupation with certain all-too-familiar and excessively hopeful "final solutions" couched in Greek and Roman roots, the two central cannots which he levies against metaphysics are sound. He was, after all, combatting both rationalism and empiricism; and the sum and substance of what metaphysics can *not* claim to be is according to Kant twofold. It cannot claim to be a system of strict deductions on a par with mathematics; and it cannot claim to be a system of empirically testable hypotheses. All of this is clearly and unambiguously summarized by Kant in the passage to which I refer.

Now, he does continue to label metaphysics, even in the sense of critique which he recommends, as a "science." The sub-title of the section is: "How is metaphysics possible as a science?" Clearly, if one persists in using the word "science" as a label confined to the practice of precisely those two methods which Kant is denying to metaphysics, one will be puzzled or even repelled. If, however, we are to grasp Kant's meaning we cannot ignore the fact that the entire argument of his first critique was designed to show that science itself requires more than deductions (in the *usual* sense) and/or testable hypotheses. When, in the present context, Kant speaks of "science" he intends in a very general sense any intellectual undertaking which is capable of providing justification of the principles upon which it proceeds. His claim that metaphysics *can* be conceived as a science is no more nor less than the claim that metaphysics as critique *constitutes* a justification of procedural principles.

We do not have to argue that Kant's own account of what we can and cannot do by way of providing theoretical justification is correct. Far from it! But amidst many errors, profound insight may emerge. Kant's insight into the proper conception of the role of metaphysics was sound. The ultimate purport of all that we have been saying in the preceding chapters is an endorsement of his view that the proper role of metaphysics is critique.

It makes an important difference, however, what we select as the object of our critique. Kant was immersed in the faculty psychology typical of his times. He assumed that the object of critique was the faculty Reason. We can no longer think in this way. Reason is not a definite object; and its procedural principles are not definite objects either. Reason is a wide range of decision practices; and its procedural principles are as various as the range of contexts within which decisions must be made. Metaphysics as critique, metaphysics as an attempt to generalize the principles involved in justification procedure, is even more complicated than

Kant supposed. This is one of many reasons why Kant's modified conception of the "deductive" character of metaphysics is utterly inappropriate. We cannot start with Aristotelian principles and proceed from there; we have to plunge into a much more confusing and fallible context.

One of the most helpful distinctions we can draw at the very outset is the distinction between critique directed toward such restricted or limited efforts as those with which we have been concerned in previous chapters. We may, for example, ask with respect to the restricted enterprise of political theory: what are the basic principles of justification procedure appropriate therein? We may ask the same kind of question concerning ethics or physics or art history or jurisprudence. As contrasted with such restricted objects of critique, we must separate off the attempt to provide an unrestricted critique of any and all effort to achieve sane or rational understanding. This will make a difference in our conception of the role of metaphysics.

For example: When a political theorist announces that all men are created equal, he is indulging in metaphysics. So is a philosopher of science who announces that there are separable causal lines. If we are right, neither is uttering provable propositions. Each is, with reference to his special problem, announcing a decision as to the rules which are governing his concept of justification. His "metaphysics" can be careful, and it can in its way be complete, though he confines himself to the problem at hand. He does not *have* to broaden his interest to accommodate all possible justification procedure in all possible contexts. But there are peculiar problems which arise to haunt those who *do* choose to broaden their interest and to try similar recommendations with unrestricted intent.

There is clearly no sharp dividing line here. The unrestricted question is a specific question by virtue of *being* unrestricted. And it would make no sense to specify as a rule governing *any* justification procedure one which did not apply in a restricted case. The distinction is most helpful by way of indicating a range. Throughout the range, talking metaphysics is a matter of issuing advice which we cannot prove one way or another, and in particular of issuing advice which in the context under consideration prescribes basic decisions as to justification procedure. We may use the very same words in markedly different contexts. Consider, for example, the expression "Time is unreal." We may consider such an expression as an example of very *bad* metaphysics; but even bad metaphysics must be shown to be bad in terms of the purpose it is designed to fulfill. The expression "Time is unreal" might well function as part of the justification of a highly specific political program—a program, let us say, of some utopian community. Defenders of the Oneida community in mid-nineteenth-century New York said this kind of thing. They were certainly not talking nonsense. They were trying to justify what they were doing—however absurd we may think the doing of it. At the same time, they were not interested in philosophy as we usually conceive of it academically. Here the expression "Time is unreal" might function with far more general intent. It might function as part of a generalized justification of either ignoring or minimizing the weight to be given to empirical evidence in deciding upon questions of *any* sort. The members of the Oneida community were not interested in this general problem; some philosophers have been; the difference is a difference in range of interest.

When a philosopher of metaphysical bent directs his attention to a question that is broad enough he pays a price. The broadest question he can ask is what constitutes appropriate justification procedure in *any* case; and if he braves a question as broad as this his every answer will involve him in a circle.

A philosopher whose interest lies in the completely general always runs the risk of thinking that he can avoid what other men cannot. Other men constantly make assumptions which they do not question; other men ask questions without sufficient awareness of what is entailed in asking those questions rather than alternative ones; other men use thought-models without examining them. The philosopher with general intent may try to place himself outside all this. He examines all assumptions; he asks questions about all questions; he suspects all thought-models. This is an admirable enough purpose, so long as he does not fancy that he can examine assumptions without assumptions, avoid the implications of his own special kinds of questioning, or dispense with thought-models altogether. However general your intent may be, your theory is still an interpretation. You cannot get out of your own skin. You are still distributing emphasis even though your purpose be a completely general study of emphasis distribution.

We may be frightened by this circularity; or we may boldly accept it as a clue to the proper conception of our task. If we are to take the latter course, we must squarely face the fact that the whole point of philosophy emerges from our own shortcomings. General philosophical problems arise precisely *because* we tackle intellectual tasks with limited equipment. Confess at once that if we were not motivated by the urge to understand what we do not already understand those problems would not arise. If, motivated by that urge, we could fancy ourselves as omniscient, or if we could fancy ourselves in possession of a perfect language tool, we might envision a time in which all our philosophical puzzles might vanish. Philosophy will never cease because such fancies are utopian.

We deceive ourselves if we formulate utopian goals. We are not and we cannot be omniscient. Our language is not perfect and it cannot be made perfect. The questions "What must we do if we are to achieve understanding?" and "What must we do if we are to be rational?" will *never* lose their force. We may increase our information, and we may increase our linguistic precision, but the need for philosophy will continue to arise from the situation we are irrecoverably in. We will always need advice beyond the limits of proof and precision.

Once more, the sword with two cutting edges: the need for such advice makes fools of those who think they can eradicate metaphysics; but it makes equal fools of those who overestimate what metaphysics can accomplish. Sensible metaphysics can never be utopian, and must always emerge from careful consideration of the predicament we are in. It is always circular and it is always fallible. Throughout the range where its persistence is assured, it can be neither more nor less than the attempt to advise as to the conditions of sound advice, to distribute emphasis as to the rules for distributing emphasis.

What will happen if we boldly reassert ourselves in the "grand tradition" in the spirit suggested by these remarks? Above all, I think, two things which I shall seek to clarify in the two closing sections:

First, that, as I have repeatedly suggested, the core of our *Weltanschauung* must emerge from careful analysis or critique. As we have ourselves been concerned with analysis or critique, there should be contained within all that we have been saying certain guideposts to responsible metaphysical talk. Our first task is thus summary with a twist. The twist is to show that within what we have already said may be found rich clues to a reasonable and responsible conception of the world. To this task the following section will be devoted.

But there is a second consequence to be faced. For if metaphysical speculation is to be rightly viewed it must be conceived as the apex of a man's thought rather than as its foundation. You cannot start by prescribing what can and cannot be done in general. This you can only learn gradually and with great effort. At no point has the grand tradition more persistently gone astray. To conceive of one's commitments on the highly general and the grandiose matters as the "foundation" of one's thought is downright wrong-headed. Such commitments must be fought for, groped for, sought. They are always suspect when viewed as a solid base from which to start. They are not where we start; they are where we are trying to arrive. Because we will never quite arrive, the highest goal of metaphysics can only be poetic. The roots of metaphysics are critique; its flower is a species of poetry. In Section III we will seek to defend and clarify this contention, and therewith draw our argument to a close.

## II. *The Nature of the World*

We *are* frightened of circularity; we are so frightened that we sometimes base our philosophies on proposals of escape. Such proposals always misfire; but certain of them merit brief comment. Though they misappropriate valuable clues, the clues are important.

It would indeed be remarkable if the central fact of our intellectual life had passed unnoticed. The circularity with which we are concerned has often been noticed. It is only too obvious that our way of interpreting determines what considerations will convince us. But if, in the face of this fact, we persist in asking how to justify one way of interpreting rather than another, two courses are open to us. We may accept the very circularity of the predicament we are in as the key to our answer; or we may seek our answer in some attempt at escape. Consider for a moment three such attempts at escape.

Perhaps the most influential of such attempts has been pragmatism. Pragmatism seeks to break the circle by appeal to purpose. But whence do purposes come? It is the way we interpret the world which determines what purposes will move us. Pragmatism rightly perceives that our purposes determine the way in which we distribute emphasis; but it slurs over the reciprocal fact. The street is a two-way street. And this means that we cannot "justify" our rational efforts by going outside of them. Purpose is not external to rational effort; and justification of one's purposes in neither more nor less rational than justification of one's interpretations themselves. There are not two things here; and when a well-known philosopher tells us that he sees no solution short of "a more thoroughgoing pragmatism" I cannot comprehend what solution he has in mind.[1] The pragmatists rightly

---

[1] Willard van Orman Quine, *From a Logical Point of View* (Cambridge: Harvard University Press, 1953), p. 46. The word "pragmatism" may of course be used in a very untechnical way as a label for the practice of keeping one's eye on matters of practical decision. In this sense Plato and Locke are perhaps the outstanding "pragmatists" in the history of philosophy. In this sense, Quine's remark may be persuasive; but it does not tell us *how* to proceed or *what* to do. If, on the other hand, Quine is using the

## THE NATURE OF THE WORLD

insist that all rational effort is a "doing"; but they unfortunately talk as though "doing" is an activity with a general description. This is part of the reason for their assumption that the single word "purpose" is in some way a cure-all for our intellectual predicament. If we are clear about the range of that word, it rather states the problem than cures it.

In recent years a complex assortment of notions propagated under the label "existentialism" have been gaining ever wider currency. Existentialism (like pragmatism) means many things; but there seems to be at least one common claim. We are told that we must break the circle of our predicament by the performance of some pre-rational and frankly unjustifiable act of commitment. Now, it is certainly the case that our manner of conceiving of the world hinges upon decisions—*many* of them. Any interpretation already commits us whether we concede it or not. But there is serious danger in the notion that any decision lies outside the scope of reason's demands. Rationality is *itself* a temper of deciding, a temper we must encourage most at precisely that point where existentialism casts its lot with the "irrational."

Empiricism has always sought to break the circle by appeal to evidence. But we know well enough that our way of interpreting will determine what we do and what we do not accept as *constituting* evidence. And no self-critical empiricist need to be told about the circularity involved in the justification of induction. But all of this has led to a tendency on the part of some empiricists to endorse "subjectivism." Here is a third attempt to escape based on misappropriation of a valuable clue. The clue now takes the form of insisting that final arbitration in all matters of theory falls upon human beings with all their interests. Where, pray, is the "subjectivism" of this? Obviously it is we with all our interests who arbitrate. The question is whether we are to arbitrate quixotically or sanely.

Each of these "escape" philosophies rests upon the truth that

---

word in any of several technical senses prescribed for example by James or Schiller or Dewey, it hangs in mid-air. Nothing Quine has said justifies *that*.

in all our thinking about the world our attempts at justification are in the end thrown back upon themselves. Over and over again, the things we do, the decisions we make, the attitudes we adopt, determine the kind of justification which counts for us. This *defines* the predicament we are in; in and of itself it provides no leverage for choosing between alternatives. Each "escape" misses fire as a consequence of trying to break the circle rather than accept it. The result is irrationalism. As though there were something inherently irrational in having purposes, or in deciding, or in being guided by our interests! To be irrational is to select a purpose without critical care, to decide without critical care, or to cling to an interest without critical care. In every case, care is a matter of internal critique, of analysis turned uncompromisingly upon itself. The choice between irrationality and rationality is a choice between dogmatic irresponsibility and scrupulous self-criticism.

Let us then accept the circle we are in. Let us neither condemn *Weltanschauung* out of hand nor burden it with the stigma of irrationalism. Let us rather seek to be as critically self-conscious as we can as to the fundamental decisions which have been forced upon us in our own effort to exercise care. Let us look upon what we have already said *as* metaphysics. This can only come, and ought only to come, by way of summary. It contains no theses to be proved; but it constitutes a point of view to be defended. It must justify itself.

In listing the following principles, it may be helpful to differentiate the relatively negative from the relatively positive. The difference is tenuous, for (as I have said before) to understand what you cannot expect to accomplish is to achieve positive insight; but we have committed ourselves to more than "cannots." We would therefore stress the difference.

A. Relatively negative principles.

1. That the world is not of such a character that we can succeed in forcing it into the strait jacket of any purely deductive system. No philosophical interpretation of the world can pose

## THE NATURE OF THE WORLD

as a mathematical demonstration. Spinoza's dream is a chimera. The power of mathematics is a demonstrable fact; equations are helpful tools. But the world is not an equation, and the power of mathematics is limited. Part of our task when we seek to understand the world is to appreciate the significance of logic and mathematics as instruments which enable us to control it; but it is madness to think that logic and mathematics can do the whole of philosophy's job. We learn something of importance *about the world* when we learn that as a model for our theories deduction is limited and esoteric.

2. That the world is not of such a character that any adequate conception of it can pose as merely descriptive. Two points are here bracketed as one. First: that, if by "descriptive" we mean empirically testable, our conception of the world must always be more than descriptive. A philosophical interpretation of the world must accommodate the fact that careful testing of empirical hypotheses continuously increases the range of our understanding and our control; but it cannot pose as itself constituting nothing more. Secondly: that, where we allow for looser senses of the word "descriptive" the word provides no panaceas. Every philosophical system "describes" in some looser sense; so does every science, every art, and every historical interpretation. The very range of our capacity to describe in looser senses is indicative of the richness of the world itself. No description can pigeonhole the world.

3. That the world is thus not of such a character as to be understood in the frame of mind generated by "ism-thinking." By "ism-thinking" I do not mean just any use of ism-words. Such words are in our vocabulary; carefully used they may serve as convenient shortcuts, especially in the often helpful task of relating what we wish to say to what has been said by others before us. "Ism-thinking" arises when ism-words are read as solutions rather than as convenient devices. "Ism-thinking" occurs wherever it is assumed that the application of general labels solves problems. Ism-thinking is a kind of linguistic bullheadedness. The antidote to ism-thinking lies in increased sensitivity to range, and

the limits of instructive generalization. We learn a most important fact *about the world* when we learn to reject all overgeneralized accounts of it.

4. Finally, that the world is of such a character that it allows us no refuge in "irrationalism." Our theories are as much a part of the world as are rocks and kangaroos and wars. We learn something about the nature of the world when we focus our attention upon the requirements of responsible theorizing. And no lesson is more important than the lesson that "irrationalism" is nothing but a misleading word. Irrationalism is the consequence of refusing to abandon mistaken models of rationality after you have discovered that they are mistaken. The *world* is not irrational; *we* are irrational when we are perversely disillusioned, when we wrongly think of our decisions as to distribution of emphasis as something other than the very essence of the life of reason.

B. Relatively positive principles.

5. That realism is a categorical premise of all rational effort. We do not have to prove that the world stands over and against our efforts to understand it. It just does; and no attempt to conceive otherwise can be expressed with sense. This fact does not itself constitute a metaphysical theory; it certainly "describes" nothing. But it is a fact which makes metaphysical speculation coercive; and it sufficiently disposes of the philosophical myth that we ought to be silent where we cannot prove.

6. That a reasonable conception of the world must make its peace with a greater complexity and a greater richness than it can summarize. Reason destroys itself by arrogance; it fulfills itself by sensitivity to range. The world is an arena within which many ways of interpreting and of distributing emphasis make sense and lead to insight. All theories are piecemeal and self-limiting. We understand the world better when we squarely face the predicament we are in. The very lifeblood of philosophy is amazement; and amazement is itself sufficient guaranty of complexity and richness.

## THE NATURE OF THE WORLD

7. That the world is both orderly and disorderly. Its order in fact lulls us into complacency. We need to cultivate amazement in the face of complacency. Do I find my shoe this morning where I placed it last night? Wonder of wonders! That in the midst of this topsy-turvy hurly-burly of a world we can depend upon such homely little facts. We live amidst an order which, if our imagination could dispel our complacency, might stun us. And yet, we are not always complacent; and there are surely limits to order. Those limits may or may not exceed the limits of our capacity for theory; but the difference between order and disorder *is nothing less than* brute.

8. That the world is such that we may *understand* more than we *know*. The search for knowledge has been a search for kinds of certainty based upon limited models. Too often in philosophy we have sought for greater certainty than that which marks what we take for granted as sane human beings. If a man settles himself in a chair and learnedly expounds his doubts as to whether physical objects "exist"; if a man drives his car across the Golden Gate Bridge and declares his serious doubt that physics describes the "real" world; if a man condemns his neighbor and yet proclaims his doubt that there is any communicable difference between right and wrong; it is to be suspected that he is somehow seeking a lesser degree of doubt than he is going to find. Philosophy should stop seeking more certainty than we need; it should seek instead the full significance of accepting such certainty as is *enough*. We "know" when we can prove the truth of propositions; we "understand" when we achieve sensitivity to the coercions of sanity. The world is precisely that *kind* of a place.

These eight principles prescribe the *Weltanschauung* to which our own critique has led. We offer it, so far as it goes, as a kind of metaphysics which can coexist in harmony with the best results that the most competent analysis can provide. The great divide between analysis and world-view is here repudiated. In its stead we offer a self-critical and fallibilist account of the basic categoricals to which the very notion of rational self-justification commits us.

Will it be said that what we offer is very thin gruel? I shall not argue that it is thicker than most. I shall merely note that we have made no effort to add poetic gusto. Once critical self-examination has done its work, the field for poetic imagination lies open. Within limits, bold poetic gusto is our most effective weapon against intellectual stagnation. Indeed, I will go so far as to add that the most utterly wrong-headed poetic imagination can sometimes serve the salutary purpose of providing the stimulus of shock. Few panaceas—and panaceas are always the fruit of poetic imagination—have been more wrong-headed than that which inspired the early *infant terrible* positivists of the present century. The shock of this panacea was the shock of metaphysical excess. It was based upon the excessive and unjustifiable advice that we consider the world as an orderly storehouse manageable solely by the rigidly controlled use of tautologies and testable hypotheses. There was something absurdly wrong-headed about this; and "logical atomism" has gradually assumed the status of a "queer" and repudiated program. But we had to *think* in order to say why. As so often in the past, we have learned most in the laborious process of shuffling back to normal after the disruption produced by profound shock.

Having conceded this, having conceded that even beyond the limits of sanity poetic gusto may justify itself, I revert to the point that we need a kind of poetry which seeks to remain sane. The sanity of metaphysics when it waxes poetic will be in direct proportion to the degree of its sensitivity to the "musts" of internal critique. Short of the desire to shock, the aim of responsible metaphysical imagination should be governed by the eight principles we have listed. Thus, the distinction between metaphysics as critique and metaphysics as poetry requires constant careful review. There is good and bad poetry; and to concede that bad poetry may have salutary effects does not rescue it from being bad. Our conception of responsible metaphysics remains a function of our conception of responsible critique.

## ULTIMATE MATTERS: RELIGION

I turn now to my final point, which is a consequence of all this: that responsible metaphysics must be conceived as the apex of our thought about the world, not as its foundation.

### III. *Ultimate Matters: Religion*

The point I have in mind must be handled with sufficient care to avoid profitless misunderstandings. To begin with, the word "foundation" introduces an ambiguous metaphor. It is often, as we have seen, associated with the deductive model of justification. But in raising the word again I do not intend to return to the argument that deduction is a limited model. Concerning that argument we have said enough. I now have in mind a different claim.

Then, too, it would be disastrous were we to be lured into an argument of the endless "which-came-first-the-chicken-or-the-egg" variety. Our entire discussion has been predicated upon the view that specific justification practices and general principles of justification procedure are interdependent. No "chicken and egg" argument as to whether we start with specific practices and end up with general principles, or start with general principles and end up with specific practices, is going to be profitable. On this matter, too, we have said enough.

But still we cannot ignore a final cry of *non possumus*. This cry may come from a variety of sources, but from none so energetic as the religious. If we feel that there can be responsible religious philosophy, we may wish to conceive of it as a species of what we have been calling responsible poetic metaphysics. And our claim has been that the very essence of responsibility here means that what is said must emerge gradually from careful piecemeal critique. The cry that will go up is the cry that this view is not only destructive of the religious spirit but is in fact the antithesis of genuine fallibilism. It will be said that we are here assuming greater potentialities for man's rational powers than any contrite fallibilist can or ought. Nowhere more vigorously than in religion do men make the claim which is most often expressed in the phrase "the priority of faith." This phrase expresses the doctrine

## THE PRESENT STATE: THE GRAND TRADITION

of man's incapacity ever to reach high enough as the result of careful critique. Can we by careful critique justify the poetry of belief in God or in the divinity of Christ? Yet these, it will be said, are rock-bottom beliefs. They are commitments of the general and grandiose kind which must come *first*.

Now, this kind of claim is by no means easily disposed of. Like all persistent claims, it rests upon its core of insight. But there is a veritable forest of ambiguity through which we must find our way. The very word "faith" has been a source of endless confusion. The plea for priority of faith may be made in all good conscience as a commendable attempt at intellectual modesty. But we must be on our guard. Try, for example, the following question: Who in a given matter displays the greater faith in his ideas; he who takes those ideas as a starting point and refuses to entertain alternative ideas, or he who is willing to subject those ideas to every test and to subject them to free and open competition with all others? If you reflect upon that question, you will be less likely to indulge in some of the more slippery uses of the word "faith" which we so often encounter.

Slippery and puzzling questions are very often the sign that we are concerned with words that have breadth of range. The word "religion" itself has tremendous breadth of range. Unless we are clear as to the range, and clear as to the point within the range upon which we seek to focus attention, we might just as well abandon all attempt to convince or to persuade. Let us therefore seek some precision as to the range of the word "religion" and the range of the word "faith." We may be surprised at our profit.

Those who pontificate about religion without explanation of their use of the word add confusion to confusion. The word "religion" is on a par with such words as "good" and "analysis" of which we have said so much. There is no one proper definition of the word, and we enter a blind alley when we try to seek one. The maximum we can do is to specify various uses of the word in a wide range. I submit six uses of the word "religion" as indicative of such range. Each is an important use. No one is "the proper" use. There are doubtless many more, but six will be sufficient to suggest the range.

1. A single definite creed associated with an established tradition such as Roman Catholicism or Presbyterianism. In this sense a man's religion consists in those beliefs which make him a Jew *rather than* a Quaker, an Episcopalian *rather than* a Seventh Day Adventist.

2. A broad historical tradition, as for example the "Hebraic-Christian" tradition. (We sometimes speak of "Christianity" with habitual vagueness as to its relation to Judaism.) In this sense a man's religion consists in those beliefs by virtue of which he belongs to the Hebraic-Christian tradition of the West rather than to such traditions as the Islamic or Buddhist.

3. A still broader conception, of those five or six *major* traditions which have had greatest impact in world history. One might note that this is the sense of the noun "religion" which John Dewey so vigorously attacked in his proclaimed attempt to free the adjective "religious." Many philosophers presently interested in generalizing the insights of East and West, who talk much of a "world religion," use the word in this way. Here the core of a man's religion is not those beliefs which differentiate him from a Presbyterian or a Teravadian Buddhist, but rather those beliefs which he *shares* with them.

4. A still broader conception arises when we include not only the major traditions, but minor ones as well. This opens the door very wide indeed. You may now speak of the religion of Hottentots and of Dobu indians. You will notice that as the scope of the word broadens the scope of its reference to intellectual content is increasingly more narrow. You find yourself reverting more and more to general similarities of social practice and custom, of behavioral response rather than of specific beliefs. You discuss matters of psychology and sociology more and more, and matters of metaphysical belief less and less.

5. It is a very short step to that use of the word "religion" which has become increasingly popular since Dewey's attack on the major traditions. It is common practice to speak of the reli-

gion of Communism or the religion of science. Dewey defined the *adjective* "religious" in the following way:

> Any activity pursued in behalf of an ideal end against obstacles and in spite of threats of personal loss because of conviction of its general and enduring value is religious in quality.[2]

An arbitrary rigidity in any distinction between a noun and an adjective is bound to be forgotten. Dewey attacked the noun and defended the adjective, but a new noun has become associated with his own adjective. The Vatican and the Kremlin are after all somewhat alike; and the behavioral responses of a devout Catholic and of a self-depriving party-cell worker are remarkably similar. So Communism, with all its atheistic and materialist metaphysic, is a "religion." If that is the way you want to use the word, I cannot deprive you of the privilege.

6. I cannot resist the urge to tell a true story. I once invited a most eminent social psychologist to address a group of undergraduates on the subject of religion. Like any good scientist, he defined his key words at the outset; and his definition of the word "religion" was remarkable. "By the word 'religion,'" he said, "I mean anything which satisfies a human need." One of the undergraduates pointed out that asparagus satisfies a human need. The distinguished visitor was not disturbed. He remarked that the need in this case was not uniquely human; that his definition needed tightening up, but that it was the job of scientific psychology to achieve greater precision as to what the uniquely human needs are. To such extremes one's serious use of the word "religion" may go! And if a man makes perfectly clear what he is trying to say, it is difficult to deny him the privilege of using any word he likes.

Perhaps enough has been said to indicate range. Now notice that at any point in the range one might make use of the word "faith." Where we mean by a man's "religion" his adherence to Roman Catholicism or to Presbyterianism, we will incline to use

[2] John Dewey, *A Common Faith* (New Haven: Yale University Press, 1934), p. 27.

## ULTIMATE MATTERS: RELIGION

the word "faith" in reference to a highly specific set of beliefs. Where we mean by a man's "religion" his devotion to ideals, we will incline to use the word "faith" in reference to generalized behavioral pattern. The more specific the reference, the more difficult it is to differentiate between the concept of faith and the concept of credal dogma.

Now, I believe that what is sound in the cry of *non possumus* which I have envisaged is something like the following: To begin with, the word "religion" is being used in a relatively specific way. It is being used in such a way that the essence of a man's "religion" consists in a certain kind of view of the world. It is being used in such a way as to prescribe that Communism and science are *not* religions. And there is much to be said for this use. There is much to be said on the side of those who insist that the Marxian *Weltanschauung* is precisely *not* a religious one, and that any use of the word "religion" which slurs over this fact is misleading. The key to an unambiguous definition, either of the noun "religion" or of the adjective "religious," is the specification of those characteristics in virtue of which a *world view* is or is not a religious one. Our modern antipathy to metaphysics, and our tendency to psychologize and sociologize our concepts, has led us to a disastrous shift in the focus of emphasis. I am not now arguing that the earlier uses of the word "religion" in the above list are proper and the later uses improper. Any use is "proper" enough so long as it is made clear and understood. But I am conceding that the earlier uses direct our attention to important matters as to which the later uses are silent and uninformative.

Granted then that we are concerned with relatively specific uses of the word religion, and remembering that the more specific the use the more difficult it becomes to distinguish matters of faith from matters of credal dogma, we will be forced to recognize something sound in the objection we are confronting. For, at their most specific, religious beliefs are certainly *not* the kind of thing which careful philosophical critique can hope to achieve. No amount of careful critique is going to reach so high as to grasp a belief in a personal God or in the divinity of Christ. The most that careful critique could accomplish is the justification of a highly general attitude toward the reasonableness of such poetry as our imaginations can produce. Most credal dogma has sprung from man's poetic imagination; in general terms critique may be receptive, but no *specific* dogma can be justified by critique.

This is what is sound in the cry of *non possumus*. But the cry was envisaged as a complaint against our restriction of the concept of rational metaphysics; and in this it misses its mark. For all that it means in the end is simply that specific credal dogma is *not* rational metaphysics. What is needed is not a revision of our conception of rational metaphysics. What is needed is a careful examination of the justification of specific credal dogma.

I submit that our key to understanding the important, the proper, and indispensable role of dogma in human life is the fact that most people do *not* devote themselves to the pursuit of reason. By this I mean that most human beings do not continuously devote their energies to self-critical examination of justification procedure. This is why dogma is an essential element in the strength of any social force or institution. This is a truth not only of religion but of politics. We are extraordinarily unrealistic whenever we condemn dogma out of hand. The democratic *dogma* is an essential element in any free nation which hopes to exert itself as an effective international force. The dogma is necessary because most people do not think. As a philosopher, Charles Sanders Peirce was no friend of dogma or of the a priori method. But Peirce clearly saw that these are the only effective and indispensable methods among unthinking men. I intend no misanthropy when I assert that most men do not devote themselves to the pursuit of reason. There are other admirable pursuits; and not all dogma is black. I intend merely to stress the point that the genuine need of specific religious creeds is not a function of the use of reason but a function of its non-use.

The philosophic quest is an esoteric one. It is the quest of those who place no limits upon the search for rational foundations. It is in *this* context that one must insist that any "religious" elements of one's thought must come as apex rather than as founda-

## ULTIMATE MATTERS: RELIGION

tion. The concern of philosophy is with those who think, not with those who do not; a concern for leaders of opinion rather than followers. In the social and political context our concern is with the self-justification of those who are in a position to guide and to instruct. There is no philosophical problem in connection with the normal attitude of the normal southerner in the matter of race relations. Any sensitive and intelligent man can understand that attitude. The problem for concern is the irresponsibility of those in a position to guide and to mold southern opinion, the demagogue senator who capitalizes upon popular opinion rather than accept the burden of enlightening it. Just so in religion. There is nothing disgraceful about the dogma of a devout communicant; but the dogmatic pretension of a priest is quite a different matter. The theologian with rational pretensions must distinguish dogmatics from justification.

There is every difference between religious dogma and a reasoned sensitivity to the possibilities of religious faith. For the former there is no place in philosophy; its honored place is elsewhere. The only hope for a religious temper in philosophy is the hope that out of long effort and after every sympathy for alternative ideas, some basic categorical emerges which justifies commitment of a special kind. Short of this, which is itself a goal to be achieved rather than a premise from which to start, the only alternative for the introduction of religion into our philosophy is high poetry. And as poetry, whatever of religion we can achieve remains apex rather than foundation. It is an insight to be sought, not a platform on which to base our proofs.

# INDEX OF PROPER NAMES

Aristotle, 84, 175, 192
Austin, J. L., 5, 65, 66n, 80n, 148
Ayer, A. J., 95, 148

Baier, K., 148n
Barth, C., 167
Berkeley, G., 24, 91, 139
Berlin, I., 89-92
Burtt, E. A., 127n

Carnap, R., 138, 142, 144, 159, 163

Descartes, R., 24
Dewey, J., 17-21, 22n, 23, 27, 36, 38, 100, 110, 197n, 205-206

Edwards, J., 115
Emerson, R. W., 34, 39-49

Feigl, H., 103, 142-144, 162, 164-166
Fichte, J. G., 39-49
Field, G. C., 96-97
Foot, (Mrs.) P. R., 84, 86-88

Goodman, N., 4

Hampshire, S., 157-160
Hare, R. M., 84-89, 96n
Hegel, G. W. F., 22, 31, 39, 161, 174
Hobbes, T., 44, 55, 56
Hume, D., 24, 83, 84, 93-94, 138, 142, 143, 145-146, 153, 175, 176-177

James, H., 107
James, W., 153, 197n
Jefferson, T., 53
Johnson, Dr. S., 91
Joseph, H. W. B., 159

Kant, I., 61-64, 71-81, 84, 92, 131, 138, 143, 146, 161, 163, 175, 176-177, 178, 183-187, 190-192
Kneale, W., 95

Leibniz, G. W., 24, 125, 143
Lenin, V., 32n
Locke, J., 24, 53, 54, 153, 196n

Mach, E., 142, 148
Machiavelli, N., 55, 56
Maritain, J., 32
Mill, J. S., 71-78, 142, 143
Moore, G. E., 84, 96-97, 99, 124, 125, 148, 149-150, 168, 170

Nowell-Smith, P., 96n, 159

Oppenheimer, J. R., 178

Peirce, C. S., 106, 150, 163, 179-180, 183-187, 208
Plato, 22, 138, 174, 175, 196n
Poincaré, H., 186
Popper, K. R., 21-28, 29, 38, 110
Price, H. H., 153
Pritchard, H. A., 98-99

Quine, W. V., 4, 138, 159, 162n, 170, 196n

Ross, W. D., 98-99
Rousseau, J. J., 54
Royce, J., 174, 184
Russell, B., 92, 138, 142, 143, 148, 166, 167, 168, 175, 179-180, 183, 185
Ryle, G., 170

Santayana, G., 188
Schelling, F. W. J., 39
Schiller, F. C. S., 186
Schweitzer, A., 28-30, 38
Spinoza, B., 24, 38, 143, 199
Stevenson, C. L., 129-131

Toulmin, S. E., 85, 148n

Warnock, G. L., 139-140
Weitz, M., 159n
Weldon, T. D., 15-17, 27, 30, 33-34, 36, 38, 46, 47
White, M., 96n, 97n
Whitehead, A. N., 170
Wittgenstein, L., 5, 79, 135, 136, 154, 167-168

211

# INDEX OF SUBJECTS

absolutism, 17, 19, 20
advice—political proposals as, 48
—conditions of sound, 49-59
—and Kant, 63-64
—ethics and, 122-123, 128
—and physics, 178
—metaphysics as, 193, 195, 202
analysis—philosophy as, 1-3, 5-6, 13
—and moral philosophy, 69, 76, 89, 97, 103, 123, 124, 128
—present state of philosophy, 137-189:
  as empirical, 147, 148-161
  as formal, 140, 144, 146, 147, 161-167
  as not talking sense, 147, 167-169
  and distribution of emphasis, 169-177
—and metaphysics, 190, 195, 198, 201
analytic, *see under* propositions
attitudes—rational, 26
—in politics, 45-46
—ethical judgments as expressing, 93-95
—and ethical disputes, 129-131

casuistry, 122
categoricals—political proposals as, 57-59, 108, 114
—general treatment of the term, 60-71
—singular, 83, 89-93, 96, 97, 99, 154, 156
—methodological, 105-106, 135, 173, 200, 202, 209
—in morals, 122, 131
—in science, 177-189 passim
categorical imperative, 61-64, 75-78, 131
Catholicism, Roman, 15, 31-32, 111-112, 205-206; *see also* Thomism
checks and balances, 55, 111, 114-116, 119, 120
Christian, 15, 32, 52, 56, 57, 109-110, 111, 114, 205
church and state, separation of, 111-114

circularity, 12-13, 105, 109, 175, 183, 193-194, 196-198
clarification, 169-170
cognitive, non-cognitive, 22, 28, 66, 145, 156, 164-165; *see also* knowledge
communism, 15, 16, 109-110, 111, 116, 206-207; *see also* Marxism
critique, 190-195, 202, 203-204, 207-208

deciding, temper of, 7, 197
decision, 8, 24, 26, 28, 46, 48, 58-59, 73-74, 76, 80, 81, 87-88, 91, 92, 100ff, 116, 118, 129, 130, 155, 177, 183, 197, 198
deduction—model of, 5, 6, 8, 10
—opposition to in political philosophy, 15, 16, 17, 20, 26-27
—vagueness of the model in political philosophy, 28-39
—examples, 43-48, 49, 50
—in moral philosophy, 62, 63, 69, 70, 74-75, 82, 83, 86, 88, 100ff
—limits of, 107-115, 170
—appropriateness of, 132, 169, 171, 176, 188
—and metaphysics, 138, 190-192, 198-199
democracy, 16, 35, 56, 109-121, 132-133, 173, 208
describing (description), 50-51, 63-64, 68-69, 97, 100ff, 147-161, 163, 170, 175, 180-183, 199
depravity, 55, 114-115, 116, 128
dichotomizing tendency (dichotomy), 2, 5, 18, 22, 23, 26, 64, 65, 81, 92, 99-106, 108, 130, 140, 157, 161, 168, 169, 176
distribution of emphasis, 7-13, 70, 80, 103-105, 130-131, 133-135, 155, 169-177 passim, 184, 188, 194, 195, 196, 200
dogma (dogmatics, dogmatism), 17, 18, 20, 48, 112, 117, 136, 167, 175, 187, 207-209
dualism, 185-187

212

## INDEX

emotive (emotion), 22-25 passim, 28, 80, 165, 171-172
empiricism, 20, 24-25, 70, 83, 88, 93, 108, 144, 148-155, 161-163, 176, 177, 190, 197; *see also* analysis, hypotheses, induction
"engineering, piecemeal," 6, 14, 15-28, 107, 110, 113, 132
entailment, 13, 32-43 passim, 48, 86, 117, 120, 167; *see also* "must"
—logical, 12, 14, 17, 32-33, 36-37, 46; *see also* deduction
equal ("All men created"), 34, 50-54, 111, 114-120, 192
existentialism (-ist), 29-30, 197

faith, 25, 188, 203-204, 206-207, 209
fallibilism (fallibility), 7, 12, 105-106, 108-109, 112, 117, 128, 131, 133, 135, 174, 175, 176, 183, 185-186, 188, 192, 195, 201, 203
fascism, 15, 111, 116, 132
foundations, 16, 75, 110, 117, 118, 120, 195, 203, 208-209
freedom, 34, 111, 118-120

game analogy, 11-12, 47-48, 119, 125, 128, 170, 181-182, 188
generalizing tendency, 9, 37, 39, 80, 93-97, 119, 136, 151-152, 192-194
—overgeneralization, 52-56, 123-131 passim, 133, 135-136, 141, 200
—general principles, 69, 82, 83, 85-86, 87, 88
"good," 55, 84, 96, 97, 121, 124-128, 140

Hegelian, Hegelianism, 20, 27n, 31-37 passim, 115
history, 26-27, 88, 99, 132, 138, 166, 174-176, 180, 192
hypotheses: empirical, testable, descriptive, etc.
—general remarks, 12, 49-53, 66, 79, 104, 106
—and political theory, 15, 17-21, 23, 26-28, 48, 56, 114, 117, 118
—and moral theory, 78, 83, 86-87, 93, 97, 130

—and analysis, 140, 145-147, 148-161, 162-163, 166, 168, 170
—and science, 182-183, 185-186, 187-188
—and metaphysics, 138, 191, 199, 202

induction—model of, 5, 10, 100ff, 176
—limits of in political philosophy, 14, 25, 26-27, 28, 29, 108, 110, 113, 116
—in moral philosophy, 69, 70, 72, 73, 74-75, 81, 83, 85-86, 87, 88
—and analysis, 132, 170, 171
—and metaphysics, 138, 150
"intellectual underpinnings," 169-171
interpretation, 8-14, 26-27, 33, 57, 127-128, 196-198, 200; *see also* distribution of emphasis
intuition (-ism), 69, 70, 76, 81-99
irrational (-ism), 7, 23-26, 29-30, 66, 88, 99, 110, 131, 188-189, 197-198, 200
ism-thinking, 5, 35, 88, 97, 99, 138, 177, 199

justification—as need, 5
—of distribution of emphasis, 7-13, 172, 173, 174-175, 176, 183
—in political theory: by induction, 15-28 passim
by deduction, 28-39
problem of, 57-59
—in moral philosophy: as "categorical," 60-71 passim
of ought expressions, 71-81 passim
by deduction, 84-89 passim
by "just seeing," 89-99 passim
as not unique, 99-106
—positive account: general theme, 107-109
in political theory, 109-121
in moral philosophy, 121-131
conditions of appropriateness, 131-136
—and metaphysics, 139-140, 190-193, 196-198, 202, 208, 209

Kantians, 27n, 190

213

knowledge, 92, 98-99, 133, 138, 142, 143, 169-171, 177, 184, 187, 201; see also cognitive

language (linguistic), 9, 22n, 27, 37, 45, 70, 77, 80, 81, 97, 101, 128, 139, 140, 143-144, 149, 154, 156-160, 164, 171, 172, 173, 194
logic, 33, 38, 46, 48-49, 140, 142, 144, 145, 146, 154, 156, 159-160, 163, 167, 168, 199

man, the nature of, 9, 14, 54-57, 60, 119, 123, 128, 131-136
Marxism, 22, 31-35, 36, 56-57, 110, 112, 115, 207; see also communism
metaphysics, 14-15, 29-49 passim, 76-78, 97, 106, 109, 111, 114, 121, 137-141, 150, 152, 157, 163, 177, 189, 190-209; see also *Weltanschauung*
models, of rationality and of justification procedure
—general remarks, 6-9, 107-108, 133, 135
—in political philosophy, 15, 16, 28, 29, 30, 110
—in moral philosophy, 63, 74-75, 81, 81-88, 123
—and analysis, 156, 161, 172, 174-176
—and metaphysics, 193-194, 200, 201
moral philosophy, 18, 29, 59, 60-109, 121-136
"must"—general treatment, 5, 7, 12, 13, 62, 105-106, 173
—in political philosophy, 30-31, 33, 36, 38, 39, 43, 46, 47
—in science, 11-12, 47, 59, 88, 170n, 173, 177-189
—and metaphysics, 202

naturalistic fallacy, 96-97, 124

objectivism, 83-84, 95-96
Oneida Community, 193
"ought," 33, 34, 39, 51, 70
—versus "is," 68-69, 71-81, 131

performatives, 65-66, 80, 81, 108, 123
phenomenalism, 89-92
Platonism, 97, 99
political philosophy, 7, 14-59, 60-61, 104, 105, 107-121, 131-133, 136, 192, 208-209
poetry, metaphysics as, 138-139, 195, 202, 203, 209
poll, principle of, 111, 116-118
positivism (-ist), 22, 30, 139-140, 145, 148, 202
pragmatism (-ist), 21, 27, 34, 88, 106n, 186, 196-197
proof, limits of, 5, 140, 174
—in political theory, 14-15, 16, 29, 109-110, 113-118
—in morals, 71-72, 75, 98-99, 121, 122
—in metaphysics, 138, 150, 194, 209
—and realism, 184, 188, 200
propositions—analytic versus synthetic, 3-4, 8, 13, 22, 62-64, 67, 97, 100ff
—not the only way of talking sense, 4, 26, 51, 54, 128, 130, 187, 188-189
—vagueness of the class, 64-70
—categorical imperative as, 62-64, 75
—ought expressions as, 77-81, 131
—general principles as, 82, 87, 88
—singular categoricals as, 89-93
—appropriate scope, 132-133, 184
—metaphysics and, 104, 123, 192, 201
Protestant, 111-112
Puritans, 34, 55, 114

realism, 183-185, 200
reductionism, 1-3, 77, 141-142, 161, 166, 174
religion, 111-112, 113, 167, 203-209; see also Catholicism, Roman; Christian; Protestant
rules—governing use of expressions, 4, 36-37, 97, 128, 151, 173
—"basic," 11-12, 47, 48, 65, 119, 170, 181-182, 188-189, 192
—"loose," 85-86
—Feigl on (as tautologies), 103, 165-166

*INDEX*

science—general, 14-15, 23, 27, 30, 47, 48-49, 58, 59, 74, 88, 99, 101-106, 123, 133, 135, 142-144, 158, 176, 177-189, 191, 206-207
—linguistic, 156-161
—social, 19-21, 22, 23, 27, 58, 113-114, 116, 132
—and state, separation of, 113-114, 116
—worship, 161-167, 178
—musts of, *see under* "must"
self-correctiveness, 107-109, 122, 137-140, 167, 169, 175
self-criticism, 1, 57, 140-141, 172-174, 184, 189, 198, 201, 208
sense data, 153-155
skepticism, also solipsism, 179, 187-188
statism, 39-46 passim
subjectivism, 83-84, 93-96, 197
sympathy, 121-122, 131, 132
synthetic, *see under* propositions

synthetic a priori, 4, 5, 62-64, 75, 100, 167, 176

tautology—and analytic, 62
—as only sensible alternative to empirically testable hypotheses, 15, 22-27 passim, 78, 79, 93, 104, 130, 138, 145, 168, 182, 183, 187, 202
—principles as, 49-53, 115-117
—rules as, 103, 164-166
Thomists, 32, 35, 36, 110, 112, 115; *see also* Catholicism, Roman
true, 64, 66, 75, 125-126, 165-166
truth, 4, 126, 174, 185-187
twilight zone, 100-104, 172-173

Vienna Circle, 142, 167

*Weltanschauung*, 13, 15, 33, 37-39, 137, 195, 198, 201, 207; *see also* metaphysics

GPSR Authorized Representative: Easy Access System Europe - Mustamäe tee 50, 10621 Tallinn, Estonia, gpsr.requests@easproject.com